Roma Activism
Reimagining Power and Knowledge

ROMANI STUDIES

Edited by Sam Beck, Cornell University

In the course of the twenty-first century, Europe has become aware that the Roma are its largest minority, with an estimated population of eleven million people. As a result, Romani Studies has emerged as an interdisciplinary field that offers perspectives derived from the humanities and social sciences in the context of state and transnational institutions. One of its aims is to remove the stigma surrounding Roma scholarship, to engage with the controversies regarding Roma identity and, in this way, counter anti-Roma racism.

Volume 1
ROMA ACTIVISM: REIMAGINING POWER AND KNOWLEDGE
Edited by Sam Beck and Ana Ivasiuc

ROMA ACTIVISM
Reimagining Power and Knowledge

❋ ❋ ❋

Edited by
Sam Beck and Ana Ivasiuc

berghahn
NEW YORK • OXFORD
www.berghahnbooks.com

First published in 2018 by
Berghahn Books
www.berghahnbooks.com

© 2018, 2020 Sam Beck and Ana Ivasiuc
First paperback edition published in 2020

Library of Congress Cataloging-in-Publication Data

Names: Beck, Sam, editor of compilation. | Ivasiuc, Ana, editor of compilation.
Title: Roma Activism: Reimagining Power and Knowledge / edited by Sam Beck and
    Ana Ivasiuc.
Description: First edition. | New York: Berghahn Books, 2018 | Includes bibliographical
    references and index.
Identifiers: LCCN 2018015940 (print) | LCCN 2018027671 (ebook) |
    ISBN 9781785339493 (eBook) | ISBN 9781785339486 (hardback: alk. paper)
Subjects: LCSH: Romanies—Politics and government. | Romanies—Social conditions.
Classification: LCC DX145 (ebook) | LCC DX145 .R587 2018 (print) |
    DDC 305.8914/97—dc23
LC record available at https://lccn.loc.gov/2018015940

British Library Cataloguing in Publication Data

A catalogue record for this book is available from the British Library

ISBN 978-1-78533-948-6 hardback
ISBN 978-1-78920-847-4 paperback
ISBN 978-1-78533-949-3 ebook

We dedicate this volume to Nicolae Gheorghe, the work he accomplished, and all the people he inspired to shape a positive Roma identity and to carry on advancing their emancipation.

FIGURE 0.1. Nicolae Gheorghe interviewing a *Romungro* in 1979. Photo by Sam Beck.

CONTENTS

❀ ❀ ❀

PART III. RENEWING ACTIVISMS

Illustrations

✻ ✻ ✻

Abbreviations

❋ ❋ ❋

ACDR	The Civic Democratic Alliance of the Roma (Romania)
AKP	Justice and Development Party (Turkey)
ANR	Romanian National Agency for the Roma
CBO	Community-Based Organization
CEE	Central and Eastern Europe
CHP	Republican Peoples' Party (Turkey)
CoE	Council of Europe
CSO	Civil Society Organization
DAHR	Democratic Alliance of Hungarians in Romania
EANRS	European Academic Network of Romani Studies
EC	European Commission
ECtHR	European Court of Human Rights
EdRom	Edirne Roman Association
ERGO	European Roma Grassroots Organizations (Network)
ERIAC	European Roma Institute for Arts and Culture
ERPC	European Roma Policy Coalition
ERRC	European Roma Rights Centre
ERTF	European Roma and Travellers Forum
ESF	European Social Funds
EU	European Union
EUJS	European Union of Jewish Students
EVS	European Voluntary Service
FBO	Faith-Based Organization

FER	Ethnic Roma Federation
FLAS	Foreign Language and Area Studies
FSG	Fundación Secretariado Gitano
GLS	Gypsy Lore Society
FERYP	Forum of European Roma Young People
GRO	Grassroots Organization
HDP	Peoples' Democratic Party (Turkey)
HVIM	Hungarian Sixty-Four Counties Youth Movement
IDP	Internally Displaced Persons
IGO	International Governing Organization
IPA	Instrument for Pre-Accession Assistance
IREX	International Research and Exchanges Board
IRU	International Romani Union
IST	Institute of Turkish Studies
LGBTQ	Lesbian, Gay, Bisexual, Transgender, and Queer
MHP	Nationalist Movement Party (Turkey)
MS	Member State(s)
NCCD	National Council for Combating Discrimination (Romania)
NGO	Non-Governmental Organization
NISR	Netherlands Institute for Sinti and Roma
NRIS	National Roma Integration Strategies
ODIHR	Office for Democratic Institutions and Human Rights
OMC	Open Method of Coordination
OSCE	Organization for Security and Cooperation in Europe
OSI	Open Society Institute
PKK	Kurdistan Worker's Party
QUANGO	Quasi-autonomous Non-Governmental Organization
REF	Roma Education Fund
RIRNM	Romanian Institute for Research on National Minorities
TOKI	Turkey's Housing Administration
UK	United Kingdom
UN	United Nations
UNDP	United Nations Development Program

Preface

Sam Beck

❀ ❀ ❀

This book was imagined in Bucharest, when I was invited to participate in a conference organized by the Roma Cultural Museum in Bucharest in 2014, "Roma Policies in Romania: Between Ethnicity and Social Vulnerability; The Perspectives of Nicolae Gheorghe." This is where I met Ana Ivasiuc, and where we discussed the importance of Roma activism and scholarship in light of controversies regarding the viability of Roma as scholars, and of activism in scholarship. We held strong views about the importance of demonstrating that the Roma were actively engaged in their struggle for recognition as scholars and in their leadership and participation in Roma liberation, resisting the powerful pressures to give up their identities no matter how they are manifested, and fighting for their dignity.

Among the individuals who come to mind who entered this struggle, Nicolae Gheorghe managed to play important roles, mediating between the political controls of Romanian communism and those of Roma groups he sought to embolden, and daring to explore their unification in the 1970s, when I was carrying out field research in Transylvania. My relationship with Romania was limited as my ability to enter the country ended (Beck 1992b), my academic career choices narrowed, and I adapted to the changing environment.

I met Nicolae Gheorghe during my first two years of doctoral research on the history and political economy of an upland Romanian community (1974–76), supported by the anthropology department of the University of Massachusetts and the International Relations and Exchanges Board (IREX). At that time, I knew him as a sociologist and a student of Romanian sociologist Henri Stahl, himself of Dimitrie Gusti's Bucharest School of Sociology. My relationship with him intensified when I was alone in the field carrying out postdoctoral research (1978–80) during my second lengthy stay in Romania. My research, supported by IREX, investigated economic specialization in Țara Făgărașului, a valley system whose ethnic Romanian population was studied by the Bucharest School of Sociology.

After inviting him to Șercaia, where I had a room with a German Saxon family, Nicolae came to visit me often, and I visited him in Bucharest. He was tall, dark skinned, black haired, and always talking fast and furious, with great passion and intellectual urgency. We had long, intense discussions about the history, culture, and future of the Roma. He taught me about the Roma and confided in me his own struggles of identity. I was stimulated by his ideas and wanted to support his efforts to create a language he could use not only to describe the Roma, the various conditions in which they were living, and the diversity of identities they held, but also, and in some ways more pressing, to reform the Roma into a cohesive body that could challenge the state to gain the rights and integrity of other Romanian citizens and to improve their lives. While the Roma were the largest non-Romanian ethnic group in the country, they had no unity. Many of the groups did not even identify as Roma. This was a particularly important point; it was a matter of developing and increasing not only Roma self-identity, but also the recognition assigned to this population by the state as a co-inhabiting nationality, a Romanian minority. The vast majority of Roma were living in abject poverty without access to resources to change this condition. We discussed the plight of African Americans and Native Americans for comparison.

The more I learned, the more I wanted to know. Yet, I was aware even in those early times that to understand the Roma, I also had to understand the social and political-economic environments in which they were situated. Romanian regions differed socioculturally. How Roma were integrated within each region by occupation, by their self-ascribed identity, the identity ascribed by other ethnic groups, their relationships with the other groups in which they were enmeshed, and their relationship with the state—this was the puzzle I was seeking to understand. My work still focused on regional economic specialization from a historical perspective as I gained a deeper understanding of the various social groups in interaction with each other.

I am forever grateful to Nicolae Gheorghe for pulling me into the study of the Roma, but even more so for modeling a kind of activist/advocacy research that I sought to implement in the United States ever since. It is a kind of research we now call public or engaged anthropology/sociology. I found refreshing the work Gheorghe was doing, not just collecting data, not just generating information to be used for writing an ethnographic research report for consumption by others with similar academic interests, not just another entry in a curriculum vitae for career and professional advancement, but perhaps accomplishing all these things while also making a contribution to the people engaged through research; he was making a difference in people's lives. The research had a purpose beyond scholarship. From this perspective, one may say that his influence continues to inspire activist academics well beyond the boundaries of Romania, where he was born, or Europe, where he carried out his activity. This powerful thought motivated us to dedicate this volume to his memory.

For some, engaged anthropology is not perceived as an academic activity at all because it is seen as a role assumed by anthropologists using academic knowledge outside academia. For others, engaged anthropology cannot be scientific because it is not neutral or value free. This is a shortsighted position because it ignores the important contribution made by feminist theory and the use of situated knowledge production and standpoint epistemology. With a few exceptions, non-Roma men have dominated Romani studies. We hope that our volume helps in bringing about change.

Engaged anthropology takes a moral stance. Engaged anthropology is not biased because it takes a social justice position. It takes advantage of this position. When playing an engaged role, the anthropologist takes a critical stand because the intent of the research, besides producing knowledge—translating and making understandable the "strange" and "different"—is to work with people to improve their lives and participate with them as allies in their struggles. This is about identifying the conditions, processes, and forces that produce unequal power relations and disparities. This is about not accepting ideological hegemonies. It is about challenging inequities and injustices. It is about activism. It is about working with the marginalized and vulnerable people in society and bringing the research back to them in an effort to improve their lives. It is about active participation in political work to promote human rights, the right to work and to earn a livable wage, the right to housing, the right to education, the right to healthcare; it is about human rights.

I was inspired by Nicolae Gheorghe, and, as I returned to the United States from carrying out research in Romania, I dedicated myself to exploring how to resolve the contradictions involved in carrying out anthropological research and being an activist in my own society (Beck 1992a). While Gheorghe focused on the particular people with whom he identified and in whose name he entered the struggle, I entered the struggle for liberation by focusing on oppressed people in my own society, who were seeking to alter their life condition, dignity, and justice. Decades-long efforts in anthropology to make scholarship public and engaged are now legitimized and led me to publish accounts to support such work (Beck and Maida 2013; Beck and Maida 2015).

This book is about research and Roma activism. I am grateful to the contributors who have added to the growing efforts of an engaged academy ready to raise into greater prominence the civil and human rights struggle in which modern day Roma are leading the charge. More broadly speaking, the contributors of this volume bring to wider attention the plight of the largest ethnic minority of Europe as one of the more marginalized people of the globe living under regimes of oppression. Too often, oppressed people are characterized as victims who must rely on government or outsiders to liberate them. It is time to recognize that even when people are positioned in contexts of poverty, or subjugated politically, economically, and spatially— all ways that oppressed people are held in place—they have the strength and will to resist and struggle for their own liberation. Outsiders have a role, if they are ready and able to contribute, but only as allies.

I am immensely grateful to Ana Ivasiuc, who has played a central and critical role in producing this volume. Her enthusiasm for this project has brought it to conclusion even when we lost contributors and had to replace them in short order and when each of us had to deal with personal matters that held us up and delayed our work. Our contributors have been extraordinarily patient as has our publisher, Marion Berghahn, whose support has been unwavering. Our editors at Berghahn, Lynn Otto and Elizabeth Martinez, have been a great support. We are grateful to all of them.

Sam Beck is the former director of the New York City Urban Semester Program and the current director of the Practicing Medicine Program at the College of Human Ecology of Cornell University. An anthropologist whose research interests focus on intergroup relations, liberatory forms of education, and activism among vulnerable populations, Beck has carried out fieldwork in Iran, Yugoslavia, Romania, Austria, Germany, and the United States. With Carl Maida, he edited *Toward Engaged Anthropology* (2013) and *Public Anthropology in a Borderless World* (2015).

Sam Beck's Roma-Related Publications and Preface References

Beck, Sam. 1979. "Transylvania: The Political Economy of a Frontier." Ph.D. dissertation. University of Massachusetts Amherst.
———. 1989. "The Origin of Gypsy Slavery." *Dialectical Anthropology* 14: 53–61.
———. 1991a. "Toward a Civil Society." *Socialism and Democracy* 13: 135–154.
———. 1991b. "Contested Space: The Symbolic Nature of the Romanian Revolution in 1990." Working Papers on Transitions from State Socialism: Cornell 6 Project on Comparative Institutional Analysis; Center for International Studies, Cornell University.

————. 1991c. "What Brought Romanians to Revolt." *Critique of Anthropology* 11 (1): 7–31.

————. 1992a. *Manny Almeida's Ringside Lounge: The Cape Verdeans' Struggle for Their Neighborhood.* Providence, RI: GAVEA-Brown.

————. 1992b. "Persona Non Grata: Ethnicity and Romanian Nationalism." In *Dialectical Anthropology: Essays Presented to Stanley Diamond,* edited by Christine Gailey, 118–145. University of Florida Press.

————. 1993. "Racism and the Formation of a Romani Ethnic Leader." In *Perilous States: Conversations on Culture, Politics and Nation,* edited by George E. Marcus, 165–186. Chicago: University of Chicago Press.

Beck, Sam, and Carl A. Maida, eds. 2013. *Toward Engaged Anthropology.* New York: Berghahn Books.

————, eds. 2015. *Public Anthropology in a Borderless World.* New York: Berghahn Books.

INTRODUCTION

Renewing Research and Romani Activism

Ana Ivasiuc

Unlearned Lessons

On 31 March 2017, the small Transylvanian town of Gheorgheni (in Hungarian, Gyergyószentmiklós) in county Harghita was the stage of a bitterly familiar scene: a mob of twenty to thirty men attacked Roma settlements, burned one house, and set ablaze straw bales in five different locations.[1] Those present inside the houses at the moment of the attack were dragged outside, and, in the middle of bystanders' applause, the women and children were beaten, while the men were forced to kneel in a line. The event, at first announced on online platforms by local journalists in Hungarian, appeared over the course of the next few days on several German-language blogs (Ecoleusti 2017; Parászka 2017; Pester Lloyd 2017), and only made its appearance in the Romanian news three days later (Ivașcu 2017).[2] The Romanian news site HotNews reported that, according to a trusted source, "several Hungarian citizens of the town wanted to teach the Roma a lesson," to put a halt to their alleged misdemeanors (Ivașcu 2017). The English-speaking community of (pro-) Roma activists learned about the events nearly one week after the facts, through an article published on the blog of the European Roma Rights Centre (ERRC) (Lee 2017). The next day, the article was circulated on the European Academic Network of Romani Studies (EANRS), where it seemed to pass unnoticed: there were no reactions to it. The event, fortunately, did not result in the loss of lives, and perhaps was therefore deemed too prosaic to wrest a reaction from the academic community. And yet, this silence signals the passing of such events in the sphere of the ordinary, the tacit acknowledgment of the normalization of violence against the Roma: nothing out of the ordinary, *just* another attack on Roma. The "lesson" is a persistent and recurrent trope in justifying anti-Roma violence, and a claim of moral and epistemological superiority, postulated from particular positions of power. It posits the non-Roma as invested with a pedagogical "white man's burden" aimed at civilizing the Roma, while infantilizing them as unruly and in need of punishment. Yet, many of those advocating for "teaching the Roma a lesson" would also, undoubtedly, in the same neoracist breath, claim that the Roma cannot be "civilized" due to their unalterable otherness (Čada 2012: 76). In turn, on the ERRC's blog written in reaction to the event, Jonathan Lee (2017) claims that "the lessons of Harghita's history of pogroms against Roma have been conveniently forgotten," reversing the blame onto lax authorities, the tacit condoning of such acts by the police, and institutionalized racism writ large.

We felt it necessary to start our volume by recounting this episode of violence to make the point that in the context of increasing violence against the Roma across Europe, the pursuit of knowledge only for the sake of knowledge seems at best indecent. However, acting on such developments without reflecting on the wider politics of activism, its own blind spots and fallouts, is at best irresponsible. Two other violent events, running on very similar scripts, are closely and critically analyzed in this volume, together with the activist responses articulated at the time (see the chapters by Chirițoiu and Fosztó). They span a period of a quarter century, which has seen antigypsyism erupt at numerous locations and following various events, but always according to the same script, involving, invariably, arson, humiliation, violence, and the leitmotif of "teaching them a lesson." Yet, as Lee (2017) underlines, but also as the chapters in this volume claim in many different ways, Roma-related research and activism seem to have their own "unlearned lessons."

This volume focuses on blind spots in Roma-related research and activism and is a search for spaces for dialogue, past the unilateral sense of "teaching" each other from positions of epistemic—or moral—superiority. Indeed, framing past missteps and yet unattained goals of activism in terms of "learning experiences" enables a space in which plural voices may articulate their views building on previous attempts by critical founders of Romani activism such as Nicolae Gheorghe (Acton and Ryder 2015: 5), whose lessons we attempt to explore in this volume. Thus, the volume is not merely about Romani activism, and does not seek to offer a comprehensive view of its historical development or of all of its contemporary forms and their varied locations; this, in itself, would be an enormous task requiring years of research.[3] Rather, the reader will discover forms of Romani activism in a piecemeal fashion, through several of the volume's chapters that offer contextualized analyses of Romani activism embedded in particular social and political dynamics. The volume is also not only about Roma-related research, or about research on activism. Rather, it is situated precisely at the confluence between research and activism, seeking to create a space for reflexivity in both.

Far from being specific to the Roma, the reflections cultivated by this collection of essays can be productively applied to the problematic of many other subaltern groups involved in forms of activism, and which, simultaneously, have been the focus of social research and policy interventions. Our volume speaks to the need to defamiliarize known forms of research and activism by embedding a recurrent practice of reflexivity in both, incessantly questioning and renewing intellectual and political commitments. Our volume is an exercise in questioning the knowledge thus far yielded and the ways in which it was produced, as well as renewing familiar forms of activism and exploring future possibilities opened by reflection.

The general context of the volume is spanned by the rise of antigypsyism (Stewart 2012); the increase of xenophobic sentiment and far-right ideologies across the Western world; the uncertainties related to the EU project after Brexit and to how this potentially paradigmatic shift will impact insecurities, mobilities, and processes of othering, including of Romani groups; the fallout of the financial crisis related to contemporary forms of predatory capitalism, violently pushing many into growing hardship and spurring competition on increasingly scarce public resources; and the hegemonic expansion of the discourse on "security" as the supreme goal to be pursued. Indeed, since roughly the nineties, Western societies have entered an era marked by the disquieting productivity of "risk" and "security" as enablers of repressive policies and structuring principles of a sociality marked by waning solidarity. This accompanied the demise of the welfare state, progressively replaced by a repressive state keen to defend rather the interests of powerful capital than of its most destitute citizens, increasingly precaritized and criminalized (Lorey 2015). In parallel, neoliberal governmentalities have colonized public discourse on—and state policies for—the poor, pathologizing and stigmatizing them while producing their undeservingness (Haney 2002). In the case of the Roma, this led to forms of "reasonable antigypsyism" (van Baar 2014), coalesced in increasingly frequent episodes of violence such as the ones described above.

Contemporaneous to these worrisome developments are discernible reconfigurations of the Romani movement. In part, such shifts follow the rejuvenation of its membership base, with emerging trends in a bottom-up youth movement with the power to reform its own discourses and practices (see Mirga-Kruszelnicka, this volume). But some of the reconfigurations of the Romani transnational movement espouse powerful top-down advocacy initiatives, which have recently materialized in the creation of a European Roma Institute for Arts and Culture (ERIAC), aimed at promoting a positive (self-)image of Roma by the Roma themselves, in order to tackle what is perceived to be the "root cause" of the exclusion and discrimination of Roma: ignorance, hatred, and mistrust. The establishment of the ERIAC, one of the most debated forms of activism at the moment, has spurred fierce confrontational discussions across activist and scholarly communities, spanning a range of concerns reflected in our volume. On the one hand, on the dimension of activism, the question emerged as to how this sort of identity politics can be reconciled, and possibly articulated, with a politics of redistribution beyond mere cultural(ist) frames (Magazzini 2016: 54). Critics of the initiative have argued that the neoliberal cultural(ist) framing of the root causes of exclusion as "matters of the mind" ignores wider political stakes and the materiality of structural racism resting rather on misdistribution than misrecognition, echoing earlier criticism to the particular forms of identity politics in which the Romani movement is vested (Kovats 2003). The creation of the ERIAC—which remains a contested initiative among Roma actors themselves—signals the institutionalization and solidification of a culturalist European Romani identity politics where Romani elites are given (have taken?) a space to produce forms of cultural "authenticity," deemed a valid tool for combating socioeconomic and political exclusion. Yet, given the politically and financially powerful support invested in the initiative by the Council of Europe and George Soros's Open Society Foundation, coinciding with the discontinuation of European funding to the European Roma and Travellers Forum (ERTF), it can be predicted that the establishment of such an institution is likely to foreclose alternative paths for an activism grounded in a politics of redistribution, rather than recognition.

On the other hand, on the dimension of knowledge production, the prominent place of Romani intellectuals in the ERIAC spurred another set of debates. There is a discernible shift in what some scholars call the "Roma Awakening": the increasing strength of Romani actors' voices in multiplying debates concerning Roma lives, including on practices within academia itself (Acton and Ryder 2015). Institutionally, this veritable critical turn was marked, in the summer of 2017, by the launch of the Romani Studies Program at Central European University, led by two prominent Romani scholars, and by the establishment of its journal, *Critical Romani Studies.* The growing numbers of Romani scholars and the way they disrupt, with increasing visibility, the narratives produced by the established core of Romani studies scholars have already started to influence academic debates by eliciting reactions (see, for instance, Stewart 2017). Partly, the current volume speaks to this shift, identifying those dynamics through which Romani academics contribute to renewing scholarship by unsettling not only discourses, but also the power mechanisms and structures underlying them. This move echoes the critique of epistemic privilege and the paramount emphasis on decolonizing anthropology (Harrison 1991), or methodologies of research with subaltern peoples more generally (Tuhiwai-Smith 1999).

The project of the ERIAC has received criticism from scholars pertaining to the EANRS, too, on basis of concerns related to the lack of legitimacy of knowledge produced outside established university and research structures, which derive their legitimacy from quality control protocols defined as scientific. The opponents of these arguments have deemed this position conservative and scientist, critiquing it for being oblivious to issues of power and epistemic privilege. Yet their arguments have often resorted to ethnic essentialism or "epistemological insiderism" (Brubaker 2016): the belief that one's perceived identity may function as to (dis)qualify the production of knowledge on particular topics from external positions. In the subtext of claims that Roma scholars are uniquely legitimate producers of knowledge on the Roma looms large the contestable idea that non-Roma scholars are less able—and in any case less legitimized—to do so, because of their "outsider" status (see also Stewart 2017). Both views construct and reify borders and the things they separate: the first between various forms and institutions of knowledge production (scientific versus nonscientific), and the second between particular identity formations seen as rigid and essential ethnic units (Roma versus non-Roma). A missing stance in this rather chunky, unsophisticated debate is what Rogers Brubaker (2016: 10) coins "a trans of beyond": "positioning oneself in a space that is not defined with reference to established categories. Such a move is characterized by the claim to transcend existing categories—or to transcend categorization altogether." The question of whether, and how, such a "trans" moment is possible in Romani-related scholarship and activism seems a timely one.

If "Romani studies" as a general topic area has been known to vest forms of scientific racism in the Gypsy Lore Society (Acton 2016), more recently, many scholars have taken up an active role in combating, through their knowledge, stereotypes against Romani groups (Tremlett 2009). But the growing interest in "the Roma" from outside Romani studies has subsequently delocalized knowledge production toward research institutions that do not necessarily have an ethnic focus. As a result, there has been an explosion of analyses of various facets of Romani lived experiences. Stewart (2013) renders an account of contemporary tendencies in Roma-related anthropological research, but the ever-increasing corpus of literature stemming from political science, cultural studies, geography, sociology, or international relations has not been structured in a similar account, and would be a near-impossible task to undertake, given the current prolific production of Roma-related research. The last decade in particular has seen the massive expansion of policy-oriented and applied research on the Roma, with major stakeholders such as the World Bank, the European Commission, or the United Nations Development Program commissioning research aimed at understanding the challenges Roma face in different contexts in order to justify various policy responses. Smaller organizations have also profited from the funds thus made available for applied, policy-oriented research. Often, the authors of these reports pendulate between institutions carrying out research—be they purely academic, looser networks of advocacy think-tanks, or smaller but "professionalized" NGOs. Some of them declare themselves activists, while others claim a more neutral stance; but the knowledge they produce is shaped in crucial ways—to our sense not fully explored yet— by their position at the crossroads between academic, activist, and policy trajectories. Importantly, the knowledge thus generated is molded by the ways in which funds are made available for the production of specific types of discourses grounded in particular visions of the Roma as a population in need of intervention (Timmer 2010; Schneeweis 2014; see also Ivasiuc, this volume).

With funds made available for Roma-related research from the policy sector, there has been an undeniable "inflation of expertise," which, understandably, regularly raises concerns of quality (Matras 2015). Some of these debates have tended to dichotomize between "neutral" and "objective" knowledge, on the one hand, and knowledge "tainted" and disqualified by activism, on the other hand; yet these rigid categorizations foreclose a more nuanced reflection on the ways in which knowledge is being produced and shaped. The simplistic division between "scientific" and "activist" research misses a number of important points. The "quietistic dream of unsullied professionalism" (Heyman 2010) may obscure the ideological roots of seemingly neutral "expert" knowledge. The production of knowledge is a social process, taking place in particular historical contexts and through dynamics replete with power and subjected to cultural trends, social pressures, and political interests. Claiming the impartiality and neutrality of knowledge attests at best a form of unpardonable naïveté regarding the ways in which knowledge is being influenced by its embeddedness in power-laden contexts, including through the meta-epistemological question of who has the power and appropriate forms of capital—symbolic, social—to legitimize the validity of research itself. Knowledge and power, we know at least since Foucault (Foucault and Gordon 1980), are inseparable. This brings us to the second point that these dichotomies miss, forcefully articulated by advocates for a public anthropology (Beck 2009; Beck and Maida 2013 and 2015): the sources of legitimacy of engaged research are grounded elsewhere than in purely epistemological criteria, requiring *not a choice,* but a constant *move* between social and epistemological commitments (Hale 2006: 105). Rather than positing engaged and disengaged forms of scholarship as antithetic, and advocating for one or the other, or superimposing critique and commitment in a single epistemological engagement, what emerges as unquestionably more productive is a dialectical move between them (Montesinos Coleman 2015), and also beyond them. This move allows for questioning the very categories and frames upon which both research and activism are predicated—again, a "trans of beyond" (Brubaker 2016). One of the meaningful messages which this collection of essays conveys is a call to move beyond simplistic dichotomies—"good" versus "bad" activism, "objective" versus "activist" research stemming from "Roma" versus "non-Roma" scholars—and to critically interrogate the contexts in which these debates and the constructed epistemological and political objects they criticize are produced, contested, and (de)legitimized, and how they further shape the assembling of knowledge. Far from being inconsequential and locked up in a putative ivory tower, the knowledge produced by scholars in positions of "experts" has the power to affect political and representational processes (Okely 1997; Willems 1997; van Baar 2011; Surdu 2015; Surdu and Kovats 2015; Law and Kovats 2018), making a compelling case for privileging reflexivity in scholarly writing.

Beyond the productivity of scholarly discomfort with prescribed categories, it is also worthwhile to reflect upon the emancipatory politics at the core of Romani activism, brimming with contradictions and identity double binds (Kovats 2003; Vermeersch 2006; Law and Kovats 2018). While some of these questions reemerge forcefully from the debates on the establishment of the ERIAC, some of the chapters in this volume directly engage with the contradictions of past and contemporary forms of activism. There is nothing of real simplicity and self-evidence in projects of emancipatory politics, and the often-ambivalent workings of activist politics should not be obscured by an uncritical taken-for-grantedness of empowerment projects' outcomes. The proliferation of the word "empowerment" itself has masked its ambiguities and the contradictory political projects in which it is embedded (Ivasiuc 2014; see also van Baar, this volume). Activism cannot do without a continuous and arduous "reflective practice" (Schon 1983), perpetually interrogating learned and unlearned lessons, and, more importantly, seeking other possible forms of being political.

Reflexivity as Practice: Arguments and Dialogues

The idea of this volume emerged during an exchange between the editors, in which an apparently simple question was posed: "How did you, as an activist, help the Roma through your research?" To this question, we found that very few unambiguous and comfortable answers could be given before carefully deconstructing every word of it. In lieu of an answer, many more questions emerged: about the possibilities and ethics of activism, the ontology of research as a tool for change, and the pitfalls of being all too certain that as activists or researchers—or both—we are *really* making a difference. None of these questions could circumvent the analysis of the complexities and ambivalence of both activism and research. What was initially requested as a relatively short and straightforward answer became a set of questions ultimately leading to an entire book project in which we set out to explore the intersection between contemporary—but also past and possibly future forms of—activism, and research involving Romani groups. Thus, the question was transformed to explore the mechanisms and phenomena that produce ambivalence in the seemingly straightforward endeavor to work with the Roma from activist and academic perspectives. Rather than aiming at building consensus, the volume is intended to unsettle certainties, to provoke questions, and to throw a "working dissensus" (see Ryder, this volume) among activists, researchers, and policy practitioners and professionals who find themselves at any of the intersections between these roles or fluctuate between their porous boundaries. The book is an attempt at bridging reflexivity and practice, and simultaneously an argument for the development of reflexivity *as practice* within both Romani activism and the academic production of knowledge. The authors set out to critically analyze key practices and current issues in Romani activism and academia, scrutinizing both established and emerging dynamics of Romani activism and the processes of knowledge production stemming from applied and academic research, and feeding into interventions of both governmental and nongovernmental actors. We explore the ambiguous legacies and contradictions of certain forms of activism, as well as of certain ways of conducting research, framing it, or aiming at transposing research into policy. But we also consider it crucial to explore, from the margins, certain openings and promises, both within Romani activism and academic research. The book is structured in three parts, each comprising three chapters entering in dialogue with each other, and with arguments gaining in complexity across the sections.

Renewing Methods, Renewing Sites

Romani activism, as a complex object of research, demands nuanced, nonbinary analyses, rooted in the historical and sociopolitical contexts in which it takes place, and critically aware of any underlying—explicit or implicit—normative or moral assumptions. In the first part, the authors make a case for in-depth ethnographies uniquely able to grasp the contradictions and ambiguities of activism and of the role of its protagonists. In this section, some of the ways in which activism has been framed in research become contested as simplistic and binary, whereas ethnographic approaches to instances of activism reveal the ambivalences and contradictions of historically and politically embedded activist stances and undertakings. The "local" emerges clearly as a paramount site demanding a lucid analysis beyond the temptation to romanticize it as the unique, authentic place of mobilization, but also beyond the tendency of the vast majority of analyses on Romani activism to overlook the "local" in favor of national or transnational contexts.

We start our volume with a sober analysis by Huub van Baar of the nexus between activism and research through the lens of the development of the Romani social movement in Europe, contemporaneous to the emergence of the "nongovernmental" as a distinct category of rule and research. The chapter sketches the historical and political context for the volume's analyses, which focus mostly on post-1989 Europe. Van Baar systematizes the last thirty years of Roma-related activism and policy-making, as well as the ways in which Roma-related scholarship analyzed these developments, in a periodization comprising three phases. The first period, van Baar argues, was characterized by the emergence of civil society organizations (CSOs) funded and organized mostly through support from Western-based donors and international governing organizations (IGOs). Many Roma activists became attached to these initiatives, and the emergence of the civil society was largely applauded as a welcome development facilitating the exercise of democracy in postsocialist contexts. Subsequently, many organizations became professionalized and progressively occupied a niche of service provision between state structures and communities. In this process of governmentalization, these CSOs sometimes forfeited their independence and had to adapt to their new position and relationship to power by making compromises to their agendas, adhering to the goals of well-defined funding streams. Scholarly assessment reflects this development in different ways: while some saw the governmentalization of CSOs as the consequence of their professionalization and a way to exert power through government structures, others analyzed it in terms of the rise of a "Gypsy industry" (Trehan 2001 and 2009; Barany 2002; Kóczé and Trehan 2009; Rostas 2009) and deplored the deviation and downgrading of activism toward mere self-interested service provision under neoliberal conditions. Finally, the third and ongoing period is marked by the "ethnic turn" of policy-making, with the instatement, in 2011, of the "EU Roma Framework" and the obligation of member states (MS) to devise national "integration" strategies. In the process, while the slogan "Nothing for the Roma without the Roma" became a mantra repeated in official documents and declarations of European Commission representatives, the participation of Roma civil society organizations in policy-making was minimized to formal consultation, with little, if any, influence.

Van Baar contends that the post-1989 development of the category of nongovernmentalism needs to be analyzed in the larger historical context in which it operates. Shaped simultaneously by both a participatory democratic and a neoliberal project focusing on the same concepts of empowerment and rights—in opposite directions, however—the Romani movement is a heteroclite and ambiguous phenomenon embedded in contemporary global political dynamics. This sharp and nuanced analysis is a welcome reminder to engage critically with developments within Romani activism, for some forms of activism contribute to the depoliticization of Romani issues by translating political vocabularies of empowerment into technocratic advocacy for individual inclusion on the labor market, seen—in neoliberal guise—as the passe-partout solution for all ailments.

Van Baar critiques certain strands of research on Roma activism for their tendency to affect a binary opposition between, on the one hand, a localism praising forms of grassroots, bottom-up, "authentic" mobilization of Roma (such as Pentecostal mobilizations), and, on the other hand, a form of universalizing activism imposing frames, practices, and vocabularies foreign to Roma "culture." He insists that forms of activism and mobilization must be analyzed in the wider historical developments in which they occur, against naïve constructions of "good" versus "bad" activism. Echoing earlier calls for ethnographic research on activism (Juris and Khasnabish 2013: 8), he calls for an anthroposociology of Roma-related activism focusing on life histories of activists, often traveling between scales and sites and, in the process, blurring or shifting boundaries.

The second contribution in the volume—Ana Chirițoiu's interrogation of the activist response to the 1993 Hădăreni conflict, in which mob violence led to the lynching of several Roma men and the burning of Roma houses—enters in dialogue with Huub van Baar's argument on several levels. Chirițoiu's account of activism in the aftermath of the conflict constitutes a prime example of in-depth analysis of activism, critically revisited over two decades later by Nicolae Gheorghe, as one of the main actors shaping the activist agenda around the case. She mobilizes her ethnographic research on the Hădăreni conflict and shows the contradictions of early activism reinterpreted—and thereby placed in a larger historical and sociopolitical perspective—by Nicolae Gheorghe. She reads the Hădăreni case as a cautionary tale of early postsocialist Romani activism and uses a historicizing approach to underline the contradictions inherent in the early post-1989 Romani movement, locked in a double bind of state opposition and transnational activism, in which local understandings and experiences were consciously effaced in favor of universal notions of justice and rights. In the process, "local knowledge" was lost between transnational strategies of the Romani movement to put Roma issues on the European political agenda as a matter of security, and to establish its own legitimacy by using universalizing human rights vocabularies. To some extent, this contributed to what Gheorghe himself (Gheorghe and Pulay 2013) characterized as a state of crisis of an activism largely estranged from "the local." Chirițoiu's analysis focuses on the process of truth-production deployed by the various actors involved in the postconflict intervention, and shows how the legitimizing use of repertoires pertaining to trauma and victimhood inhabits a "structural contradiction between humanitarian 'emotions' and strategic 'procedures.'" Through her refined, ethnographically informed analysis, "the local" reemerges, with clarity and in all its complexity, as a pertinent analytical site of research on political activism and its discomfitures.

Notwithstanding the multiplication, over the last thirty years, of ethnographic research sites—from multisited (Marcus 1995) to digital (Pink et al. 2015) ethnographies—"the local" remains for anthropologists a relevant site of research, a locus of knowledge production that deserves to stand central to scholarly investigation of forms of activist mobilization. "The local" features precisely at the core of László Fosztó's chapter. He focuses on the analysis of incongruities between activist agendas and local understandings of conflict, identity, and coexistence. Nicolae Gheorghe remains at the core of both activist mobilization and critical appraisal of the forms activism embodied, but moves on to a more scholarly reflection on the role of local knowledge in the process. Fosztó recounts his own experience of activism "from the margins" on two occasions, both involving Gheorghe and other activists and scholars, and both having at the core a conflict, either physical (the violent clashes and destruction of Roma property in Harghita county in 2009) or symbolic (the battles between proponents of "Rom" or *țigan*—in Romanian, "Gypsy"—as the "correct" ethnonym for the Roma). Analytically, Fosztó stresses the advantage of embedding inquiries on activism in the wider dynamics of state transformation, for, as he rightly claims, activism is almost always driven by attempts to transform the state. He also calls for nuanced understandings of both "state" and "activism," which seem all too often to be placed in the inescapable roles of the "good" activists versus a reified "bad" state.

By following closely the diverse threads of meaning woven in the case of the Harghita conflict, Fosztó shows how Nicolae Gheorghe, together with anthropologist Gergő Pulay, came to understand the various ways in which meanings became "lost in translation." The interpretation of the pro-Roma activist response as an anti-Hungarian, provocative manifestation, the refusal of the local communities to allow activists to meddle with the conflict, and the self-identification of the *Romungre* (Hungarian-speaking Roma residing in a predominantly Hungarian area of Transylvania) involved in the conflict as Hungarians, rather than Roma, unsettled simplistic and binary framings of the events in terms of "ethnic" conflict between Hungarian oppressors and Roma victims. While unveiling how local understandings differ in substantial ways from activist agendas, these misinterpretations also raised questions about the pertinence of activist discourses on Roma victimhood and universalistic human rights vocabularies, and signaled the need to call for an alternative discourse on "shared responsibility" and for a dialogue with local forms of knowledge (Gheorghe and Pulay 2009). As a result of a common, thorough reflection on the events by activists and scholars, new ways of engagement emerged as alternatives to contemporary forms of activism, and the role of critical scholars in the process was key to reaching nuanced understandings.

Fosztó advocates for nuanced understandings also in the second, symbolic, conflict recounted in his chapter, rejecting partisan positions on the necessity to impose one or another "correct" ethnonym. The reflexive encounters he narrates speak of the paramount meaning of local knowledge and the necessity, contra a "one-size-fits-all" approach, to allow for space for self-identification. Fosztó's analysis is a persuasive argument on the urgent need to permanently intersect scholarly reflexivity and activism, while allowing for researchers to shape their own posture either as fully engaged activists or as critical observers "from the margins," or, indeed, anywhere in between.

Renewing Epistemologies

The sober tone of the first part is followed in the second section by contributions with a clearly more engaged resonance, advocating for epistemological renewal within Romani studies. The three chapters of this part are critical of some of the current dominant dynamics in Roma-related research, and propose crucial shifts of perspective to enable and generate renewed kinds of scholarship better attuned with activist engagement. The contributions of this section take stock of scholarly literatures outside the narrow field of Romani studies and address wider issues of power relations within institutions producing knowledge.

Andrew Ryder explores the debates around the epistemological implications of conducting engaged forms of research, especially by Roma academics. In recent years, the EANRS, as the main forum of exchange among academics involved in researching Roma issues, has been the stage of telltale battles announcing a decisive transformation: power and the legitimacy of current hierarchies are being contested by Roma researchers increasingly joining the ranks of Romani studies academics and unsettling notions of objective, neutral knowledge. In many ways, this is a war already fought elsewhere and in earlier times: the birth of public anthropology as knowledge serving the aim of building a just world (Beck 2009; Beck and Maida 2015) bears testimony to the force of the idea that the potential of research should be used for emancipatory goals. The antithetic argument maintains faith in the illusion of objectivity, claiming that engaged research necessarily implies biased premises on which it is judged improper to construct meaningful knowledge. At stake are, unmistakably, definitions of "meaningful": while for adepts of scientism, meaningful knowledge is objective, detached and neutral, for activist researchers, the meaningfulness of their knowledge is derived from its usefulness to bring about transformative change. Through a factional conversation creatively staged, Ryder reenacts the dialogues within the EANRS, deliberately polarizing the positions on this debate so as to render the fracture all the more striking. He comments on the opposition between scientism and critical research by stressing how the first favors the detachment of academics from the object of their inquiry, whereas the latter values embodied knowledge from the standpoint of the researched, blurring, in the process, the boundary between researchers and the people whose lives they investigate—and thus also between research and activism. Ryder emphasizes that research is shaped in crucial ways by institutional and economic factors, and comments on the example of EU-funded research, which, in the case of Roma-related knowledge production, risks reinforcing existing problematic power relations. On the one hand, while the participation of Roma in research is a trendy buzzword in applications for funding, it appears to be more often than not tokenistic; on the other hand, the bureaucracy inherent in the process of accessing EU funds acts as to favor professionalized NGOs above community-based organizations (CBOs), which might have a broader Roma participation. Yet the chapter ends on a more optimistic tone: while noting the recent motion proposed by Thomas Acton and Yaron Matras within the Gypsy Lore Society, recognizing that the institution has not been immune to prejudicial attitudes toward the Roma and committing itself to "promote knowledge of and engagement with Romani communities," Ryder is confident that the access of Romani scholars to the community of Romani studies will promote a paradigm shift toward more engaged forms of research, and predicates that diverging views should enter into a constructive dialogue.

Taking up the topic of the ingression of scholars of Romani background in academic circles, Angéla Kóczé's chapter uses autoethnography and accounts of other Roma women in academia to expand on the adversities they encounter in their attempts to build scientific and professional legitimacy among peers. The women she interviews emphasize the painstaking labor of shaping a space for themselves—as Roma and as women—and creating themselves "from scratch, in environments where one is not supposed to exist," for, until very recently, in the research equation, Roma were objectified as researched subjects, and never in the powerful position of those who actively shape knowledge. Kóczé thus deeply unsettles a readership engaged in the ethnographic investigation of Roma lived experience, by contesting its position as research object solely and claiming the legitimacy to generate knowledge on its own terms.

To make sense of the struggles Roma women face in academic environments and to chart the hierarchies and the power relations imbued with racism and sexism, which their presence unsettles, Kóczé mobilizes feminist and critical race theory, emphasizing the intersectionality of the positions her interlocutors occupy, as women and as Roma. She delivers a poignant critique of mainstream Romani studies by building further on Romani and Black feminist scholars who pointed out racist and sexist epistemologies at work, as well as power imbalances in academia itself. She criticizes the choice of Romani studies to work with the analytical category of "ethnicity" instead of "race," showing how the emphasis on Roma as an "ethnic" group renders racism invisible, thus debilitating a critique of the hierarchies though which the Roma are constructed as an inferior "culture," in what Balibar (1991) termed "neo-racism." For Kóczé, as for her interlocutors, race is, to the contrary, a very practical issue: in academia, the racialization of Romani scholars amounts to their inferiorization and infantilization, often depriving them of the legitimacy to shape the way in which knowledge is created. She ponders on the pivotal role of these women in transgressing borders, a metaphor fitting at once the act of an insurgent trespassing of invisible but powerful boundaries into the headquarters where knowledge is assembled, and the permanent back-and-forth crossing of the porous—and often completely dissolved—border between academia and activism. In line with earlier arguments underlining the intrinsically dialogical character of Romani feminism (Kóczé 2008), she emphasizes the role of Roma women in academia as skillful "passers" between worlds, in a position from which they "seek to create a politics of possibility" not only by connecting them, but also by playing a paramount role as mentors of the emerging generation of Romani activist-scholars.

To a large extent, the contributions by Ryder and Kóczé can be read as reactions to the institutional debates in Romani studies about the engagement of Romani scholars, exemplifying marvelously how academic literature, rather than being produced by neutral actors in aseptic and "objective" environments devoid of power relations, is carved in crucial ways by debates and power struggles in the scientific community: as the locus where knowledge is generated is itself composed of a social fabric rife with power struggles, knowledge cannot be detached from the context of its production.

The interconnectedness between knowledge and the environment of its own genesis is also one of the arguments in the last chapter of this section. In line with the first section's emphasis on the usefulness of ethnographic research methods, while continuing to question some of the strands of Romani activism, Ana Ivasiuc critiques the pervasive narrative of victimhood and entrapment transpiring from militant advocacy discourses and "gray literature" coproduced by certain NGOs and powerful donors, which sometimes also percolates through in academic writings. Using observations from her experience as research coordinator in a Roma NGO, Ivasiuc contextualizes the production of the victimhood narrative, by showing how and why this discourse is manufactured at the heart of the development apparatus in which CSOs, forced to compete for funds, are compelled to fabricate a discourse based on buzzwords and tropes of victimhood, which simultaneously constitutes a practice of accessing funds. This narrative impels a pessimistic bias, which sometimes bends the interpretation of research data, altering the process of selection of quantitative findings to stress the shortfalls and inadequacies of the Roma. She shows how the emphasis on the "lacks" and "deficits" of Roma, simultaneous to the neglect of their forms of agency, is a perverse form of Orientalism sustaining paternalistic policy interventions and feeding the wider discursive needs of the development apparatus. Building on her ethnographic study of the conflicts within the implementation of a World Bank–sponsored community development project, Ivasiuc discusses forms of agency in which Roma groups engage, suggesting a renewal of activist epistemologies within and through gray literature attentive to these forms of agency.

Renewing Activisms

The last section of the volume explores some of the promising "margins" potentially able to renew Romani activism.

In her chapter, Margaret Greenfields argues that besides activism for the empowerment of Roma, and high quality research providing "moral and practical arguments for change," the third crucial element likely to bring about the betterment of Roma lives is appropriate policy. While the volume addresses the first two dimensions extensively, her contribution specifically deals with the underresearched nexus between Roma-related activism, research, and policy, with a marked emphasis on the latter. She emphasizes the need for pragmatism in channeling change through the institutional paths of policy-making, with clear rules defining which types of knowledge are relevant to policy makers and which are likely to be shelved as irrelevant. Greenfields uses quantitative data provided by the EANRS on its membership composition to show the unmistakable underrepresentation of policy as an area of expertise among researchers dealing with Roma issues. Noting the increase—in both demand and supply—of policy reports and advice on Roma-related issues throughout Europe, she suggests that although scholars are involved in significant numbers in providing policy consultancy to various national and transnational bodies, many of them lack the training, experience, and insights into the policy-making machinery that would enhance the chances of their knowledge to be incorporated effectively into successful measures. She suggests that activist scholars should become familiar with policy environments in order to "translate their research into policy outcomes," and that the constraints of the policy-making process should be taken into account when imparting policy advice. While she acknowledges that pertinent criticism to policy-making has been formulated both within the anthropology of policy literature and by Romani studies scholars, she advocates for a pragmatic, closer association between activist research and policy-making, specifically on the latter's terms. Greenfields argues that there is a gap between academics and policy makers and contends that scholars can bridge this gap not only by attuning their recommendations to the requirements of policy makers in terms of theoretical models, terminology, and pragmatism, but also by attending to the "packaging" of their knowledge, for instance by refraining from expressing "too great a criticism of the administrative regime's actions," and also by using clear tools to showcase their recommendations, such as case studies. Greenfields makes the case for confronting policy makers with the concrete problems encountered by their "end-users," and provides a telling example of how she involved Gypsy and Traveller activists, as well as homeless activists, in a training she organized with policy makers in the United Kingdom, in which knowledge was coproduced and policy makers were practically confronted with the issues they had to solve through policy. Finally, advocating for "practice-based approaches to critical thinking" in policy advice, Greenfields warns against the dangers of "overthinking" and complexifying beyond measure the knowledge presented to policy makers, arguing that such approaches are likely to stall intervention or reduce it to substandard practice, and that the ethical choice of activist researchers should ultimately lie in opting for what "works" in policy toward the practical improvement of the living circumstances of its "end-users." For activist researchers to whom this is a paramount, immediate aim, Greenfields thus opens up the terrain of practical research activism through policy advice.

From Europe's margins, Danielle V. Schoon investigates in the next chapter the case of Turkish *Romanlar,* whose activism stands in stark opposition to universalizing, European-based forms of identity politics activism. Schoon's argument thus provincializes European Roma activism, questioning its universalistic assumptions and revealing the different logic at play in the formulation of collective identities and demands of Turkey's *Romanlar,* analyzed in its wider historical and political context. The chapter starts from the double observation that, on the one hand, representatives of the *Roman-*

lar were absent from the mass protest movement of Gezi Park in May 2013, yet that, on the other hand, their presence was assumed. Using this example, she explicates the theoretical and political challenges that the case of activists for the rights of the *Romanlar* in Turkey pose to European scholars and activists. To understand the dynamics of *Roman* activism in contemporary Turkey, Schoon embeds her analysis in the historical genealogy of the republican conception of difference and citizenship, in which commonness based on shared Islam overrode ethnic, linguistic, or cultural differences, constructed as illegitimate and threatening to nation building. It is within this framework that the *Romanlar* historically claimed their right to equality. In recent times, Turkey's republican conception of citizenship stood under tension, notably from pressures by the international community, and in particular the EU, to shift toward the framework of minority rights.

Yet *Roman* associations, indifferent or even hostile to international pressures for the recognition of minority rights, have opted for a different strategy, in which class, rather than cultural differences, is underscored, allowing them to formulate policy claims to address inequality in terms of poverty. Schoon argues that this strategy should compel both scholarship on Romani issues and Romani activism to rethink critically the categories upon which European Romani activism has built its identity politics, including, crucially, the category of "civil society," which works to merely reconfigure, rather than dissolve, existing power relations. The example of the Turkish *Romanlar,* who practice fluid, contextual identities in the idioms available to them in a "politics of the governed" (Chatterjee 2004), underscores their agency in the process of forging political subjectivities that contrast, in many ways, the ones largely prescribed by European Romani activism. In the subtext, the argument that a conscious renewal of scholarship and activism could not come into being without the scrutiny of the margins of "mainstream" possibilities is compelling.

We end our volume appropriately with the examination of an emerging form of militancy, at once challenging and rejuvenating current trends, namely Roma youth activism. In her chapter, Anna Mirga-Kruszelnicka illustrates how the emerging Roma youth movement shares common characteristics epitomizing a renewal of Romani activism, defying its established patterns while contesting it from the margins. She begins her argument by painting with large brushstrokes a current "panorama of Romani affairs" as background against (in both senses of the word) which youth activism takes shape. She contends that the increase of interest among international organizations to develop policies for the Roma, and the booming of both Roma and non-Roma civil society organizations incorporating Romani issues on their agenda, together with the availability of funding for related interventions, led to ambiguous dynamics. The inflation of "expertise" in Roma-related

policy dialogues, as well as the cooption of professionalized NGOs as deliverers of government services, have often worked to cement old hierarchies
or create new ones—such as the subalternization of grassroots organizations
(GRO) to professionalized organizations, and the former's subsequent diminished access to funding. Thus, despite the increased attention to Romani
issues on political agendas nationally and supranationally, nongovernmental actors did not substantially challenge existing power imbalances. To the
contrary: an overpopulated domain became rife with tensions over funding,
expertise, and legitimacy, and the cooption of Roma NGOs has often signified in practice that the role of these organizations in mobilizing, organizing,
and engaging with Roma communities has been neglected or squarely abandoned in favor of bureaucratic compliance with donors' demands for reports
and grants applications.

Against this gridlock, Mirga-Kruszelnicka depicts the emergence of the
Roma youth movement as a persuasive and energetic contender, capable to
challenge existing dominant trends on a number of levels. Through the analysis of its identity discourses and practices of association, Mirga-Kruszelnicka
argues that the Roma youth agenda marks a paradigm shift and a significant
departure from current forms of activism. First, with regards to the particular configuration of a Romani identity uprooted from frames of stigmatization, victimhood, and subalternity, the Roma youth movement promotes a
positive identity grounded in ethnic pride, and distinctly aims at constructing narratives of self-esteem and empowerment. Second, Roma youth activism engages with "the grassroots" to a significant extent, framing Roma
communities as a resource and consciously challenging the gap between the
established organizations and their constituencies. In the process, they forge
new forms of activism away from service provision and tokenistic participation, toward robust frames of community engagement sustaining the development of political consciousness. Third, youth activism aims at broader,
more inclusive coalition-building processes, in which not only Roma participate, but also non-Roma and actors with perceived common political
interests, such as other minorities, thereby reconnecting and intersecting
Roma activism with wider social movements in an attempt to build larger
interest-based alliances. While Roma youth activism is exposed to a number
of challenges, Mirga-Kruszelnicka contends that the paradigm shift signified
by its emergence is paramount to understanding the future possibilities of a
rejuvenation of Romani activism.

By bringing together all the various strands of debates both within research on Roma issues and within Romani activism, the volume lays bare
the cracks and tensions of their intersection, pointing toward spaces of
moderate renewal or radical ruptures in both. And to formulate our intent
in the familiar language of the gift, the volume's impulse is to return the gift

to the people and the institutional nodes in the Romani movement that have allowed or encouraged the contributors to examine current developments through research, in the hope that activists and researchers will find it useful to reflect upon the legacies of Roma-related research and activism explored in the volume, and, by developing critical reflexivity, to be part of a meaningful renewal of both. Ultimately, the volume speaks of activism as a mode of research (Juris and Khasnabish 2013: 8), but also of research as a vital posture of engagement.

Ana Ivasiuc is an anthropologist affiliated with the Centre for Conflict Studies at the Philipps University in Marburg, Germany. Through her past activity as a research coordinator within a Romani NGO in Romania, she has conducted research at the confluence between Romani activism and academia. After obtaining her Ph.D. in 2014 from the National School of Political Science and Public Administration in Bucharest, she joined a Roma-related postdoctoral research project at the Justus Liebig University in Giessen. She is the winner of the 2017 Herder–Council for European Studies Fellowship.

Notes

1. A note on terminology is in order when writing about "the Roma" as if the label denoted a coherent and self-evident whole. Some of the contributions of the volume approach "the Roma" in their many identitary manifestations: Hungarian Roma, or *Romungre* from Transylvania; Turkish Muslim *Romanlar*; Gypsies, Roma, and Travellers from the United Kingdom, etc. Some others speak of "the Roma" as a more vague and general umbrella term. The editors' choice has been to let the authors use the term that they saw fit, in a bid to reflect the heterogeneity of "the Roma" under this single label. Whereas many scholarly works include a discussion on the preferred terminology and opt for various strategies of labeling, often concurring with political views on the (in)correctness of particular terms, we have preferred to leave out such discussions, treated more in detail in other works (among many others, Vermeersch 2005; Tremlett 2009; Agarin 2014; Law and Kovats 2018). Within the volume, Fosztó's chapter deals with the naming battles in the Romanian context, offering insights into the political stakes of such controversies. While being aware both of the heterogeneity of groups artificially brought under the label "Roma," and of the politics of labeling, on the one hand, and identity production, on the other hand, this discussion is beyond the scope of the volume. For linguistic parsimony, we will use "Roma" to mean the constellation of groups self-identifying as Roma, Gypsies, Sinti, Manouches, Kaale, Romanichals, etc., and Roma/Romani as the alternating forms of the corresponding adjective.

2. There are some inconsistencies in the different accounts of the events in the Hungarian, German, and Romanian press. I am grateful to László Fosztó for pointing this out to me.
3. For an overview of the politics of Roma in Europe and a sophisticated analysis of its complexities, see Law and Kovats 2018.

References

Acton, Thomas. 2016. "Scientific Racism, Popular Racism and the Discourse of the Gypsy Lore Society." *Ethnic and Racial Studies* 39 (7): 1187–1204. doi:10.1080/01419870.2015.1105988.

Acton, Thomas, and Andrew Ryder. 2015. "From Clienthood to Critique: The Role of Nicolae Gheorghe as Mediator and Catalyst in the Roma Awakening." *Roma Rights: Journal of the European Roma Rights Centre* 1: 5–18.

Agarin, Timofey. 2014. "Introduction." In *When Stereotype Meets Prejudice: Antiziganism in European Societies,* edited by Timofey Agarin, 11–25. Stuttgart: Ibidem.

Balibar, Etienne. 1991. "Is There a Neo-Racism?" In *Race, Nation, Class: Ambiguous Identities,* edited by Etienne Balibar and Immanuel M. Wallerstein, 17–28. London: Verso.

Barany, Zoltan. 2002. *The East European Gypsies.* Cambridge: Cambridge University Press.

Beck, Sam. 2009. "Introduction: Public Anthropology." *Anthropology in Action* 16 (2): 1–13. doi:10.3167/aia.2009.160201.

Beck, Sam, and Carl Maida, eds. 2013. *Toward Engaged Anthropology.* New York: Berghahn Books.

———, eds. 2015. *Public Anthropology in a Borderless World.* New York: Berghahn Books.

Brubaker, Rogers. 2016. *Trans: Gender and Race in an Age of Unsettled Identities.* Princeton, NJ: Princeton University Press.

Čada, Karel. 2012. "Social Exclusion of the Roma and Czech Society." In *The Gypsy "Menace": Populism and the New Anti-Gypsy Politics,* edited by Michael Stewart, 67–79. London: Hurst.

Chatterjee, Partha. 2004. *The Politics of the Governed: Reflections on Popular Politics in Most of the World.* New York: Columbia University Press.

Ecoleusti. 2017. "Antiromaistischer Pogrom in Gheorgheni/Rumänien." [Anti-Roma pogrom in Gheorgheni/Romania]. Ecoleusti blog. Accessed 3 April 2017. https://ecoleusti.wordpress.com/2017/04/01/antiromaistischer-pogrom-in-gheorghenirumanien-31-3-2017/.

Foucault, Michel, and Colin Gordon. 1980. *Power/Knowledge: Selected Interviews and Other Writings, 1972–1977.* New York: Pantheon Books.

Gheorghe, Nicolae, and Gergő Pulay. 2009. "Raport de analiză a violenţelor împotriva romilor din Ungaria şi România." [Analysis report of Anti-Roma violence in Hungary and Romania]. Bucharest: unpublished manuscript.

———. 2013. "Choices to Be Made and Prices to Be Paid: Potential Roles and Consequences in Roma Activism and Policy-Making." In *From Victimhood to Citizenship: The Path of Roma Integration; A Debate,* edited by Will Guy, 41–100. Budapest: Kiadó.

Hale, Charles R. 2006. "Activist Research v. Cultural Critique: Indigenous Land Rights and the Contradictions of Politically Engaged Anthropology." *Cultural Anthropology* 21 (1): 96–120.

Harrison, Faye, ed. 1991. *Decolonizing Anthropology: Moving Further toward an Anthropology for Liberation.* Washington, DC: American Anthropological Association.
Heyman, Josiah M. 2010. "Activism in Anthropology: Exploring the Present through Eric R. Wolf's Vietnam-Era Work." *Dialectical Anthropology* 34 (2): 287–93.
Ivasiuc, Ana. 2014. "Empowering the Roma: Lessons from Development Practice." Dissertation, National School of Political Science and Public Administration, Bucharest, Romania.
Ivașcu, Mihai. 2017. "Incident între romi și maghiari la Gheorgheni." [Incident between Roma and Hungarians in Gheorgheni]. *HotNews,* 3 April 2017. Accessed 11 April 2017. http://www.hotnews.ro/stiri-esential-21696928-conflict-intre-romi-maghiari-din-gheorgheni-ungurii-incendiat-casa-mai-multe-bunuri-dupa-doi-min ori-etnie-roma-furat-30-000-lei-din-masina-unui-batran-din-localitate.htm.
Juris, Jeffrey, S., and Alex Khasnabish. 2013. "Introduction: Ethnography and Activism within Networked Spaces of Transnational Encounter." In *Insurgent Encounters: Transnational Activism, Ethnography and the Political,* edited by Jeffrey S. Juris and Alex Khasnabish, 1–36. Durham, NC: Duke University Press.
Kóczé, Angéla. 2008. "Ethnicity and Gender in the Politics of Roma Identity in the Post-Communist Countries." In *Violence and Gender in the Globalized World: The Intimate and the Extimate,* edited by Sanja Bahun-Radunović and Julie Rajan, 175–88. London: Ashgate.
Kóczé, Angéla, and Nidhi Trehan. 2009. "Racism, (Neo-) Colonialism and Social Justice: The Struggle for the Soul of the Romani Movement in Post-Socialist Europe." In *Racism Postcolonialism Europe,* edited by Graham Huggan and Ian Law, 50–76. Liverpool: Liverpool University Press.
Kovats, Martin. 2003. "The Politics of Roma Identity: Between Nationalism and Destitution." *OpenDemocracy.* Accessed 27 May 2017. http://www.opendemocracy.net/people-migrationeurope/article_1399.jsp.
Law, Ian, and Martin Kovats. 2018. *Rethinking Roma: Identities, Politicisation, and New Agendas.* London: Palgrave Macmillan.
Lee, Jonathan. 2017. "Roma Burned from Their Homes as Lessons Go Unlearned in Romania." *ERRC* blog. Accessed 8 April 2017. http://www.errc.org/blog/roma-burned-from-their-homes-as-lessons-go-unlearned-in-romania/165.
Lorey, Isabell. 2015. *State of Insecurity: Government of the Precarious.* Translated from German by Aileen Derieg. London: Verso.
Magazzini, Tina. 2016. "Cultural Institutions as a Combat Sport: Reflections on the European Roma Institute." *The Age of Human Rights Journal* 7: 50–76. doi:10.17561/Tahrj.N7.9.
Marcus, George E. 1995. "Ethnography in/of the World System: The Emergence of Multi-Sited Ethnography." *Annual Review of Anthropology* 24 (1): 95–117.
Matras, Yaron. 2015. "Europe's Neo-Traditional Roma Policy: Marginality Management and the Inflation of Expertise." In *Romani Worlds: Academia, Policy and Modern Media,* edited by Eben Friedman and Victor A. Friedman, 29–47. Cluj-Napoca: Editura Institutului pentru Studierea Problemelor Minorităților Naționale.
Montesinos Coleman, Lara. 2015. "Ethnography, Commitment, and Critique: Departing from Activist Scholarship." *International Political Sociology* 9: 263–80.
Okely, Judith. 1997. "Some Political Consequences of Theories of Gypsy Ethnicity: The Place of the Intellectual." In *After Writing Culture: Epistemology and Praxis in Contemporary Anthropology,* edited by Allison James, Jennifer L. Hockey, and Andrew Dawson, 224–43. London: Routledge.

Parászka, Boróka. 2017. "Bis alles Feuer fängt." [Until all catches fire]. *Pusztastranger* blog. Accessed 3 April 2017. http://pusztastranger.blogspot.de/2017/04/bis-alles-feuer-fangt.html.

Pester Lloyd. 2017. "Selbstjustiz, Rassismus oder Bandenkrieg?" [DIY Justice, Racism or Clan Feud?]. *Pester Lloyd,* 3 April 2017. Accessed 3 April 2017. http://www.pester lloyd.net/html/1714pgromromarum.html.

Pink, Sarah, Heather Horst, John Postill, Larissa Hjorth, Tania Lewis, and Jo Tacchi. 2015. *Digital Ethnography: Principles and Practice.* London: Sage.

Rostas, Iulius. 2009. "The Romani Movement in Romania: Institutionalization and (De)mobilization." In *Romani Politics in Contemporary Europe,* edited by Nando Sigona and Nidhi Trehan, 159–85. New York: Palgrave Macmillan.

Schneeweis, Adina. 2014. "Communicating the Victim: Nongovernmental Organizations Advocacy Discourses for Roma Rights." *Communication, Culture and Critique* 8: 235–53. doi:10.1111/cccr.12077.

Schon, Donald A. 1983. *The Reflective Practitioner: How Professionals Think in Action.* New York: Basic Books.

Stewart, Michael, ed. 2012. *The Gypsy "Menace": Populism and the New Anti-Gypsy Politics.* London: Hurst.

———. 2013. "Roma and Gypsy 'Ethnicity' as a Subject of Anthropological Inquiry." *Annual Review of Anthropology* 42: 415–32.

———. 2017. "Nothing about Us without Us, or the Dangers of a Closed-Society Research Paradigm." *Romani Studies* 27 (2): 125–146.

Surdu, Mihai. 2015. *Expert Frames: Scientific and Policy Practices of Roma Classification.* Budapest: Central European University Press.

Surdu, Mihai, and Martin Kovats. 2015. "Roma Identity as an Expert-Political Construction." *Social Inclusion* 3 (5): 5–18.

Timmer, Andria. 2010. "Constructing the 'Needy Subject': NGO Discourses of Roma Need." *PoLAR: Political and Legal Anthropology Review* 33 (2): 264–81.

Trehan, Nidhi. 2001. "In the Name of the Roma? The Role of Private Foundations and NGOs" In *Between Past and Future: The Roma of Central and Eastern Europe,* edited by Will Guy, 134–49. Hatfield: University of Hertfordshire Press.

———. 2009. "The Romani Subaltern within Neoliberal European Civil Society." In *Romani Politics in Contemporary Europe,* edited by Nando Sigona and Nidhi Trehan, 51–71. New York: Palgrave Macmillan.

Tremlett, Annabel. 2009. "Bringing Hybridity to Heterogeneity in Romani Studies." *Romani Studies* 19: 147–68.

Tuhiwai-Smith, Linda. 1999. *Decolonizing Methodologies: Research and Indigenous Peoples.* London: Zed Books; Dunedin: University of Otago Press.

van Baar, Huub. 2011. *The European Roma: Minority Representation, Memory and the Limits of Transnational Governmentality.* Amsterdam: F&N.

———. 2014. "The Emergence of a Reasonable Anti-Gypsyism in Europe." In *When Stereotype Meets Prejudice: Antiziganism in European Societies,* edited by Timofey Agarin, 27–44. Stuttgart: Ibidem.

Vermeersch, Peter. 2005. "Marginality, Advocacy, and the Ambiguities of Multiculturalism: Notes on Romani Activism in Central Europe." *Identities* 12: 451–78.

———. 2006. *The Romani Movement: Minority Politics and Ethnic Mobilization in Contemporary Central Europe.* Oxford: Berghahn Books.

Willems, Wim. 1997. *In Search of the True Gypsy: From Enlightenment to Final Solution.* London: Frank Cass.

PART I

❋ ❋ ❋

RENEWING METHODS, RENEWING SITES

CHAPTER 1

❁ ❁ ❁

NEOLIBERALISM AND THE SPIRIT OF NONGOVERNMENTALISM

Toward an Anthroposociology of Roma-Related Engagement and Activism

Huub van Baar

The fall of socialism has inaugurated a new chapter in the history of Roma-related activism and has coincided with the diversification, strengthening, and deepening of the Romani social movement in and beyond Europe (Vermeersch 2006; van Baar 2011a). One of the profoundly new conditions under which the post-1989 movement has taken place has been the Europeanization of the representation of the Roma. What I have called "the Europeanization of Roma representation" designates, first, the post-1989 problematization of the Roma in terms of their "Europeanness"; second, the classification of heterogeneous groups scattered over Europe under the umbrella term "Roma"; and, third, the devising of Europe-wide programs dedicated to their rights, inclusion, development, empowerment, and participation (van Baar 2011a: 153–89). Historically, those who are called, or call themselves, "Roma" have often been considered a "non-European" minority, with origins outside of Europe, "dangerous" for "progress" and "civilization" in Europe. Yet, since the fall of Central and Eastern European state socialism, the Roma have been reclassified as a "European minority" to be respected and included as "true Europeans."

This development toward Europeanizing the Roma's status and representation represents a unique case, as no other minority has become the target of such wide-ranging processes of Europeanization, nor of the large-scale development programs that have been launched by state-related institutions, international governing organizations (IGOs) such as the European Union (EU) and the World Bank, and a wide range of civil society organizations (CSOs). The Europeanization of Roma representation has enabled (at least) some of the Roma—primarily Romani activists engaged in governmental boards, advocacy groups, activist networks, and grassroots movements—to become critical players in the public and political debates about their status and in the large policy fabric that has been built around them. By developing their own heterogeneous social movements across and beyond Europe, Romani actors have entered the post-1989 political scene as active agents, rather than passive "victims" of how others have continued to represent them (Vermeersch 2006; van Baar 2011a; 2013). Increasingly, they are not just the objects and subjects of discourses, programs, and instruments of inclusion, development, and participation. The Europeanization of Roma representation could be understood as a shift from considering the Roma as the externalized outsiders against which Europe defines itself to representing them as the internalized outsiders to be integrated as participating "true Europeans."

At the same time, this shift does not represent a decisive, but only a highly ambivalent, turn toward considering the Roma as "true Europeans" (van Baar 2011a; 2015). Current practices, such as the ongoing expulsion of Romani migrants from France and Europe-wide manifestations of antigypsyism, show that the Roma frequently still end up in the symbolic or administrative cloud of "non-Europeans." Despite the institutionalized promises of inclusion and European citizenship, both at home and in the European countries into which the Roma have migrated since 1989, they continue to be dealt with differently than other national and EU citizens. Thus, they "need to put in additional efforts to be regarded as equal and full citizens of the states where they live and the 'Europe' to which they belong" (van Baar 2011a: 18).

The ambivalences inherent to the Europeanization of Roma representation, and particularly the trend of the last decade toward a deterioration, rather than improvement, of the situation of many Roma, have encouraged several scholars and activists to reflect on the role that Roma-related activism has played in generating these ambiguous results. This chapter focuses on the post-1989 development of the heterogeneous Romani social movement and takes stock of the rise and impact of "nongovernmentalism," that is the emergence of the "nongovernmental" as a category of rule and research in Roma-related policy-making and scholarship. The focus on nongovernmentalism does not imply that I seamlessly identify it with Roma-related activism or the Romani social movement, as if these are just three terms for one and the same phenomenon. Yet, many activists associate or align themselves with a more or less organized form of the "nongovernmental." Therefore, the "nongovernmental" could be considered as a kind of interface of activist and scholarly attitudes toward desired or required societal change. Thus, rather than discussing varieties of activism that have been developed since 1989, or examining the discourses and practices that have emerged in informal and formal manifestations of the Romani movement, this chapter focuses on the nexus of activism and research through the lens of the emergence of the category of the "nongovernmental."

I will distinguish three phases in the post-1989 period in which the policy relevance and scholarly appraisal of the role of CSOs have been discussed along different lines. First, I will discuss the reasons of the rapid rise, in the immediate aftermath of 1989, of civil society organizations, which include nongovernmental, faith-based, and grassroots organizations (NGOs, FBOs, GROs). This European pattern followed a more global one, according to which researchers and national and international policy makers considered CSOs as potentially effective partners and channels in attempts at challenging the "authoritarian" remainders of postauthoritarian regimes and transforming them into liberal democratic, economically sustainable, and "minority-friendly" states that would be able to address more effectively issues of poverty, development, and inequality.

This first phase, in which a relatively positive image of CSOs and their capabilities to "make a difference" dominated, would quickly be followed by a second phase in which, at the policy front, CSOs have increasingly been "governmentalized." The governmentalization of civil society designates a trend in which the professionalization of CSOs is occurring hand in hand with their attachment to the more formal and institutionalized governmental structures at state and suprastate levels, thereby often (though not necessarily) diminishing their activist independence (van Baar 2011a). Accordingly, the scholarly assessments of CSOs have also become more mixed with, at the one end of the spectrum, those who consider the institutionalization of activism as an inevitable result of the activists' professionalization and their aim at exercising power within official governmental structures and, at the spectrum's other end, those who understand this governmentalization as a troublesome reduction of CSOs to mere service deliverers or, even worse, puppets of an omnipotent and destructive neoliberalism. At the policy level, this second phase was coinciding with the trend in which the largest donor of Roma-related development programs, the EU, mostly shifted its support toward the direct funding of its candidate member states' governments, even though many other donors continued to fund Roma-related CSOs directly. This trend took place at the same time as negotiations about the EU access of these states continued and, finally, led to the eastward enlargement of the Union in 2004 and 2007. Some donors stopped their funding of Roma-related CSOs in the new EU members directly after these entered the EU, which required some of these CSOs to shift their activities more eastward to those countries that are (still) not EU member states.

We can distinguish a third phase that has started relatively recently with the "ethnic turn" in EU policies. This turn designates the move in EU support for the Roma toward the explicit devising of policies for Roma, a shift from generic to specific Roma-related policies that is particularly embodied by the 2011 launch of the so-called EU Roma Framework (European Commission 2011a). Apparently against the idea behind this framework, in many EU countries CSOs have been sidelined or deliberately excluded from the processes toward the development, implementation, and evaluation of the so-called National Roma Integration Strategies (NRIS) that these states were encouraged to devise in this framework's context. Consequently, we are currently facing, it seems, a phase in which Roma-related CSOs have increasingly less to say about how Roma policies are (to be) envisioned, designed, implemented, and assessed.

This chapter discusses the ways in which we could explain this post-1989 development, including the rise of nongovernmentalism and its development toward the current, third phase. Simultaneously, I will reflect on the ways in which researchers have assessed the rise and impact of nongovernmentalism, particularly vis-à-vis the abilities of CSOs to impact political and policy debates, agendas, and transformations. I will argue that, in Roma-related scholarship, the assessment of the emergence of the "nongovernmental" as a category of rule and research has frequently and primarily been led by a largely counterproductive idea that we need to be either "for" or "against" CSOs. In line with the approach to the Romani movement that I have discussed elsewhere (van Baar 2011a; 2012b; 2013), therefore, I call for a critical "anthroposociology" of Roma-related activism and nongovernmentalism, in which these phenomena are interrogated in their historical and interdisciplinary settings and assessed not so much in moral terms but, rather, vis-à-vis their critical potentiality to make a difference to the situation of the Roma and to the ways in which we see and study them.

Roma Activism and the Post-1989 Governmentalization of Civil Society

In the aftermath of 1989 and until well into the 1990s, Western (European) governments, donors, and IGOs primarily perceived new and already established Roma-related CSOs as entry points into postauthoritarian societies in Central and Eastern Europe and as actors who could (possibly) effectively

challenge authoritarian legacies and the ways in which these were considered to impact issues such as the discrimination, poverty, and marginalization of the Roma. Initially, relatively well-established, Western-based
NGOs with a background in advocacy work that had begun in the 1960s and
70s—most notably, Minority Rights Group International, Amnesty International, and Helsinki Watch (later Human Rights Watch)—as well as new
associations such as the Project on Ethnic Relations and the Open Society
Institute (OSI), played an important role in bringing to the fore the violations of the rights of Central and Eastern European Roma. In their reports
of the early and mid-1990s, which were considerably based on information
received from domestic Romani activists and scholars, as well as from local or national advocacy and dissident groups that were already established
during the socialist era, these CSOs presented the situation of the Roma as a
"human emergency" (van Baar 2011b; 2018). Indirectly, these informal and
more formally organized local groups of activists, intellectuals, and other
advocates played a crucial role in how, through the vital and indispensable
link of several of these international NGOs, the Roma gradually emerged
onto the agenda of IGOs, the EU in particular (Ram 2010; van Baar 2011a).
At about the same time, established and new Western-based CSOs with a
background in community building, local development, microfinancing and
poor relief—among them several FBOs—started to fund (usually) small-
scale initiatives dedicated to improving the living circumstances of Central
and Eastern European Roma.

Both in the case of advocacy work and in that of several development projects, IGOs and larger donors such as Cordaid, OSI, and Western (European)
ministries of foreign affairs and development assistance started to perceive
of (the founding and funding of) these local civil societal initiatives as tools
to put pressure on postauthoritarian governments and their approaches to
Romani minorities. Somewhat similar to how CSOs were seen in the 1980s
in the broader framework of development in the Global South, in the European Roma-related context, these "nongovernmental" channels were often
represented as "having a set of comparative advantages in relation to public
sector agencies such as cost effectiveness, less bureaucratic operating styles,
closeness to communities and reduced prevalence to corruption" (Lewis
2005: 211). Thus, one of the characteristics of the rise of nongovernmentalism was, David Lewis (2005: 211) suggests, the somewhat naïve and conservative idea that CSOs were "essentially private, non-state protectors of
the public interest." At the same time, in the case of the Romani movement,
a distinction between this first phase and a second one, in which civil society has increasingly been governmentalized, is difficult to make. This difficulty relates to the global conditions under which the post-1989 support for
Roma-related CSOs had started.

The post-1989 Romani movement has been confronted by a dilemma that has largely emanated from a "perverse confluence" (Dagnino 2008) of two different processes, related to two different political projects: a participatory democratic project and a neoliberal one. The Romani movement has profoundly been influenced by postsocialist processes of democratization, which have coincided with the development of new public spaces; new forms, subjects, sites, and scales of citizenship; decentered forms of governance and the increased participation of civil societal actors in decision-making linked to public and policy issues. Dissident movements with roots in opposition against communist regimes, human rights and social movements that appeared in the West since the 1960s, and the momentum of 1989 have contributed to the emergence of this participatory process aimed at developing and deepening democracy, including the building of a stronger, viable civil society.[1]

At the same time, the Romani movement has been influenced by the neoliberal project (see also below, where I discuss the governmentalization of civil society more explicitly). Postsocialist state and civil society building and the transition from plan to market economies in Eastern and Central Europe have coincided with sweeping and intense processes of neoliberalization (van Baar 2011a). The participatory democratic and the neoliberal projects have ambiguously flown together:

> The perversity lies in the fact that, even if these projects point in opposite and even antagonistic directions, each of them not only requires an active and proactive civil society, but also uses a number of common concepts and points of reference. In particular, notions such as citizenship, participation and civil society are central elements in both projects, even if they are being used with very different meanings. (Dagnino 2008: 55)

The uncomfortable merging of these two political projects complicates a reading of the Romani movement along straightforward lines of empowerment, emancipation, and human and minority rights articulation. The participatory project and its focus on collective responsibilities, disputing exclusionary mechanisms, and rendering delicate societal problems public tend to be displaced. Indeed, the neoliberal project limits societal participation to individualistic market inclusion—for instance, through activation policies (van Baar 2012a). Accordingly, a democratic agenda tends to be translated into a technocratic, social inclusion one, in which minorities such as the Roma are naturalized as "problem groups" that are individually, or at the community level, held responsible for solving the problems they face. The socioeconomic, political, and historical trajectories that have contributed to the marginalization of many Roma tend to be depoliticized through privatizing, territorializing, and culturalizing these problems. Due to the narrow focus on the ethnicized individual or community, on particular (usually segregated) localities, and on cultural and behavioral patterns of work, consumption, or mobility, complex contexts of marginalization have often been overlooked and depoliticized. As a consequence of these neglects and reductions, it has often been suggested that it is a "Roma (inclusion) problem" that needs to be solved (van Baar 2011a: 243–44).

Accordingly, there is an important difference between, on the one hand, the Romani movement and other social movements in Central and Eastern Europe and, on the other hand, social movements in parts of the world where participatory democracy had been established longer ago. The way in which civil societies have been revived and woven in postsocialist Central and Eastern Europe has roughly taken place at the same time of the global "NGO boom" and the changing of roles that CSOs were going to play in policy-making. These changes took place in the context of influential transformations of the structures of capitalism, including new approaches to poverty, security, and development (van Baar 2011a; 2018). Moreover, neoliberal concepts and practices have transnational "roots," including some in pre-1989 Central and Eastern Europe (Bockman 2011). In some countries, most notably in Hungary, the impact of neoliberalization has already become tangible since the 1970s (Haney 2002). For these reasons, the simultaneity of the post-1989 rise of nongovernmentalism with the neoliberalization of states, markets, and societies in Central and Eastern Europe makes it more difficult to distinguish or phase the participatory democratic and neoliberal projects, particularly regarding the Roma's situation.

Until late into the 1990s, and partly as a consequence of Cold War East-West relations and the related Western distrust of state authorities in Central and Eastern Europe, the direct Western support for Romani minorities in Central and Eastern Europe mainly consisted of establishing and supporting small-scale CSOs. The steadily growing number of Roma-related CSOs, mainly funded by Western donors, became a major channel for the initial development of, and support for, the (more formal) Romani movement. At the same time, the restructuring of Central and Eastern European states and their institutional infrastructures led to a major change of state–civil society relations. The "strengthening of civil society" and the post-1989 restructuring of the state were parallel, largely interconnected processes, if not, to a large extent, leading political projects. Partially and incoherently, these processes contributed to the decentralization of formerly authoritarian socialist state structures, to the privatization of formerly state-owned sectors, to the reform of welfare regimes, and to the development of various kinds of private-public partnerships. Thus, the support for Romani and pro-Roma CSOs on the one hand, and for democratic state and market reform on the other, coincided with an unprecedented transformation of state–civil society relationships and with a partial transfer of state responsibilities to existing, but most of all newly developed, civil society actors (for an extensive discussion of these transformations, see van Baar 2011a).

These complex changes in the structures, patterns, tools, and forms of governance did not involve a deregulation, but, rather, a *re*-regulation of government that has been accompanied by a blurring of the boundaries between state, market, and civil society (van Baar 2011a: 163–74). This has certainly been not only an outwardly driven process governed by Western actors or IGOs, but a complex process supported by various kinds of governmental actors, including local and national ones in the region. As part of these processes of state–civil society transformations, IGOs, foreign donors, and state authorities in Central and Eastern Europe have been looking for reliable Romani civil society partners with whom they could build up formal and informal partnerships.

In some cases, these emerging dialogues between state and pro-Roma or Romani civil society actors have had their roots in late socialist economic crises and the need for restructuring the socialist plan economy and reducing the costs of the then existing Roma assimilation programs. In 1984, for instance, the Hungarian authorities argued that "the integration [of the 'Gypsies'] is restricted by our difficult economic situation . . . a consequence of which is that we must now consider the Gypsy population as playing an important role in the construction of a new consensus" (quoted in Kovats 1997: 57). Martin Kovats (1997) clarifies that allowing the Roma to play a role in socialist Roma policies was largely motivated by socioeconomic difficulties, rather than by a desire to establish Romani minority self-governance and to allow the Roma to impact political and policy developments. He also puts forward that this ambiguity has not disappeared with the fall of socialism and with the post-1989 development of important new representational structures, such as, for instance, the minority self-government system in Hungary. He states that the introduction and building of policy dialogues with tactically chosen members of the Romani minority represent state strategies to postpone the development and implementation of the socioeconomic policies that were and are still needed to improve the situation of the Roma.

Kovats's observations on the ambivalent effects of these policy dialogues can be put into the perspective of the perverse confluence of the two political projects. State actors that have been involved in the (partial) transfer of their responsibilities to civil society actors potentially consider Romani or Roma advocacy CSOs as the relatively ideal and trustworthy partners for (assisting with) the implementation of policies. These CSOs are seen as agents who are operating in the proximity of Romani communities and who have developed knowledge and expertise about the local situation. From the viewpoint of national or international governing organizations, these features make such CSOs relatively ideal intermediaries between governments and state or suprastate institutions on the one hand, and Romani minorities and "grassroots" communities on the other. Since the 1990s, much has been expected of the "strengthening of civil society" through supporting and establishing CSOs and mobilizing or improving their "local" connections and forms of expertise. For those Romani or pro-Roma CSOs that have been approached by—or have approached—governmental offices, foreign donors, or IGOs, taking up such roles in policy delivery is most often not a question of choice and, more often than not, represents a challenge. Yet, these involvements have also had more ambivalent effects.

The governmentalization of civil society by state and international governmental actors embodies a complex attempt to loosely but effectively attach CSOs to the state and suprastate institutional frameworks of governance. These processes of governmentalization have also led to the development of so-called "quasi-autonomous NGOs" or QUANGOs. Indeed, a substantial number of new civil societal structures, and private-public partnerships in particular, are the result of how states themselves, while mobilizing neoliberal techniques of government, have established NGOs and other quasi-autonomous bodies (autonomous from the state or other donors) to carry out tasks that were formerly directly organized by state authorities. Examples of such quasi-autonomous bodies are the national agencies that have been established for Roma minorities in the Czech Republic and Romania, or the Netherlands Institute for Sinti and Roma (NISR) that existed between 2009 and 2012 (cf. van Baar 2011a: 240–41; 2014b).

How this governmentalization of civil society has taken place at the international level and how it has been articulated and promoted by various IGOs have hitherto been largely underresearched. As I have argued elsewhere (van Baar 2011a: 8–16, 163–89), the World Bank's "good governance" and the EU's governance agendas, for instance, are dedicated to how the mobilization of civil societal actors should contribute to new participative and deliberative forms of global and European governance and to democratizing decision-making. The European Commission (2007a: 26), for example, puts forward that CSOs could be considered as "centers of expertise" that "capitalize on their knowledge of communities by becoming trainers and advisors for mainstream providers or governmental authorities." Within the EU, the governmentalization of civil society relates to a longer tradition of trying to bring "Europe" closer to its citizens. Particularly since the early 1990s, the EU has launched various kinds of "proximity policies" to improve participatory democracy and limit the EU's much discussed democratic deficit(s). The desire to bring the EU closer to its citizens was one of the reasons for initiating the influential subsidiarity principle in the early 1990s:

"We affirm that decisions must be taken as closely as possible to the citizen. Greater unity can be achieved without excessive centralization. . . . Bringing to life this principle—'subsidiarity' or 'nearness'—is essential if the [European] Community is to develop with the support of its citizens"[2] (Council of the European Union 1992: 5).

In the context of its new governance agenda, the EU has introduced several new discourses, mechanisms, and tools that are intended to bring decision-making closer to EU citizens. Lifelong learning, activation, and the so-called "Open Method of Coordination" (OMC) are examples of what can be conceptualized as neoliberal governmental technologies of proximity:

Technologies of proximity refer to all those discourses and practices which imagine democracy in terms of positive experiences of local engagement, participation, and connection. Proximity is affirmed at the level of the citizen body: democratic life is seen to benefit from a certain closeness and connection between citizens. It is also affirmed between citizens and the formal institutions of political authority: people should feel "closer" to government. (Walters and Haahr 2005: 76)

The tools that have been developed at local, national, and supranational levels to increase the role of Romani and pro-Roma civil societal actors in decision-making can also be considered from the angle of the articulation of these technologies of proximity. Several Romani and pro-Roma activists have moved into closer collaborations with national or supranational political institutions or even into their official bodies to help foster a wide range of Roma-related development programs (dealing with issues such as social inclusion, security, participatory initiatives, empowerment, active citizenship and remembrance, community building, community policing, etc.).

This development, in which CSOs have been increasingly governmentalized in the national and supranational contexts of Roma-related policy-making, has gone together with a different perception of the role of CSOs. IGOs, but also governments, have begun to see CSOs "not so much as alternatives to government but viewed [CSOs] alongside states and markets, where they not only delivered services but also formed part of a broader 'third sector'" (Lewis 2010: 333). This development represents a two-way process, in which, on the one hand, CSOs have become more dependent on state and suprastate actors, regarding the funding, content, and diversity of their work. Most notably, CSOs have become more dependent on contracts for service delivery or research-related activities formulated by governments and IGOs. Since the requirements of these contracts have often been rigid and demanding, smaller and less influential CSOs can frequently not easily meet these terms. Consequently, the more professionalized CSOs have often been the only ones that have had a serious chance to make such contracts with governments and IGOs. The latter two actors have also been in a more powerful position to manage the boundaries between the sectors in the three-sector model. Under these circumstances, the difficulty of continuing CSO work has particularly affected smaller, less "professional," less mainstream, and more "ideological" CSOs. As a result, this development has also led to less diversity among the CSOs that have succeeded continuing their activities in the field of Roma-related activism, service delivery, and development or community work.

On the other hand, the governmentalization of civil society has required CSOs to become more active and more inventive in advocacy work and lobbying in relation to what they consider as their key objectives. Particularly the stronger CSOs, such as those that are unified in the transnational activist network of the European Roma Policy Coalition, have mobilized the growing links with IGOs—and also with governments—to become more active in seeking to generate more attention to what they consider as crucial to making a change at international, domestic, and local levels, in relation to issues such as empowerment, participation, litigation regarding human and minority rights, the combating of antigypsyism and Romaphobia, gender, participatory action research, and "community" or "grassroots" development.

The tensions between CSOs on the one hand and IGOs and governments on the other, as well as the ambiguous impact of the governmentalization of civil society on CSOs, have become more visible and more explicit since the ethnic turn in EU policies regarding the Roma. To a large extent, the launch of the EU Roma Framework can be considered the outcome of years of lobbying and the perpetual call of some, particularly international, CSOs for the development of more effective, more specific, and less generic policy instruments to improve the situation of the Roma throughout Europe, and to make EU countries more directly and more effectively responsible for this improvement and the combating of all kinds of phenomena that have hitherto impeded this process.

Yet, one of the conclusions that has been drawn (European Roma Policy Coalition 2012; European Roma Rights Centre 2013), is that, in the majority of EU countries, CSOs have been excluded from the development, implementation, and official evaluation of the National Roma Integration Strategies (NRIS), even while the active inclusion of Roma and civil society actors in these processes has been one of the Framework's requirements.[3] Even in those cases in which Roma and civil society actors were consulted, their consultations have had almost no effect on the content of the NRIS documents and their policy articulation and implementation (if the latter has taken place at all). Equally importantly, topics that CSOs consider crucial to making a significant change—such as Roma participation in the development, implementation, and monitoring of policies, the combating of anti-gypsyism, gender equality, empowerment, a human rights-based approach, adequate budget allocation, and the adoption of effective accountability, co-ordination, and monitoring tools—are missing or inadequately incorporated in the NRIS (European Roma Policy Coalition 2012). Moreover, the strong focus on domestic affairs regarding education, health care, housing, and em-ployment—which is already part of the EU Roma Framework itself—has led to a neglect of the transnational dimension of migration or to addressing migration one-sidedly with regard to particular priority areas, such as social security, public order, and crime (van Baar 2014a; 2014b; van Baar, Ivasiuc, and Kreide 2019). Last but not least, the development of the NRIS has re-vealed more explicitly the ambiguity of how state actors involved in Roma policy-making have defined and demarcated the identity category "Roma," seemingly to dovetail the desired policies and their target groups (Matras 2013; van Baar 2014b). Thus, as a result of the ambiguous ways in which the EU Roma Framework has been incorporated in the present-day Roma-related political and policy landscapes, we are facing a period in which Roma-related CSOs have increasingly less to say about how Roma policies are (to be) envisioned, designed, implemented, and assessed.

Scholarly Assessments of Roma-Related Nongovernmental Engagements

More than a decade ago, the anthropologist Paloma Gay y Blasco (2002: 174) suggested that, based on her fieldwork among Gitanos in Spain, we could distinguish between three main Roma/Gypsy diasporic modalities, each of which would involve "a particular way of conceiving 'the Gitanos/Gypsies/Roma' . . . as a community as well as a distinctive pattern of sociopolitical relations." Her three modalities involve "a non-convert, non-activist and kin-oriented; a convert and communitarian; and an activist and universal-izing" modality (Gay y Blasco 2002: 174). She largely bases the delineation of each of these modalities on the portrayal of the latter two. While the ac-tivist modality would be "premised on non-Gypsy models of personhood—by which all persons become entitled to the same human rights, effectively working as equally valuable units of humanity," the convert, communitarian (Pentecostal) modality would fully maintain "the Gitano belief in two kinds of persons, Gitanos and others, who are endowed with incommensurable moral differences and who are therefore differently positioned in the world" (Gay y Blasco 2002: 181).[4] At the beginning of Gay y Blasco's (2002: 173) article, where she introduces and puts into context her three modalities, she states that "even today, when Roma activists are increasingly drawing on the political discourses of the dominant society to call for the full extension of human rights to Gypsies everywhere, there is little grassroots support for [their] appeals."

Gay y Blasco's general, and in many respects also generalized portrayal of the diverse ways in which Roma approach the "world" could be considered as characteristic of how several scholars have assessed phenomena of Roma-related activism and nongovernmentalism. Gay y Blasco's distinction between the three diasporic modalities does not necessarily imply a rejection of one of these modalities. Yet, her uniformized account of activism and its distance from grassroots support clearly hints at a normative critique of what she describes as the "activist and universalizing" modality. This combination of a generalized idea of activism with a normative or even moral, rejectionist critique of some kinds of activist activities and organizations has become a recurrent element in several scholarly analyses of Roma-related engagements with the nongovernmental.

Nidhi Trehan (2001: 138–41: 2009a: 163–75) and Zoltan Barany (2002: 279–81), for instance, have been among the first who warned against the rise of what they call the "Gypsy industry." This industry would have turned more professionally organized activism into an "ethnobusiness" in which some—primarily pro-Roma and Romani elites as well as human rights and development experts—would make money and careers while they leave the situation of the poor Roma largely unaffected. This "industry" would also cover, or overlap with, several other phenomena, such as the increased managerialism in the Roma-related third sector, the co-option of Romani activists by more professionalized CSOs ("NGOization"), the lack of democratic or grassroots constituencies of CSOs, a growing gap between Romani "elites" and "grassroots," and the neglect of "local knowledge" (Trehan 2009b: 65). More recently, several scholars have joined Trehan and Barany in their critique of these trends (e.g., Nirenberg 2009; Rostas 2009; Sigona and Trehan 2009; Voiculescu 2013). Additionally, Elena Marushiakova and Veselin Popov (2011) have critiqued what they call "NGO science"—that is, the dissemination and policy implementation of what they consider "biased knowledge" that has been produced within and by some influential NGOs.

Elsewhere, I have argued that the phenomena and mechanisms that these scholars have described and analyzed—and that some of them have attributed to neoliberalism writ large—could be considered as the ambiguous consequences of the governmentalization of civil society (van Baar 2011a: 153–74, 233–47). Yet, if we take seriously the rather radical blurring of state–civil society relations central to this governmentalization, we should also be critical of the implicit or explicit suggestion in the narratives of many of these scholars that we deal with clear and clearly distinguishable oppositions between elites and grassroots, the represented Roma and the Roma's representatives, top-down and bottom-up approaches to their situation, external expertise imposed on the Roma and local knowledge developed by them, and NGOization and grassroots (or community) empowerment.

Undoubtedly, we have to be critical of several of the developments that these scholars have examined. Yet, the attitude of some of them to criticize both these developments and the civil society actors or organizations that are involved in "NGOization," "NGO science," or the "Gypsy industry" more generally, tends to throw the baby out with the bathwater, and, moreover, often results in opting for disputable alternatives of localism. Indeed, those who reject many of the more organized forms of Roma-related activism because these would be based on the imposition of external knowledge or even of "non-Gypsy paradigms of identity and personhood" (Gay y Blasco 2002: 185) often and implicitly assume that the local, community-based, Romani grassroots, or neo-Protestant alternatives are not implicit in these larger, more ambiguous trends. In contemporary Roma-related scholarship, we rarely find scholars who, in the nineteenth-century tradition of George Borrow, openly defend the existence, then or now, of a "pristine" Romani culture that has been endangered by a "predatory" outside world. Nevertheless, some of the scholars who have adopted a critical or even rejectionist attitude toward Roma-related activism and nongovernmentalism rely on a form of localism that tends to "essentialize the local as discrete places that host relatively homogeneous communities or, alternatively, constitute sites of grassroots mobilization and resistance" (Mohan and Stokke 2000: 264; see also Davoudi and Madanipour 2015). The glorification of local community as the site where Romani activism or resistance should start and be mobilized privileges a notion of politics in which the main aim seems to be, somewhat naïvely, to "carve out spaces of empowerment where ordinary people can define their lives outside the imprisoning architecture of developmentalism" (Corbridge 2007: 185).

Similarly, networks of neo-Protestant communities might provide "an alternative space for social organization that avoids the domination of non-Roma representatives" (Fosztó and Anăstăsoaie 2001: 362). Yet, any naïvely positive appraisal of the role of neo-Protestant communities as alternatives to activist and advocacy networks, or as cases in which agency and participation are unproblematically embedded, disregards the ways in which these (neo)religious practices are also—and ambiguously—implicated in processes of neoliberalization (Comaroff 2012; Freeman 2012; Dillon 2013). A differentiation of CSOs—ranging from professionalized, relatively small, and activist NGOs to faith-based associations and grassroots organizations or groupings—can be firmly grounded in actual practices. Yet, any suggestion that we could easily apply a kind of "ethical" yardstick to this diverse spectrum of CSOs would radically reduce its complexity and fundamental hybridity. This picture resembles the common view, expressed by the most fervent critics of the "Gypsy industry," of NGOs as sometimes "representing the depoliticized 'end-points' of once vibrant social movements, which have lost their once-radical edge" (Lewis 2010: 339).

A rejectionist attitude toward CSO practices omits the fact that the inability or inadequacy of CSOs to maintain a specific activist stance often has a cause that is largely beyond their reach (van Baar 2011a: 174–88, 233–69). This attitude also, and indirectly, assumes that CSOs are a kind of tabula rasa on which diverse kinds of desired activities and responsibilities—such as empowerment, participation, and community building—could be projected (Lewis 2005). To a large extent, therefore, this scholarly approach neglects the politico-sociological context of CSOs. Moreover, it also tends to reduce dramatically the agency of those who work in the critiqued CSOs and thus their anthropological dimension.

Toward a Critical Anthroposociology of Nongovernmentalism

Instead of adopting rejectionist stances toward some CSOs or developing easy binaries or differentiations regarding their affinities or rationales, I would like to call for a critical anthroposociology of Roma-related nongovernmentalism and activism that discusses these phenomena beyond the attitude of being "in favor of" or "against" (some kinds of) CSOs. In this final section, I draft a rough agenda of this critical anthroposociology, which is also based on some promising studies that have recently been published.

One of the central elements of such an anthroposociology involves a careful analysis of what I have called "traveling activism" (van Baar 2011a; 2013). With this notion, I have drawn attention to the significance of how various discourses, strategies, and techniques of activism are translated across space and (ethnic, gender, class, etc.) difference. Indeed, activists "travel" through disjunctive circuits, and the diverse forms of coalition building that arise from these interactions and mediations can serve as a productive source for enacting their activist agenda. Traveling activism overlaps and interacts with what, in Roma-related scholarship, others have discussed as processes of "brokerage" (Voiculescu 2013; Ivasiuc 2014), a term that has its origin in development studies. Looking at activism from the point of view of brokerage, Lewis (2010: 342) argues, the work of activists

is to mediate and "broker" the relationship between their disparate everyday work practices on the one hand, and the organizing ideas of policy on the other, in the pursuit of stability, coherent meaning, and order. This process of brokerage

simultaneously subverts and destabilizes the three sector model [of state, economy, and the third sector], because the process makes apparent many of the relationships and activities that operate across sector "boundaries"—including the
boundary separating government and non-government—and, in so doing, blurs
and complicates policy assumptions about these boundaries.

Analyzing practices of traveling activism, or processes of brokerage, requires
the developing of careful, in-depth, and thus time-consuming ethnographies of how everyday practices of activism and CSOs function and of how
their main actors, and those with whom they interact in their professional
lives, frame and perform their activism. Recently, some have developed vital
examples of such ethnographies, which show and confirm the complexities,
opportunities, and ambiguities of the everyday realities of Roma-related
activism (Chu 2008; Ivasiuc 2014; Ryder et al. 2014). Moreover, Cerasela
Voiculescu (2013) has argued that we can extend this debate to everyday
sceneries of Romani life and communities. She has clarified that both practices of activism and those of neo-Protestantism, patronage, and clientelism
could be seen in the wider context of diverse and interacting webs of power
relations that reveal that mechanisms of brokerage are also, and powerfully,
implicated in allegedly "marginal" religious, economic, and political practices of everyday Romani life.

I have reserved the term "traveling activism" for those practices of brokerage that are particularly related to the emergence and, seen from a historicizing perspective, revitalization of nongovernmentalism and activism
(without suggesting that these practices are not situated in a more complex
constellation of power relations). Moreover, the attribution of "traveling"
to activism relates not only to mobility within the discursive and nondis-
cursive contexts of the contested sphere of the "nongovernmental," but also
to activists' practices of "boundary crossings" (van Baar 2011a: 264–67).
Indeed, in the course of their life histories, many activists who have initially
associated or aligned themselves with the "nongovernmental" have crossed
the contested boundaries of the third and public sectors. While some activists have started to work for governments, others have left professionalized
CSOs to commit themselves to forms of grassroots engagements or (radical) public action. Understanding these practices of boundary-crossings
and their impact requires a more extensive examination of "the types of
relationships and forms of power that link structures and processes across
the sectors. How are these constructed, both by individual agency and by
broader contextual aspects of politics, history, or culture?" (Lewis 2008:
564). Using life histories in social policy research is a relatively new phenomenon, while it has been a common commitment of anthropologists.
Analyzing "anthroposociologically" the life histories and careers of activ-

ists who have crossed, or maybe even shifted and blurred sector boundaries can teach us more about the ways in which CSOs and state institutions "are linked through hidden personal relationships, resource flows and transactions, which become more visible at particular historical junctures" (Lewis 2010: 342).

Huub van Baar is an assistant professor of political theory at the University of Giessen in Germany where he coordinates the research project "Between Minority Protection and Securitization," funded by the German Research Foundation (DFG) within the program Dynamics of Security: Forms of Securitization in Historical Perspective (2014–21). He is also senior research fellow of the Amsterdam Centre for Globalisation Studies at the University of Amsterdam. He is the author of *The European Roma: Minority Representation, Memory and the Limits of Transnational Governmentality* (2011) and, together with Ana Ivasiuc and Regina Kreide, the coeditor of *The Securitization of the Roma in Europe* (2019).

Notes

1. In the history of the Romani movement, nongovernmentalism is no new phenomenon, but goes back to, at least, the nineteenth century (Mayall 2004).
2. According to the principle of subsidiarity, the EU may only act "where member states agree that action of individual countries is insufficient. The principle serves the functions of, on the one hand, setting up a division of competence between the EU and member states and on the other, endorsing the primacy of the member states in some domains, one of which is social policy" (Daly and Silver 2008: 551).
3. Allen et al. (2015) have shown that this trend is also relevant regarding Roma-related CSOs in EU candidate member states.
4. In equally overgeneralized terms, Gay y Blasco (2002: 184) claims that "Roma activists . . . draw on non-Gypsy academic theories and take up the notion that Gypsies come from India. In claiming for all Roma a land of origin and also a shared history of persecution and nomadism, Roma activists begin to move away from the performative model of identity to the same emphasis on historical and biological continuity that lies at the core of dominant Euro-American ethnotheories."

References

Allen, Richard, Steven O'Connor, Melita Petanovic, and Nicoleta Bițu. 2015. *Thematic Evaluation of IPA Support to Roma Communities*. Brussels: European Commission.

Barany, Zoltan. 2002. *The East European Gypsies.* Cambridge: Cambridge University Press.

Bockman, Johanna. 2011. *Markets in the Name of Socialism.* Stanford, CA: Stanford University Press.

Chu, Margalit. 2008. *Integration, Erasure and Underdevelopment: The Everyday Politics and Geographies of Gitano NGOization.* Ph.D. dissertation. University of Minnesota, Minneapolis.

Comaroff, Jean. 2012. "Pentecostalism, Populism and the New Politics of Affect." In *Pentecostalism and Development: Churches, NGOs and Social Change in Africa,* edited by Dena Freeman, 41–66. New York: Palgrave Macmillan.

Corbridge, Stuart. 2007. "The (Im)Possibility of Development Studies." *Economy and Society* 36 (2): 179–211.

Council of the European Union. 1992. "Birmingham Declaration: A Community Close to Its Citizens." Brussels: Council of the European Union.

Dagnino, Evelyn. 2008. "Participation, Citizenship and Democracy." In *Can NGOs Make a Difference? The Challenge of Development Alternatives,* edited by Anthony J. Bebbington, Samuel Hickey, and Diana Mitlin, 55–70. London: Zed Books.

Daly, Mary, and Hilary Silver. 2008. "Social Exclusion and Social Capital: A Comparison and Critique." *Theory and Society* 37 (5): 537–66.

Davoudi, Simin, and Ali Madanipour, eds. 2015. *Reconsidering Localism.* London: Routledge.

Dillon, Michael. 2013. "Politics of Truth and Pious Economies." In *The Biopolitics of Development: Reading Michel Foucault in the Postcolonial Present,* edited by Sandro Mezzadra, Julian Reid, and Ranabir Samaddar, 165–89. New York: Springer.

European Commission. 2007. *Handbook on Integration for Policy-Makers and Practitioners.* 2nd ed. Brussels: European Commission.

———. 2011. *An EU Framework for National Roma Integration Strategies up to 2020.* Brussels: European Commission.

European Roma Rights Centre. 2013. *National Roma Integration Strategies: What Next?* Special issue, *Roma Rights: Journal of the European Roma Rights Centre,* 1–61.

European Roma Policy Coalition. 2012. *Analysis of the National Roma Integration Strategies.* Brussels: European Roma Policy Coalition.

Fosztó, László, and Marian V. Anăstăsoaie. 2001. "Romania: Representations, Public Policies and Political Projects." In *Between Past and Future: The Roma of Central and Eastern Europe,* edited by Will Guy, 351–69. Hatfield: University of Hertfordshire Press.

Freeman, Dena, ed. 2012. *Pentecostalism and Development: Churches, NGOs and Social Change in Africa.* New York: Palgrave Macmillan.

———. 2012. "The Pentecostal Ethic and the Spirit of Development." In *Pentecostalism and Development: Churches, NGOs and Social Change in Africa,* edited by Dena Freeman, 1–38. New York: Palgrave Macmillan.

Gay y Blasco, Paloma. 2002. "Gypsy/Roma Diasporas: A Comparative Perspective." *Social Anthropology* 10 (2): 173–88.

Haney, Lynne. 2002. *Inventing the Needy: Gender and the Politics of Welfare in Hungary.* Berkeley, CA: University of California Press.

Ivasiuc, Ana. 2014. "Empowering the Roma: Lessons from Development Practice." Dissertation, National School of Political Science and Public Administration, Bucharest, Romania.

Kovats, Martin. 1997. "The Good, the Bad and the Ugly: Three Faces of 'Dialogue'—The Development of Roma Politics in Hungary." *Contemporary Politics* 3 (1): 55–71.

Lewis, David. 2005. "Individuals, Organisations and Public Action." In *A Radical History of Development Studies,* edited by Uma Kothari, 200–221. London: Zed Books.

———. 2008. "Using Life Histories in Social Policy Research." *Journal of Social Policy* 37 (4): 559–78.

———. 2010. "Political Ideologies and Non-Governmental Organizations." *Journal of Political Ideologies* 15 (3): 333–45.

Marushiakova, Elena, and Veselin Popov. 2011. "Between Exoticization and Marginalization." *Behemoth* 4 (1): 51–68.

Matras, Yaron. 2013. "Scholarship and the Politics of Romani Identity: Strategic and Conceptual Issues." *European Yearbook of Minority Issues,* ECMI, 211–45. Leiden: Martinus Nijhoff.

Mayall, David. 2004. *Gypsy Identities 1500–2000: From Egipcyans to Moon-men to the Ethnic Romany.* London: Routledge.

Mohan, Giles, and Kristian Stokke. 2000. "Participatory Development and Empowerment." *Third World Quarterly* 21 (2): 247–68.

Nirenberg, Jud. 2009. "Romani Political Mobilization." In *Romani Politics in Contemporary Europe,* edited by Nando Sigona and Nidhi Trehan, 94–115. New York: Palgrave Macmillan.

Ram, Melanie H. 2010. "Interests, Norms and Advocacy: Explaining the Emergence of the Roma onto the EU's Agenda." *Ethnopolitics* 9 (2): 197–217.

Rostas, Iulius. 2009. "The Romani Movement in Romania." In *Romani Politics in Contemporary Europe,* edited by Nando Sigona and Nidhi Trehan, 159–85. New York: Palgrave Macmillan.

Ryder, Andrew, Sarah Cemlyn, and Thomas Acton, eds. 2014. *Hearing the Voice of Gypsies, Roma and Travellers: Inclusive Community Development.* Bristol: Policy Press.

Sigona, Nando, and Nidhi Trehan, eds. 2009. *Romani Politics in Contemporary Europe.* New York: Palgrave Macmillan.

Trehan, Nidhi. 2001. "In the Name of the Roma? The Role of Private Foundations and NGOs." In *Between Past and Future,* edited by Will Guy, 134–49. Hatfield: University of Hertfordshire Press.

———. 2009a. *Human Rights Entrepreneurship in Post-Socialist Hungary.* Ph.D. dissertation. University of London.

———. 2009b. "The Romani Subaltern within Neoliberal European Civil Society." In *Romani Politics in Contemporary Europe,* edited by Nando Sigona and Nidhi Trehan, 51–71. New York: Palgrave Macmillan.

van Baar, Huub. 2011a. *The European Roma: Minority Representation, Memory and the Limits of Transnational Governmentality.* Amsterdam: F&N.

———. 2011b. "Europe's Romaphobia: Problematization, Securitization, Nomadization." *Environment and Planning D: Society and Space* 29 (2): 203–12.

———. 2012a. "Socio-Economic Mobility and Neo-Liberal Governmentality in Post-Socialist Europe." *Journal of Ethnic and Migration Studies* 38 (8): 1289–304.

———. 2012b. "Towards a Politics of Representation beyond Hegemonic Neoliberalism: The European Romani Movement Revisited." *Citizenship Studies* 16 (2): 285–94.

———. 2013. "Travelling Activism and Knowledge Formation in the Romani Social and Civil Movement." In *Roma Education in Europe: Practices, Policies and Politics,* edited by Maja Miskovic, 192–203. London: Routledge.

————. 2014a. "The Emergence of a Reasonable Anti-Gypsyism in Europe." In *When Stereotype Meets Prejudice: Antiziganism in European Societies*, edited by Timofey Agarin, 27–44. Stuttgart: Ibidem.

————. 2014b. "Participatie, veiligheid en beeldvorming van Romaminderheden." [Participation, security, and representation of Roma minorities]. *Justitiële Verkenningen* 40 (5): 86–98.

————. 2015. "The Perpetual Mobile Machine of Forced Mobility: Europe's Roma and the Institutionalization of Rootlessness." In *The Irregularization of Migration in Contemporary Europe: Detention, Deportation, Drowning,* edited by Yolande Jansen, Robin Celikates, and Joost de Bloois, 71–86. Lanham: Rowman & Littlefield.

————. 2018. "Contained Mobility and the Racialization of Poverty in Europe: The Roma at the Development-Security Nexus." *Social Identities: Journal for the Study of Race, Nation and Culture* 24 (4): 442–458.

van Baar, Huub, Ana Ivasiuc, and Regina Kreide, eds. 2019. *The Securitization of the Roma in Europe.* New York: Palgrave Macmillan.

Vermeersch, Peter 2006. *The Romani Movement: Minority Politics and Ethnic Mobilization in Contemporary Central Europe.* Oxford: Berghahn Books.

Voiculescu, Cerasela. 2013. "Questioning Mentalities of Governance: A History of Power Relations among the Roma in Romania." Dissertation, University of Edinburgh, Edinburgh.

Walters, William, and Jens-Henrik Haahr. 2005. *Governing Europe: Discourse, Governmentality and European Integration.* London: Routledge.

CHAPTER 2

✿ ✿ ✿

EMOTIONS AND PROCEDURES

Contradictions of Early Romani Activism in a Postconflict Intervention

Ana Chirițoiu

Introduction

Hădăreni (in Hungarian, Hadrév) is a Transylvanian village of about eight hundred inhabitants, 80 percent of whom are Romanian ethnics, with Hungarian and Roma accounting for about 10 percent each (INS 2011). On 20 September 1993, a fight broke out there between four locals: one Romanian ethnic and three Roma. The son of the Romanian man came to his father's defense, and was stabbed by one of the other three during the scuffle. He died shortly afterward. A number of non-Roma villagers chased the three Roma, who then sought refuge in a nearby house. Some of those present urged them to come out and proceeded to set the house ablaze. By this time, the police had also arrived at the scene, but could not—or, according to some witnesses, would not—stop the violence. Two of the men inside the house surrendered for fear they might burn alive, and were lynched by the crowd. The third one burned to death inside the house. The mob then set fire to more than a dozen houses belonging to Roma families, and chased some of their residents out of the village. Riot troops were stationed in the village for weeks on end, to prevent further escalations of the conflict.

While this was not the first instance when Roma were targeted by mob fury, chased out of their homes, and saw their properties set on fire—indeed, there are estimates that about thirty similar riots took place in early postsocialist Romania—the Hădăreni case stands in memory as the most gruesome one. This refers both to casualties and damages, and to the erratic manner in which Romanian institutions dealt with its consequences, legal and otherwise. In fact, Roma rights activists describe it as the pinnacle of the "conflict epidemics" targeting the Roma in Romania, stating that "the Hădăreni *pogrom* . . . has come to stand, for many, as the paradigmatic event of the post-1989 Roma Rights world" (European Roma Rights Centre 2001, my emphasis).

The broad recognition that the case acquired abroad owes largely to the intense lobbying that several civic organizations undertook with international bodies so as to pressure the state into punishing the culprits and compensating the victims of the conflict. One of the most prominent organizations that supported the Hădăreni case throughout its convoluted history was Pro Europa League, a human rights NGO based in Târgu-Mureş (in Hungarian, Marosvásárhely), the seat of Mureş County.[1] Another one was the Ethnic Roma Federation (henceforth FER)—an umbrella organization which joined together several emerging NGOs dedicated to the protection of Roma rights, located in Bucharest, and led at the time by Roma sociologist and activist Nicolae Gheorghe.

As the case immediately reached international attention, the Romanian government allocated some money for the reconstruction of the damaged houses, most likely due to foreign pressure.[2] However, the money ran out long before the houses were finished, and many of the people who had been made homeless during the riot remained in the same situation, or benefited from only minimal rehabilitations. As for the legal proceedings, in the face of a lingering trial that had not produced any prosecutions for three years, Pro Europa League assisted twenty-five victims to sue the Romanian state in the European Court of Human Rights (ECtHR). The plaintiffs were represented by lawyers of the European Roma Rights Centre (ERRC), a Budapest-based NGO that specialized in strategic litigation. The case was concluded in 2004, when the ECtHR mediated a friendly settlement between the government and eighteen of the applicants; the other seven applicants started a new case, which was settled one year later with the resolution that the Romanian state would pay the applicants various sums of money. These diverging solutions escalated the tensions between the plaintiffs.

The measures outlined in the friendly settlement that had concluded the first case were written down in a comprehensive community development program designed by the National Agency for the Roma (ANR), and overseen by the United Nations Development Program (UNDP). The program was allocated an estimated one million dollars over several years, and was meant both to tend to those whose properties had been destroyed in the conflict, and to redress interethnic relations in the village. Thus, it came to include a large number of various institutional actors, ranging from several ministries and local institutions to a plethora of NGOs. In practice, the program ran with various difficulties for almost two years, until 2009, when the financing got stuck in bureaucratic procedures and was stopped altogether. By that time, although some of the formulated objectives had been attained—such as the building of a kindergarten in the village, and the refurbishment of the school and of the community center—the program was generally conceived of by most of its stakeholders, and in particular by its local beneficiaries, as having failed.[3]

As for the causes of this failure, the explanations are as divergent as they are numerous. This chapter, however, does not purport to assess their truth or to evaluate the intervention in policy terms, but rather to recount the Hădăreni case as a cautionary tale of early Romani activism.[4] In doing so, I build on the narrative of the case as elaborated by Nicolae Gheorghe, one of the movement's leading figures, two decades after the fact, in his interview to me in May 2013 and in his published assessment about how the "Roma victimhood" paradigm failed to address the plight of the Roma on both a micro and macro scale (Gheorghe and Pulay 2013). Additionally, my analysis is informed by discussions with other actors in the case, and by my own observations from the field. Drawing on these (often diverging) narratives, the present chapter contributes to a discussion about the prominence of humanitarianianism within the Romani movement in early postsocialism, and its consequences for the Romani movement. I argue that this strand emerged under the double bind of state critique and transnational politics, which pressured the movement's ideologues-cum-practitioners to convert local experiences into more universal notions. By the time of my dialogue with Nicolae Gheorghe in 2013, it had long been evident that this contingent mode of framing accumulated inner contradictions and alienated itself from its local publics.

Against this background, the chapter examines the tensions generated among the actors of the intervention by such legal notions as "truth" and "justice" emerging from various accounts of this case. It shows that, being riddled with ambiguities and contradictions, the very epistemology of the intervention is symptomatic for the misunderstandings and half-truths in which the reparation process became stranded. The analysis focuses primarily on the truth-production process involved in this intervention, and shows that the humanitarian notion of "trauma" (Fassin and Rechtman 2009) and the consequent political repertoire of "victimhood" employed to legitimize this intervention dwell on a structural contradiction between humanitarian "emotions" and strategic "procedures."

The structure of the argument is as follows: in the next section I draw some lines between the main findings of several fields, such as the critique of humanitarianism, the politics of the Romani movement, and ethnic conflicts, and relate them to Nicolae Gheorghe's main arguments in his last text published in 2013, in which he reexamines his role within the Romani movement. Then, I recount some of the parallel lives of the Hădăreni case as told by various actors, especially locals, to contrast them with the official, or principled, narrative emerging from politics. Building on these narratives—political, civic, and vernacular—I argue why this case can be read as an early cautionary tale of Romani activism. Finally, I delve into the tensions between local relations and the activists' agenda, and build on Gheorghe's account of how Romani activism took shape under the double bind of national and transnational politics, more specifically in the interstices created by these often-diverging fields.

"Victimhood" versus "Local Knowledge"

The notion of victimhood has been subjected to strenuous scrutiny both under the rubric of the critique of humanitarianism and in the field of Romani studies, questioning its phenomenological universality and its political effectiveness alike. Echoing Arendt's discussion of the politics of compassion that are kindled by the Christian postulate regarding the sacredness of life itself, Fassin (2012: 8) begins his compelling critique of humanitarianism by asking "What . . . is gained and what lost, when we use the terms of suffering to speak of inequality, when we invoke trauma rather than recognizing violence . . . more generally when we mobilize compassion rather than justice?" The question is similarly implied by research that tackles the local effects of humanitarian governance and its contingencies (Fassin and Pandolfi 2010; Bornstein and Redfield 2011), or that shows how it reproduces and strengthens, rather than destabilizes, state apparatuses (Zigon 2013).

As far as Romani studies are concerned, numerous contributions explore why the project of Roma emancipation failed, or rendered unintended results, or both (Jenne 2000; Sobotka 2001; Klímová-Alexander 2005; Vermeersch 2006, 2012; Liebich 2007). Other authors propose to move beyond the binary of failure and success, and instead examine the political lives that such programs developed in relation to their circumstances (van Baar 2011; see also van Baar, this volume). Many of these analyses dwell on contradictions similar to the ones exposed by Nicolae Gheorghe, between emotional humanitarianism and pragmatic, political strategizing, as well as between "local knowledge" and activist interventions. Sigona and Trehan (2009), for instance, note that as the marginalization of Roma citizens is addressed in humanitarian terms, which then become "NGOized," the singling out of the "Roma" category as a group in need of special attention can easily backfire and provide discursive material for the burgeoning antigypsyist political agenda throughout Europe (see also Stewart 2012).

Borneman (2002: 286) makes a similar claim in his discussion about reconciliation after ethnic cleansing, stating that "ethnicization is a politics of repetition" that "is more likely to lead to a perpetuation of, rather than a departure from, violence." Thus, in order to avoid violence, the belligerents need to develop a shared moral community by recourse to the creation of affinity, through truth-telling and mutual acknowledgment of loss, and to legal retribution—both of which, he insists, function when accountability is embedded in the law. In his criticism to Borneman's piece, however, Sampson (2003: 184) dismisses the efficacy of truth-telling in itself. Instead, he states that "it is not the truth as such that sets us free, but rather the practice of truth-assessing and the public frameworks created by such assessments," thereby postulating that societies run on hidden transcripts or social lies rather than on truths. Elsewhere, Sampson (2002: 181, 185) similarly argues that it is primarily the task of impersonal institutions to enforce "a higher morality" and "lift community conflicts out of the quagmire of personal vendetta or ethnic revenge and into the realm of justice." Borneman's (2002) reply, in turn, emphasizes that institutional mediation is not enough to achieve the rebuilding of social ties, and needs to be complemented by an effective, bottom-up practice of affiliation and accountability.

In a similar vein, Toma's (2012) take on some comparable so-called ethnic conflicts in Romania suggests that it might be more accurate to analyze these phenomena as processes that are socially embedded in the daily fabric of their locality, rather than as discrete events. Moreover, the author shows that to label them as "ethnic" is to restrain their alternative readings, since the two main narratives that emerge from this interpretation, one that emphasizes the victimhood of the Roma, and one that outlines their criminality, get locked in a zero-sum game between diverging interests. Thus, rather than focus on the "last drop" that prompts the conflict and try to find the culprits there, Toma's suggestion is to look at how the glass gets full before it is spilled, and to talk about the "shared responsibilities" for this process, as well as for future resettlement.

Nicolae Gheorghe and Gergő Pulay (2013) made a similar argument in their contribution to the volume *From Victimhood to Citizenship: The Path of Roma Integration,* edited by Will Guy. The chapter is a hybrid between engaged anthropology, policy critique, and memoir, and was edited by Pulay, an anthropologist, based on several interviews with Gheorghe about Romani activism, and his role therein. Its core claim is that the movement arrived at a moot point and needs to undergo some changes, which should be inspired by a responsible critique of its essentially liberal underpinnings. Central to these changes should be the notion of "shared responsibilities," also proposed by Toma, by which Gheorghe and Pulay seek to capture the tension between the universality of human rights that Romani activism builds on, and the messy and occasionally "controversial" realities of microsociality. They dub the latter "local knowledge"—that is, a closer account of local relations between Roma and majority populations (Gheorghe and Pulay: 89ff.), and illustrate it precisely by recourse to the interethnic conflicts in the early 1990s, such as the one in Hădăreni (Gheorghe and Pulay 92–93).

Referring to these early days of Romani activism, Gheorghe and Pulay show how "local knowledge" got lost in the symbolic struggles between civil society and the state, together with its potential to fuel mediation, rather than confrontation. While Gheorghe was well aware of the historical origins of this intransigence, namely civil society's mandate to "dismantle the institutional frameworks of the Communist regimes" (in Gheorghe and Pulay 2013: 48) or to "confront governments" (77), he was also of the opinion that "instead of becoming zealots in the defence of human rights, we should be finding more accommodating ways of proceeding as intermediaries" (93). Indeed, throughout the chapter, he is adamant that it is mediation, rather than vindication, that helps rebuild social ties. The choice between these two strategies speaks to different political philosophies that I leave for others to explore; what I would like to note here is that this notion of mediation, with its emphasis on the contingency of social ties, calls into question the egalitarian axiom of humanitarian politics.

The present chapter dwells on these dividing lines between humanitarian principles, their political practice, their local effects or lack thereof, and their resulting inconsistencies through a case study of an intervention that the Romani rights movement generated and built on in order to establish its legitimacy. My analysis, then, dwells on the dialectical relations between these planes, emphasizing their overlaps, continuities, and unavoidable contradictions, emphasizing how, and to what effects, "the local" got lost between the blurred lines of transnational politics. By this, I seek to suggest a way out of the analytical, moral, and practical void of the "victimhood" paradigm that has come to epitomize humanitarianism in general, and much of Romani activism in particular (see also Ivasiuc, this volume).

The Hădăreni Case as a Cautionary Tale of Romani Activism

In May 2013, Nicolae Gheorghe took part in a debate at the Open Society Foundations occasioned by the release of the collective volume *From Victimhood to Citizenship: The Path of Roma Integration*. In his interventions in the debate, as well as in the book chapter he co-authored with anthropologist Gergő Pulay (Gheorghe and Pulay 2013: 44), Gheorghe unequivocally stated that Roma civil society finds itself in a state of crisis in terms of legitimacy, political mobilization, and approaches. He substantiated this claim by arguing that liberal, human rights–oriented interventions designed over the previous twenty years to address the various phenomena lumped together under the label of "Roma exclusion" had obviously failed to meet their goal. Moreover, he expressed strong doubts about the paradigm of Roma victimhood that he and others helped put forth in the beginnings of the post-1989 Romani movement, arguing for the renewal of its previous liberal underpinnings so as to accommodate "controversial issues" (Gheorghe and Pulay 2013: 43) that might otherwise continue to backfire in the form of antigypsyism.

Having been one of the earliest and most influential animators of the Romani movement in Eastern Europe, Gheorghe saw it as his own responsibility to provide a retrospective assessment of its trajectory, and to urge young activists to work with people "the way they are, not the way we want them to be."[5] Feeling that his assessment regarding the "victimhood" paradigm was relevant to my own conclusions about the Hădăreni intervention, and knowing that Gheorghe had played a prominent role in the early days of the case, I approached him after the debate and asked if he could find some time to talk about this in more detail. He agreed, and we scheduled an encounter on the following day, shortly before his departure from Budapest. It was the first and last time we met.

The following morning, I arrived at his hotel and found him in the lobby, parting with earlier visitors.[6] We agreed on a thirty-minute meeting, but ended up speaking well over one hour, incessantly switching between inside stories, blunt overarching assessments, minute technicalities, and subtle personal thoughts. By then, I was well aware that it was next to impossible to find two identical accounts of the case, so it came as no surprise that neither were ours. The two decades that had passed since the conflict that occurred in September 1993 in Hădăreni were rife with court verdicts, interventions, disruptions, and failures, all of which had prompted misunderstandings and mutual suspicions among the many actors involved in the case throughout this time.

While it is tempting to blame these incongruities on the failure of the case, the present chapter challenges this causality, and shows instead that such contradictions were inherent to the entire intervention, so they are not to be ascribed to its failure or success. Moreover, they epitomized broader tensions between their various levels—the local, the national, and the transnational—and their diverging repertoires, specifically that of "emotions"—the humanitarian lexicon of victimhood, trauma, and compassion—and the procedural and institutional repertoire, which entails pragmatic political strategizing.

Throughout our discussion, Gheorghe essentially reconstructed the story of the early days of postsocialist Romani activism in Romania through the archaeology of the Hădăreni case. Before providing an overview of the projects that he had intended in the community, and that failed one by one, Gheorghe proceeded to draw a *mise en abîme*. He recalled a previous story that had happened when he and other activists organized a march for Roma rights in a small province town in northern Romania, only to find out afterward that the participants had been lured to the scene by the promise of humanitarian help, not by the prospect of marching for their rights. By way of concluding, he exclaimed, half bitterly and half amused, "It was only dreams."

Then, as if startled by his own fatalistic tone, he moved on to more pragmatic explanations. He exemplified in minute detail how these "dreams" became stalled by incidents in the lives of local actors or by choices they made, and how the projects initiated by FER and others for the reconstruction of the community swayed with these personal trajectories and with the existing relations among the locals, which activists had tried to play down. This division between activists' "dreams," as he repeatedly labeled their initial aspirations or principles, and their subjects' self-interestedness became something of a trope in our dialogue: at times, Gheorghe articulated it bitterly, as if people, with their individual motivations and biographic accidents, had deliberately gotten in the way of his vision and thereby had stalled their own emancipation.

At other times, however, Gheorghe disclosed his admiration for what he called "people's pragmatism," by which he understood their ability to rebuild their own lives where both the state and the NGOs failed (them), and to navigate or mitigate their circumstances. The Roma in Hădăreni had not been poor before the conflict, nor did they remain poor for much longer afterward, as they themselves often pointed out. "Pragmatism," however, meant not only their capacity to achieve prosperity again, but also their capacity to orient themselves in the complex process of reparations and to learn how to petition the humanitarian gaze cast upon them in the hope of obtaining reparations. However, in the end, as Gheorghe admitted, it was essentially the broader village population on the whole that stood to gain from the compensations, while most of the Roma, whose houses are still not thoroughly rebuilt to this day, obtained only a little bit of money at most. Moreover, he believed that for the victims of the conflict, it was the enticement of financial "compensations" that ultimately prevailed over notions of "justice," "development," or "rule of law" that the activists were trying to inspire in them. This incongruence of interests essentially widened the gap between what he called "the subjective or moral feeling of justice" and punitive justice to be deployed by the state, further eroding any solidarity between the victims of the conflict.

While the incongruence that Gheorghe described between the subjective feeling of justice and formal justice was something that I also observed during my fieldwork in Hădăreni, I doubt that it was solely the consequence of reducing the reparation process to mere financial compensation. Rather, I argue that it was but one of the manifest contradictions inherent to the intervention. Indeed, the notion of "victimhood" is the main currency on the international market of humanitarian projects—a contentious notion, that was sometimes disputed or contested, and at other times priced, auctioned, and hollowed. Moreover, under the promise of the financial reparations, which arrived late and did not appear to have followed any particular logic in the eyes of the locals, the dissensions between various families or even members of the same family in Hădăreni grew wider, and were epitomized in mutual accusations and suspicion, and an unquenched sense of having been wronged. This result can largely be attributed to the incoherent manner in which the reparations have been distributed. Further than this, however, I see no necessary incongruity between "financial compensations" and the "rule of law," and argue that, if the locals manifested more interest in the former, it was not only out of mere pragmatism, but rather because they might have felt that the battle to impose the latter was not their own. In the next section, I turn to the epistemic and political dimensions of this battle carried out in their name, to show how it eluded "the local," and how this caused "the local" to elude it in their turn.

Local Meanings of "the Law"

Gheorghe admitted that the general sense of frustration, including his own, that the intervention stirred owed partly to his colleagues' and his own uncompromising activist approach, which he later compared to "an occupying force sent by the EU" akin to the "earlier invasions by Communist cadres" (Gheorghe and Pulay 2013: 89). Not only was their zealous insistence to impose their own cosmopolitan agenda at the expense of "local knowledge" disproportionately authoritarian, but it also threatened to disturb the "informal deals" that governed local sociality, which often caused the locals to become suspicious toward the activists, instead of cooperative. For instance, Gheorghe recalled that the local history was loaded with animosities between distinct Roma families, which had resulted in a homicide barely two weeks before the conflict, and which is likely to have stirred the non-Roma locals' grudges toward the Roma as elements of disorder and misconduct. Moreover, by way of tracing the "local knowledge" that the activists chose to ignore at the time, in our interview Gheorghe clarified that it had not been the entire Roma population in the village that came under attack during the conflict. In fact, he said, various families were targeted differently, and some of those targeted had problematic criminal records—which the authorities then used to intimidate the victims from starting a lawsuit. Apart from the family of the three Roma men who were killed in the conflict, almost all other families were inclined to settle with state representatives outside court. Gheorghe admitted that at the time he was disappointed with this inclination of the people he had thought of as victims to negotiate with their oppressors.

It was largely due to the intransigence of István Haller of Pro Europa League, he said, that there was a lawsuit at all. However, later on he understood that for most of the locals the stake was not so much that of "punitive justice," in the institutional sense, but rather a sense of moral reparation, and observed disappointedly that, throughout the process, the two came not only to diverge from each other, but even to become contradictory.

My Roma interlocutors in the village confirmed that the local history had never been as straightforward or uncomplicated as it was presented in activist narratives, and eagerly ascertained that it was only because "certain Gypsies" had been unlawful that the whole group was made to suffer. To demonstrate how peaceful village life was, they would point out that there were no separate living areas divided along ethnic lines in the village, and that people of all three ethnicities willy-nilly mingled in their daily lives, especially back when Roma and non-Roma worked together at a nearby factory that employed most of the workforce in the area.

At the same time, Roma and non-Roma locals alike would launch themselves into extensive commentary about the unreliability of justice and the local police, each side suspecting that these institutions were favoring the others. The justifications given by those found guilty for the crimes committed during the conflict can be read to this effect. Specifically, they argued that their actions had been triggered by the fact that the police had failed to react to the lawbreaking perpetrated by the Roma—who would let their horses graze on the land of the non-Roma—and so they felt compelled to take justice into their own hands, in vigilante fashion. In reality, neither the police nor other institutions countered such pseudo-civic initiatives decisively, while nationalist organizations lobbying the area at the time were kindling them explicitly, enhancing the unsubtle ethnic nationalism of Ceaușescu's regime with "grassroots" actions directed against the country's largest remaining minorities, Hungarians and Roma.

Thus, as documented by human rights activist and legal expert István Haller (1998), who has monitored the Hădăreni case closely since its inception and made repeated instrumental contributions to it, the state institutions that were supposed to deliver justice were either captured by dubious, discretionary elites, or caught in the confusion of adapting to a new world. In short, they handled the Hădăreni case in a manner that appears both idiosyncratic and dismissive, primarily by delaying the legal proceedings, but also by avoiding labeling the conflict as "ethnic."[7] Instead, official narratives maintained that it was a "local" and "social," rather than "ethnic" affair—a hypothesis that also gained some sociological support (see, for instance, Zamfir and Zamfir 1993). The pragmatic implication of this label, however, was that the Roma were at least partially responsible for their own plight and, indeed, Haller (1998) chronicles a series of judicial documents in which the causes for the conflict were simply attributed to the victims themselves.

Thus, in terms of their strategizing, Gheorghe and other activists had little choice but to refute the "local" label, and emphasize the "ethnic" one, partly out of activist fervor, partly for the sake of strategic thinking, and partly because the former drew dangerously close to the "blaming the victim" approach that was the main working hypothesis of the police and the state. In his 2013 reflections, Gheorghe speaks at large about how such conflicts "present a challenge in raising questions about responsibilities within Roma communities," (Gheorghe and Pulay 2013: 91) as they have the potential of strengthening stereotypes about "Gypsy crime," especially when the state institutions that are supposed to deliver justice in fact act on these stereotypes. Accurate though it might have been, to put forth his idea of "shared responsibilities" was politically risky, particularly at a time when the very raison d'être of civic activism was to oppose state ideology (see also Fosztó, this volume).

On the other hand, this strategy alienated the local community from the intervention, and ultimately left local Roma to their own devices when it came to managing the broken social ties that had been damaged by the conflict. Further tensions ensued from the civic entrepreneurs' insistence on overlooking "local knowledge" as if it were a compromise that might have tainted their ideals. Scaling up the way in which locals of either ethnicity felt betrayed by institutions that each suspected of favoring "the others," activists similarly accused the state (and occasionally each other) of favoring adverse interests, and sought redress by recourse to higher fora. The stakes, then, eluded the local, and became transnational.

Liberal Dissidence and Other "Political Games"

It is necessary, at this stage, to turn to some contextual explanations in support for my earlier claim that civic engagement in the early 1990s could flourish only in opposition to the state. To begin with, the liberal notion of human rights had a distinctly dissident overtone in late socialism and early postsocialism alike. To advocate for human rights in the face of a malevolent or "mendacious" government—as Haller (2010: 23) would call it—continued to remain dissident practice. In fact, some of the most prominent dissidents in Eastern Europe before 1989, who defined themselves as liberals and advocates of civil society even before the regime change, embraced human rights activism in the early 1990s. This served to oppose a political establishment that they saw as a noxious prolongation of the communist nomenclature, in terms of personnel and practices alike. Their opposition was significantly sustained by symbolic and financial resources from foreign organizations (for an account of how this junction between foreign capital and local hierarchies worked on the ground in post-postsocialist societies, see Sampson 2002). In this context, as a human rights activist, Haller (2010) was denouncing a certain criminalization of the state in essentially moral terms, particularly with regard to the monopoly that a captured state exercised over justice, which, in liberal thought, stands at the core of the state.

To illustrate, in the interview that István Haller granted my colleagues and me in the summer of 2012 about the Hădăreni case, as well as in his written contributions, his focus rests almost exclusively with the procedural vices of the case, essentially leveling critique against the practices of the political establishment that collided with or eluded the law. Although his straightforward tone is hardly punctuated by any epithets or exaggerations, his articles (Haller 1998; 2005) produce indignation even with the umpteenth rereading. Neatly documented from a wide array of sources, they portray a detailed image of how, in the hands of the state, the Hădăreni case became nothing short of a farce, albeit a tragic one. All in all, they read as a legal equivalent of Jacques Carelman's surrealist *Catalogue of Unfindable Objects*—that is, an absurd collection of facts—with the sobering difference that the absurdities inventoried by Haller do exist and have impacted numerous lives in various ways. I enumerate only a few: the declaration of a policeman sounds as if quoted from a TV gag ("I cannot provide an explanation for the inconsistencies between my declarations. . . . I think I spoke the truth each and every time"); the village mayor takes notice of the villagers' requirement that the mother of two of the Roma men who died during the conflict should not return to the village, so he advises her that "in case the money [for reconstruction] will be allocated, the inheritors should build their house wherever they see fit" [i.e., not in the village]; the suspects for murder and destruction who got detained three years after the events were released shortly from police custody under the official justification "that they can cultivate their land"—which, as Haller notes, came as a surprise even to them, since they were not agricultural workers; one villager who called the police to report the event recalled that "the policeman told me to mind my own business . . . swore at me and hung up on me"; in a rally held shortly after the events in the village, the head of the county office of the party in power congratulated the villagers for their deed, and so forth (Haller 2005: 66–85). This is, clearly, the matter-of-fact chronicle of a world turned upside down.

The redress, then, could only consist in implementing "the rule of law" upon a state gone berserk. Indeed, the lawyer of the victims notes in an address to the law court that since politics continue to prevail over the penal law, support needs to be sought from international organizations in order to solve the case (Haller 1998). Thereby, civil society partakes in the political game and enters an open competition with the state by duplicating the work of the juridical and resignifying it. Its legitimacy to denounce state abuses and to correct them relies on moral grounds: first, on the liberal tenet that governance needs to be rooted in objective justice, and second, on the similarly liberally inspired notion of the universality of human rights.

In this context, the activists' framing strategy, which Gheorghe summarized as "zealotry" in our interview, and the discarding of uncomfortable "local knowledge" entailed a significant element of strategic thinking that had to overlook poverty, marginalization, or other "local data" in favor of higher stakes to be played out against captured state institutions. He made this very explicit in our discussion:

> We insisted that these were interethnic conflicts, pogroms—maybe we exaggerated, I can make my own self-critique, but we premeditated it, in order to raise the profile of these local conflicts. . . . The police also insisted that these were all local conflicts. . . . So, once again, we did this as a political platform, for which we are—or I am—responsible, but our main concern was how to put an end [to the conflicts]. And the second point—and maybe we erred about this as well—was how to raise the profile of the Roma problem on the agenda of the OSCE as a matter of security, not a matter of poverty or human rights, but as a matter of ethnically motivated violence. Hădăreni occurred after four, five, or six previous conflicts. So we labeled it early on, without paying attention to local conditions.[8]

Several topics stand out in this dense self-critique: first, "raising the profile" of the conflicts on the international agenda, was designed—and could only be effective—in stark opposition to the platform put forth by national institutions. The conflict in Hădăreni, as an epitome of the ones that preceded it (and the several ones that followed more than a decade later), was only relevant on the international agenda as long as it was problematized as "ethnic," rather than "local," as various state actors maintained. "We knew all along that this was *also* a social conflict," Gheorghe disclosed in our interview, but it did not serve their purpose at the time to admit it. Indeed, while in practice the ethnic and the social are not necessarily opposed, in the context of international negotiations with malevolent national institutions they acquired antagonistic meanings and lost their local relevance as they gained a "political" one—that is, as they were used to legitimate one practice over another one.

Second, the topic of securitization comes in as a double bind: if Roma come under attack because they are profiled as societal threats ("public security"), to besiege them physically and institutionally becomes a threat to their very existence ("human security"). What this case clearly illustrates, as argued by Haller (2010) and Gheorghe and Pulay (2013) is that, as long as the gap between these notions is not addressed by state policies, it becomes the breeding ground of vigilantism.

Third, in his attempt to "raise the profile" of Roma issues on the international agenda, Gheorghe made reference to another international trope of trauma: the Holocaust. In our conversation, he recalled that one of their initiatives in relation to Hădăreni was to buy the building of the synagogue in the closest town, which was abandoned since the local Jewish population became extinct, and to use it to host "the museum of the plight of the Roma." The initiatives could not be realized for lack of funding, but still serve as a powerful example of how Romani identity formation that has suffering at its core aptly mobilizes a politics of memory to establish its genealogy in relation to the earlier plight of the Jews (van Baar 2015). As Gheorghe put it, "Holocaust as an operator . . . allows us to portray the plight of Roma communities as part of a greater historical narrative" (in Gheorghe and Pulay 2013: 45).

This issue of framing and its consequences remains relevant today, and invites questions about how far activist human rights narratives can downplay or ignore "local knowledge" before they become alienated from their subjects and distort their initial purposes, or, differently put, how much popular sentiment activism can accommodate before becoming confounded with the hegemonic point of view that it seeks to challenge. This chapter inevitably gives a very partial response to these broad questions, but it is meant to encourage pondering upon them.

The Forcible Lesson of "Universal Standards"

As I already discussed, the endeavor to label the conflict and to create a paradigm for the Romani movement found itself in a double-bind situation in its early beginnings. On the one hand, this choice was conditioned by the national political context, which the movement had little choice but to oppose; on the other hand, its main reference was the transnational humanitarian standard, which not even its local proponents were familiar with quite yet, as Gheorghe admitted in his conversation with me:

> How does one reconsider the reconstruction of a community starting from local knowledge, and not only from the universal standards that you need to apply because the ECtHR said so? Very well, they provide the standard, but there is also room for local knowledge, relations, vicinity, the sort of things that sociologists and anthropologists research, and this is something that we ignored back then. It was a different historical moment. The universal standard had to be im-

posed. It had to be made clear that both the state and the citizens needed to learn something new, because we [activists] didn't know what human rights meant either, what the European Convention of Human Rights was, it was a lesson to be learned forcibly.

This loose description, punctuated by strong terms such as "need to," "standard," "imposed," or "forcibly," speaks to the geopolitical context in which these lessons were being delivered, and more broadly speaking to the relations of power in the emerging eastern European politics. Several authors writing about postsocialism explore this this topic, emphasizing particularly the role that nongovernmental organizations play as they transgress the national state and seek to address higher fora by means of supranational litigation (Creed and Wedel 1997; Sampson 2002). By way of contextualizing the emergence of the Romani movement in the aftermath of the Hădăreni conflict, Gheorghe reminded me that the conflict occurred very shortly before Romania became a member state of the Council of Europe, in early October 1993, and was supervised through the so-called "Halonen mechanism,"[9] which granted special attention to the treatment of minorities. Evidently, the case loomed large over this topic, and civic entrepreneurs were thus provided with an opportunity to legitimize their evolving agendas and practice them in the testing ground that emerged in the interstices of transnational negotiations.

It has long been noted that the international framework of human rights, together with the institutions that defend them, presented an opportunity for the members of the emerging Romani movement to pursue their project of Roma emancipation (Klímová-Alexander 2005; see also van Baar, this volume). In our interview, Gheorghe was adamant that the case had a significant strategic dimension in this sense: "We insisted that this was a pogrom and that justice be administered," he recalled, and then added, "The idea that we would go to Strasbourg [the headquarters of the ECtHR] was there all along. . . . It was somehow an aim to go all the way with this case. It was clearly a political issue."

In this context, the "politics" of the Romani movement stands for anti-state politics, and essentially consists of finding a way to promote the civic agenda though high-stake negotiations, which requires undergoing the elusive process of framing that I discuss above. Interestingly, as Gheorghe pointed out in one of the quotes above, what was lost—or maybe sacrificed—in this double-bind in which civic activism found itself in its early days was precisely its local inspiration and ultimately its local relevance. Hence, Gheorghe insisted that "reviving Roma civic activism cannot be achieved simply by confronting governments—as we did from the 1990s" (in Gheorghe and Pulay 2013: 77), but instead needs to "acknowledge controversies *within* Roma communities" (Ibid.: 46, emphasis in original) and ultimately allow for in-

ternal debates and contradictions to emerge in public, as a means to escape
the Manichean epistemology that has characterized public debates on and
interventions for Roma thus far.

Epilogue: Emotions, Procedures, and Accommodating Contradictions

Two decades after the conflict, Gheorghe still seemed split as to whether
he should emphasize the strategic part of his approach, or the emotional
one, while pointing out the whole time how the two had in fact shaped each
other: "We dramatized the conflict," he told me. "Hădăreni became a sym-
bol and in a way we overdramatized it, because it marked the end of this
conflict epidemic." However, a few minutes later he hesitated: "[And yet]
people had been burned alive . . . our exaggerations aside, this was a fact
that made an impression." Our discussion was going in circles: the gruesome
facts of the conflict made an impression not only on the members of FER,
but also on the representatives of international bodies—all the more so as
they failed to make an impression on Romanian authorities. Emotions were
being conveyed through procedures, up to the highest echelons of European
politics. "It all became very personal and subjective, it involved us as persons," he recalled. And yet, in the end it was all about procedures: the two
cases were judged by the ECtHR on procedural grounds, not on substantial
ones, simply because Romania had not yet ratified the European Convention of Human Rights at the time of the conflict. This detail, it seemed to me,
hindered the sense of moral reparation that Gheorghe had hoped for.

A government representative who agreed to give me an interview on
condition of anonymity contested precisely this hybridization between
emotions and procedures in the activist approach to the Hădăreni case. He
criticized journalistic approaches driven by "sensationalism" and "specula-
tion," as well as activists who let themselves be taken over by their emotions
rather than by "facts." Pointing out that "justice won't fix social relations,"
he advised me to keep to the procedural aspects. Moreover, before I vent
my indignation about the government not fulfilling its duty to rebuild the
remaining two houses, he said, I should notice that these houses have no
property papers, and none of the activists who claim interest in the case has
assisted the victims to get them. At one point he even stated bluntly, "We're
not discussing emotions here. We're discussing my right to go to the ECtHR
because I feel that I've been wronged by each and every court of law in Romania." Emotions are a slippery matter, he concluded, that more often than
not impede upon the notion of justice, by taking away its immutability and
turning it into a matter of sentiments and subjectivity.

It might seem paradoxical to hear this argument for immutable justice while knowing that this was precisely what activists who had opposed the government for two decades were demanding from the state in this very case. And yet, as Gheorghe's narrative made clear, in the elusive early 1990s—"after all, almost everything seemed confused in Romania during the 1990s," Gheorghe admits (Gheorghe and Pulay 2013: 92)—this unwieldy mix of emotions and justice was one of the few registers that human rights activists had at their disposal in order to counter the negligent or outright hostile practices of the state. Thus, the extent to which "emotions" are still at the core of the Romani movement up until this day needs to be accounted for not only in terms of strategizing, but also by reference to the broader context in which its politics play out. At the time when the Hădăreni conflict was addressed, activists did their best to get "emotions" and "procedures" to coincide, and have justice and reparation fit together, as goes humanitarian ideology. And yet, in the course of the intervention, the two grew ever more apart, the same way in which various other pairs of words (e.g., "ethnic" and "local") became opposites, and each of them acquired a life of its own.

Toward the end of the interview, as he warned me not to attempt to look for solutions, Gheorghe saw that the contradiction between "emotions" and "procedures" could only be resolved artificially—literally through art: "At that time, I was dreaming to [organize] a theater play about Hădăreni . . . as a way to express all those tensions that cannot be captured in court decisions, reports, all that . . . for the entire community to take part in, to lead to a kind of catharsis, liberation through theatre." This abrupt change of register, from political strategizing to the abstract catharsis granted by theater, signals not only to Gheorghe's disappointment that his and others' approaches to the case had failed—that much was clear when our conversation took place. More significantly, however, it points to how a change of epistemology was needed in the Romani movement in order to escape from the zero-sum game between "victimhood" and "criminality," and to exorcise the accumulated contradictions that kept haunting the process. Bearing in mind, with this case study, that the repressed always returns, a new epistemology of the Romani movement and of Roma studies more generally should perhaps figure out how to accommodate uneasy truths, controversies, and contradictions, rather than repress them.

Ana Chirițoiu is a Ph.D. candidate in social anthropology at the Central European University in Budapest, working on a thesis about kinship among Roma in an urban setting in Romania. Her previous research concerns ethnic politics in Dobrogea, an ethnically mixed region in southeast Romania. During her work for a Roma-rights NGO based in Bucharest, she became acquainted with the "Hădăreni" case, which she then researched more closely during her second MA program, at CEU.

Notes

This chapter draws on research completed in 2013 at Central European University's Department of Sociology and Social Anthropology, under the supervision of Dan Rabinowitz and Vlad Naumescu. I thank them both for their support and sharp critique. Thanks are also due to John Clarke, Prem Kumar Rajaram, Michael Stewart, and Viola Zentai for bibliographical suggestions and stimulating comments. Gergő Pulay facilitated my interview with Nicolae Gheorghe, and made meaningful contributions to this research throughout its various stages. I thank him for that. Moreover, I am grateful to the editors of this volume, Sam Beck and Ana Ivasiuc, for their interest in my work and for their patience, and to Huub van Baar for his meticulous reviewing of my chapter. Lastly, my gratitude goes to the people of Hădăreni, who generously welcomed me into their homes and told me their stories.

 1. Pro Europa League had also been active during the negotiations that followed the 1990 conflict in Târgu-Mureş between Romanian and Hungarian groups, when state institutions had similarly postponed deploying justice to the perpetrators of the violence.
 2. For instance, the U.S. State Department discussed the case in its proceedings (Congressional Record vol. 139, no. 153), and Amnesty International and the UN committee on Economic, Social and Cultural Rights took stands on the situation of the Roma in Romania.
 3. Given that the Hădăreni case spans more than two decades, my account inevitably overlooks many of its defining moments, so it needs to be emphasized that it is not my intention to provide a detailed description of the events. For a comprehensive factual summary of the case, see for instance Haller 2007.
 4. I have previously contributed to a policy evaluation of the case, as part of a research team mandated by the National Agency for the Roma in 2012 to evaluate the results of the community development program financed (intermittently) by the Romanian state, in consequence of the ECtHR decision from 2006 (see Ivasiuc et al. 2012). It was in this capacity that I first visited Hădăreni in August 2012. One year later, during my M.A. studies, I decided to pursue a more in-depth, ethnographically-informed analysis of the local effects of the postconflict interventions and returned to Hădăreni in April 2013. My interview with Nicolae Gheorghe that I draw on in this chapter took place in early May 2013, shortly after my field research in the village.
 5. Unless otherwise indicated, the quotes are taken from my interview with Gheorghe.
 6. One of the visitors he met that day was journalist John Feffer, whose interview with Nicolae Gheorghe similarly retraces the early days of Romani activism. See John Feffer, "Toward a Roma Cosmopolitanism," blog post, 24 March 2014, accessed 1 May 2016, http://www.johnfeffer.com/toward-a-roma-cosmopolitanism/.

7. One needs to bear in mind that the conflict in Hădăreni was occurring a mere sixty kilometers away from and three years after the March 1990 conflict in Târgu-Mureş between Romanian and Hungarian groups, which was tackled in decidedly ethnic terms by state institutions (László and Novák 2016).
8. A similar statement about how crucial strategizing was is recalled also in the chapter coauthored by Gheorghe and Pulay (2013: 92): "At that time our main agenda was to protest about discrimination, so we claimed these pogroms targeted Roma communities in general, even though we noticed that mob violence was not directed against entire Roma communities in an undifferentiated way and were also told by non-Roma and police that distinctions were made. However we did not want to publicize negative aspects in case it spread the idea that all Roma are criminals. Retrospectively I regret we did this, although at that historical moment it seemed wiser not to mention these kinds of local knowledge. . . . Roma activists, backed up by international human rights organizations, framed their protest in terms of pogrom and discrimination, while portraying Roma as victims."
9. The so-called "Halonen mechanism" refers to the Council of Europe's Assembly Order No. 488 (1993) which monitored the conditions for Romania's membership to the CoE, and takes its name from the Finnish president at the time, Tarja Halonen, who had a significant contribution to the shaping of this document.

References

Berbec-Chirițoiu, Anamaria. 2013. "Carnivalesque Compassion: The Symbolic Economy of a Humanitarian Intervention in a Village in Transylvania." Master's dissertation, Department of Sociology and Social Anthropology, Central European University. Accessed 22 September 2016. http://www.etd.ceu.hu/2013/berbec_anamaria.pdf.

Borneman, John. 2002. "Reconciliation after Ethnic Cleansing: Listening, Retribution, Affiliation." *Public Culture* 14 (2): 281–304.

European Roma Rights Centre. 2001. "Victims of Romanian Mob Violence Appeal for Justice to Strasbourg Court." News release. 20 January 2001. Accessed 9 October 2016. http://www.errc.org/article/victims-of-romanian-mob-violence-appeal-for-justice-to-strasbourg-court/245.

Fassin, Didier. 2012. *Humanitarian Reason: A Moral History of the Present Times.* Berkeley, CA: University of California Press.

Fassin, Didier, and Mariella Pandolfi, eds. 2010. *Contemporary States of Emergency.* New York: Zone Books.

Fassin, Didier, and Richard Rechtman. 2009. *Empire of Trauma: An Inquiry into the Condition of Victimhood.* Princeton, NJ: Princeton University Press.

Gheorghe, Nicolae, and Gergő Pulay. 2013. "Choices to Be Made and Prices to Be Paid: Potential Roles and Consequences in Roma Activism and Policy-Making." In *From Victimhood to Citizenship: The Path of Roma Integration; A Debate,* edited by Will Guy, 41–100. Budapest: Kiadó.

Haller, István. 1998. "Cazul Hădăreni" [The Hădăreni case]. *Altera* (7).

———. 2005. "Procesul Hădăreni" [The Hădăreni trial]. *Altera* (28).

———. 2010. "The Mendacious Government: Implementation of the Romanian Pogrom Judgments." *Roma Rights: Journal of the European Roma Rights Centre* 1: 23–28.

INS: Institutul Național de Statistică. 2011. "Populația stabilă pe județe, municipii, orașe și localităti" [Population and housing census]. Accessed 1 May 2016. www.recensa mantromania.ro.

Ivasiuc, Ana, Cătălina Olteanu, Ana Chirițoiu, Andrei Constantin, Tudorel Andrei, Marius Profiroiu, Georgiana Giba, and Ioana Ploeșteanu. "Raport de evaluare a programului 'Hădăreni'" [Evaluation report of the 'Hădăreni' program]. Accessed 13 January 2016. http://www.anr.gov.ro/docs/rapoarte/Raport%20de%20evaluare%20a%20 programului%20Hadareni_ro_en.pdf.

Jenne, Eric. 2009. "The Roma of Central and Eastern Europe: Constructing a Stateless Nation." In *The Politics of National Minority Participation in Post-Communist Europe,* edited by Jonathan P. Stein, 189–212. London: M.E. Sharpe.

Klímová-Alexander, Ilona. 2005. *The Romani Voice in World Politics: The United Nations and Non-State Actors.* Aldershot: Ashgate.

László, Márton, and Zoltán C. Novák. 2016. *Provocarea libertății: Târgu-Mureș, 16–21 martie 1990.* [The challenge of freedom: Târgu-Mureș, 16–21 March 1990]. Cluj-Napoca: Editura Institutului pentru Studierea Problemelor Minorităților Naționale.

Liebich, Andre. 2007. "Roma Nation? Competing Narratives of Nationhood." *Nationalism and Ethnic Politics* 13 (4): 539–54.

Sampson, Steven L. 2003. "From Reconciliation to Coexistence." *Public Culture* 15 (1): 181–86.

———. 2002. "Beyond Transition: Rethinking Elite Configurations in the Balkans." In *Postsocialism: Ideals, Ideologies, and Practices in Eurasia,* edited by C. M. Hann, 297–316. London: Routledge.

Scott, James C. 1972. *Comparative Political Corruption.* Englewood Cliffs, NJ: Prentice-Hall.

Sigona, Nando, and Nidhi Trehan, eds. 2009. *Romani Politics in Contemporary Europe.* New York: Palgrave Macmillan.

Sobotka, Eva. 2001. "Limits of the State: Political Participation and Representation of Roma in the Czech Republic, Hungary, Poland and Slovakia." *JEMIE* 1 (winter).

Stewart, Michael. 2012. "Populism, Roma and the European Politics of Cultural Difference." In *The Gypsy "Menace": Populism and the New Anti-Gypsy Politics,* edited by Michael Stewart, 3–23. London: Hurst.

Toma, Stefánia. 2012. "Segregation and Ethnic Conflicts in Romania." In *The Gypsy "Menace": Populism and the New Anti-Gypsy Politics,* edited by Michael Stewart, 191–213. London: Hurst.

van Baar, Huub. 2008. "The Way Out of Amnesia? Europeanisation and the Recognition of the Roma's Past and Present." *Third Text* 22 (3): 373–85.

———. 2011. *The European Roma: Minority Representation, Memory and the Limits of Transnational Governmentality.* Amsterdam: F&N.

———. 2015. "Enacting Memory and the Hard Labor of Identity Formation." In *The Identity Dilemma: Collective Identity and Social Movements,* edited by Aidan McGarry and James Jasper, 150–69. Philadelphia: Temple University Press.

Vermeersch, Peter. 2006. *The Romani Movement: Minority Politics and Ethnic Mobilization in Contemporary Central Europe.* Oxford: Berghahn Books.

———. 2012. "Reframing the Roma: EU Initiatives and the Politics of Reinterpretation." *Journal of Ethnic and Migration Studies* 38 (8): 1195–212.

CHAPTER 3

❁ ❁ ❁

ENCOUNTERS AT THE MARGINS
Activism and Research in Romani Studies in Postsocialist Romania

László Fosztó

This chapter is based on my personal experiences of working in Roma-related research within the Romanian Institute for Research on National Minorities (RIRNM), an institute founded by the Romanian Government in 2007, the same year Romania joined the European Union as a member state. RIRNM has the mandate "to conduct inter- and multidisciplinary studies and research with regard to the preservation, development and expression of ethnic identity, as well as about social, historical, cultural, linguistic, religious or other aspects of national minorities and of other ethnic communities living in Romania."[1] Thus, the institute is par excellence a site of applied social research at the service of ethnic communities, policy-making bodies, and decision makers. Returning to Romania after finishing my studies abroad, I joined the RIRNM; this offered me the opportunity to continue fueling my academic interest in minorities, and it brought me into more systematic contact with activists and social mobilizers, some of whom were Roma. Living and working in Transylvania, I acquired a good sense of cultural boundaries, ethnic and class differences, past and present social injustices; while maintaining sensitivity to human rights abuses I encountered or noted threats to the personal dignity of the people with whom I worked, I never considered myself an activist of any sort. This was, on the one hand, a personal inclination: I felt my capacities were more suitable for analysis than intervention. On the other hand, I considered that given the Romanian context, where a strong generation of Roma and pro-Roma activists was already emerging, I could contribute more by doing social research, since this is what I was trained for. My interactions and encounters in this field during the past decade strengthened my conviction that the solid contribution of researchers is more needed than ever.

The analysis below will discuss these encounters in the context of social and institutional transformations within the postsocialist Romanian state. My starting point is that, in spite of the widely held view that Roma activism is best understood as part and function of "civil society," it is more useful to put the state back into the equation and investigate the dynamic interactions among activists, representatives of the state, academics, other sympathetic or less-than-sympathetic outsiders, and society at large. More specifically, I argue that activism is at least partially driven by intentions to transform the state. Activists aim to "correct" the shortcomings of state institutions, monitor and litigate the abuses of the authorities, and improve the social inclusion of the Roma population. Therefore the state, which routinely operates in these domains, is an important frame of reference for these processes. Moreover, in some cases, the state apparatus can accommodate activism (for example, part of the educational system can be put to the service of language activism); in some other cases, as I demonstrate in my ethnography below, institutions can become sites for contestation and struggle between different actors taking roles as bureaucrats, stakeholders, experts of different statuses, or activists, in a complex web of relationships and in shifting sequences.

In what follows, after a brief literature review, I discuss two episodes of my engagement with Roma-related activism. My involvement in these events can be described as marginal, since I was a rather passive newcomer in the domain of activism, working in a regional center (Cluj-Napoca; in Hungarian, Kolozsvár) far from the capital city—the main site of Roma-related activism in this highly centralized country. The moments I refer to were, first, an initiative that aimed to stop and prevent the occurrence of ethnic violence in Transylvania (2009–10), and, second, the events surrounding the public debates in 2010–11 around one of the legislative initiatives to change the official ethnonym of Roma from "Rom" to *țigan* (Gypsy) in Romania. The term *țigan* is pejorative in Romanian society and the term "Rom," according to Romanians, causes confusion between Romanians and Roma. These events are connected by the presence of recurrent issues and returning actors, among them the sociologist and activist Nicolae Gheorghe, whom I first met in 2008 during an event organized in Cluj. Part of the analysis is inspired by his ideas.

Attracted by "Civic Spirit" between Projects, Service Providers, Watchdogs, and the State

While important elements for a general historical and contemporary description of Roma activism in Romania are available, a comprehensive overview is yet to be written.[2] Such a history should encompass a broad range of initiatives on behalf of the Roma or emerging within the Roma communities, also as responses to the growing number of targeted interventions. There are some persistent definitional uncertainties. I will start with the most important one: it is rather difficult to define what exactly Roma activism is.

The common-sense understanding is that activism among, and on behalf of, the Roma has to do with nongovernmental organizations (NGOs) and their "projects." Viorel Anăstăsoaie and Daniela Tarnovschi (2001) edited a volume about the projects on Roma between 1990 and 2000, offering an overview of the impressive NGO scene of the 1990s. Iulius Rostas (2009: 182), in a chapter on the institutionalization and mobilization of Roma, also focuses exclusively on the NGOs and deplores the growing bureaucratization of Roma associations, while calling for "the genuine spread of a self-help civic spirit as an alternative to 'NGOization.'" This call remains vague and undefined, as it remains unclear how this process could be enacted. These approaches routinely overlook the influence of religious movements[3] or the mobilizing impact of artistic and musical expressions (for a critical approach see Pulay 2014). Moreover, NGOs, as frames and sites for activism, are presented in opposition to the state, which is a binary oversimplification. As a counterexample, Gheorghe Sarău (2013) offers an overview of the language movement, which is arguably a rather successful area of Romani activism, which became institutionalized within a state actor—the ministry of education. A particular form of national and international NGO is the "watchdog" organization, for which I will provide an example in my first case study. I will show below how the state/NGO opposition can become problematic.

A second observation is that Romani activism cannot and should not be interpreted only narrowly within any single state, since the Romani movement challenges the confines of individual nation-states, even if there are particularities observable in each case. Thus, as a consequence of its transnational character, the Romani movement poses methodological challenges to empirical studies. While the events tackled by activism are clearly localized in communities or institutions, they are also connected to other sites and processes, which complement their description and interpretation. Indeed, academic work has previously connected the different sites and scales of Romani activism, showing the complexity of the processes through which activism "travels" (van Baar 2009; 2017). Doing fieldwork on activism or with activists, however, requires hands-on engagement in the local context, in order to elicit details of local knowledge and identify the structures underpinning these forms of knowledge (for a critical example of why local knowledge is crucial, see Chiriţoiu, this volume). At the same time, one should be aware of the broader significance of these events and interpret them with reference to the processes which unfold in-between locations (see Fosztó 2003a).

Issues connected to this process were addressed by anthropologists in other contexts; in discussing the relationship between activism and anthropology with reference to his own work on the U.S.-Mexico border, Josiah Heyman (2010: 291) summarizes a set of assumptions that also inform my own approach in the current chapter. He concludes,

> The ethic of ethnographic solidarity is insufficient without an analysis of the historical power placement and fields surrounding our specific ethnographic subjects. Second, we must examine thoughtfully our possible engagement with states and politicians. . . . We cannot, in our current social arrangements, assume that the state is inherently and uniformly an evil institution (e.g., Taussig 1991), nor markets and businesses either. Likewise . . . we should not assume a naïve, power- and history-innocent analysis of poor and low-power communities nor of organizations and activists involved with them.

In most of my previous work on mobilization in Roma communities, I focused on the role of religion and ritual practices rather than on that of NGOs and state institutions.[4] This is partly due to the existing practices in my—mainly rural—field sites, where associations or foundations and civic activism were barely visible, while the presence of religious activists (missionaries, pastors, preachers) and the regular calendar of religious activities offered a structured domain for my inquiries. The religious groups I worked with (Pentecostals) are remarkably autonomous, independent from state support, and instead of being nationally based, they are organized in transnational networks. In addition to this decisive empirical observation, there was a conceptual limitation coming from my own background, being myself a member of a Hungarian ethnic group (Szekler) living in Romania.[5] I had taken for granted the idea that minority activism coming from "the community" might only be supported by its "own" institutions, such as ethnic churches (Fosztó 2006), and ideally independently from—or even in opposition to—the state. It took me some years to realize that while some minority groups practice ideologies and rituals of independence and autonomy, these practices interact intensely with, and often rely on structures and institutions provided by, the state. This realization made me also more reflexive about my own position within a governmental research institute.

Sam Beck (1993) argued that the socialist system in Romania not only preserved, but actively produced, ethnic distinctions, and that therefore we need to contextualize the formation of Romani ethnic identity as part of a broader process. The social and institutional processes of producing distinctions became even more intensive after the fall of the socialist regime. Partly as a response to societal processes, and partly due to international pressure, a number of new institutions emerged within the postsocialist state to deal with issues of ethnic and cultural diversity, and social and ethnic differences, or to combat racism and discrimination. The emergence and workings of these institutions need to be described and interpreted as context for the encounters that are the focus of this chapter.

As I show in the next sections, the state should not be seen as a homogeneous actor, not even as an actor in itself. It is better viewed as a bundle of social relationships controlling a set of rules, exercising real and imaginary powers (see Trouillot 2001). Its structure is layered in various ways, central authorities might have different understandings and intentions than local institutions, and there are geographical, regional disparities in access to resources and capacity to penetrate local social relationships. The state provides a domain for orientation and navigation for individuals, and a good part of what activists do is a particular form of participation in this domain. The role of the activist is performed by a wide range of individuals, employees of the public or nonprofit sector, self-employed, social workers, local politicians, journalists, lawyers, pastors, students, professors, or other academics. The activist's role is relational, defined by interactions, often bound to situations and "taking position." An anthropological analysis of activism, like Huub van Baar's contribution in this volume also suggests, should offer an understanding of the motivations and positioning of the actors who perform activist roles within and without the frames maintained by the state, but almost always with reference to it.

On Ethnic Conflicts and Shared Responsibility

In mid-summer 2009, a series of events happened that threatened to escalate into a wave of violent ethnic conflicts in a number of rural multiethnic Transylvanian settlements. These violent events emerged after a long, relatively peaceful period, which characterized the relationship between Roma and local ethnic majorities. As members of RIRNM, my fellow researchers and I felt compelled to respond to this situation. We were aware that during the early years of postsocialism in Romania a high number of clashes between Roma and ethnic Hungarians or Roma and ethnic Romanians had taken place, which often resulted in property destruction (the burning of houses) and even casualties (for a comprehensive account of one of these events, see Ana Chiriţoiu's chapter in this volume).

But, by the mid-1990s, these conflicts stopped and ethnic tensions changed in character. These changes may be attributed at least partly to emerging Roma activism and the involvement of international human rights organizations (Fosztó and Anăstăsoaie 2001). Intervening institutional actors, police, and other state authorities transformed the tensions between local groups: while violent conflicts between locals were more typical of the first decade, police raids in Roma settlements or other abuse of power by authorities became more characteristic during the 2000s (Toma 2012: 192). Also, there was a transition from the early postsocialist, almost exclusively rural, clashes to more urban forms of conflict epitomized by the evictions of urban Roma settlements by local authorities. Some of the earlier cases remained legally unsolved; court cases dragged on for decades, or even when a final court decision was made, it was not enforced (see Haller 2009; also Chirițoiu, this volume). During this relatively peaceful period, between 1995 and 2009, the belief that these earlier tensions were "solved" was widely shared and the few new instances of ethnic violence involving Roma were perceived as isolated cases. This understanding was seriously challenged in June–July 2009.

On 31 May 2009, an extended conflict, involving large groups of locals in Sânmartin (in Hungarian, Csíkszentmárton) occurred; on 9 July 2009 a second instance of violent confrontation happened fifteen kilometers away, in Sâncrăieni (in Hungarian, Csíkszentkirály), both in Harghita county. Both cases involved fighting among local Roma and Hungarians (Szeklers). In the first case, the property of Roma was damaged by a local crowd; in the second, a group of the local majority burned a stable belonging to a Roma family, and a horse was killed in the fire (see the localization of the events on map 3.1). The motives that sparked the violence were different: accusations of theft from the fields in the first, and a conflict in the bar—which ended in a knifing—in the second. In both cases the intervention of the military police (in Romanian, *jandarmeria*) was necessary to restore peace.

There were similarities between these two cases—for instance, in both cases village authorities laid down so-called "protocols": sets of rules for peaceful cohabitation drafted by the local ethnic majority (Szekler Hungarians) and agreed upon, under the pressure of the moment, by representatives of the local *Romungre* (in Hungarian *magyarcigányok,* or "Hungarian Gypsies"). The protocols prescribed measures aimed to restrict, discipline, and supervise the behavior of the local Roma community. For example, Roma who do not own or rent pastures should give up keeping horses; Roma should vaccinate and chain their dogs; they should stop stealing crops from the fields, make sure that their children go to school regularly, etc. Each expected action point had a well-defined deadline.

These "protocols" contained prejudiced statements about the Roma, and even if the local councils approved them, their legality and effects later became sources of much controversy. A group of vigilante villagers in Sânmartin paid regular "monitoring visits" to the area of the village inhabited by Roma to see if they indeed sold their horses or if they were respecting other rules "instituted" by the local council. A part of the local Roma took refuge in the nearby forest, and a Roma-led human rights organization, Romani

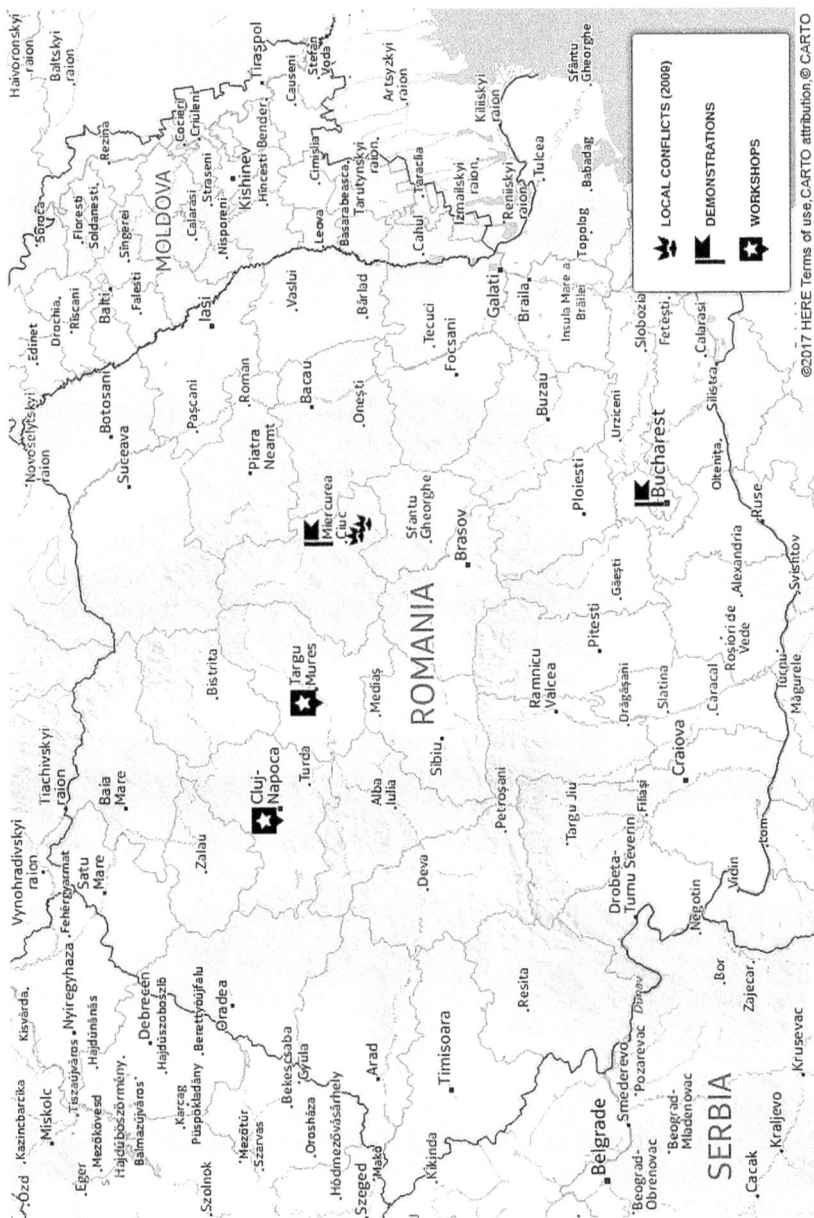

Map 3.1. The locations of the events described in the chapter. Map by the author, © CARTO, © OpenStreetMap contributors.

CRISS, visited the villages repeatedly, prepared reports about both events (Romani CRISS 2009a; 2009b), and ran an advocacy campaign suggesting that Roma who left their houses should be considered as internally displaced persons (IDPs) according to the international law.[6]

Some weeks after the events, on 20 July, the RIRNM organized a round-table discussion with researchers, journalists and human rights experts. The results were published shortly both in Romanian and in Hungarian (Sipos 2009a; 2009b). The main arguments in this discussion explained the economic background of these conflicts and suggested the role state institutions should play in managing local social tensions. We also developed an understanding of the long history of local customary law and self-regulation, including the internal social control in Szekler villages (Hungarian, *falutörvények*), which can be seen as a prototype of these "protocols."[7]

The bulk of local and regional Hungarian language newspapers downplayed the significance of the conflict and emphasized how the process of reconciliation progressed as a consequence of the protocols. One exception was an article by Tímea Bakk-Dávid (2009), working for a leading Hungarian language news portal, who visited the field and published a balanced report, including photographs documenting the damage done to the houses of the Roma. The article soon attracted a massive wave of negative comments from the readers, to such an extent that the Transindex portal felt compelled to disable commenting (Bakk-Dávid 2009a). An opinion piece by Boróka Parászka, another Hungarian journalist with a distinctive voice, attracted even more outrage. She not only criticized the passivity of the state institutions, but also blamed local inhabitants for being active perpetrators or silent accomplices. To give emphasis to her conclusions, she labeled the perpetrators of violence "animals" (Parászka 2009). As a consequence, sixteen mayors in Harghita County, Szeklerland, led by the president of the county council, sent to the National Council for Combating Discrimination (NCCD) a complaint against the journalist for discriminating against the Hungarian community. The head of the NCCD, a Hungarian himself, dismissed the complaint as being "absurd and ridiculous" (S.M.L. 2009).

On 23 July 2009, at the initiative of Romani CRISS, about fifty to sixty people representing a coalition of Roma associations organized a protest in front of the central office of the Democratic Alliance of Hungarians in Romania (DAHR) in Bucharest.[8] The protesters handed over a list of "eleven commandments for the Hungarians." According to a press article (Safta 2009), these included demands such as "obligatory schooling and educating the children and adults to enable each Hungarian to learn the proper pronunciation of twenty Romanian words such as *stork, cabbage, badger, foal, cheese*";[9] "a (proper) civilized everyday conduct, unlike Hun behavior" and "giving up wearing mustaches, as this facial architecture has been patented by Roma ancestors." These echoed Romanian stereotypes of Hungarians (stubborn, intolerant, violent, and stupid), and this sarcastic Roma response to the Szekler Hungarians' "protocol" was not lost on the amused broader public.

The same coalition of Roma organizations intended to visit the villages and organize protests there, but local mayors refused to grant them permission to do so on the grounds that local inhabitants, including the Roma, did not want peace disturbed by their interference. The intention of the local community to keep out the activists was rather clear.[10] To prove claims of reconciliation, the local authority gathered and presented signatures from members of the local Roma community in the form of a message faxed to the organizers of the demonstration. While one can question the validity of the signatures, particularly having in mind the limited literacy and lack of knowledge of the Romanian language of some of the signatories, and the social pressure to which they were subjected at that moment, we should not dismiss the possibility and significance of a local process of reconciliation that these signatures represented.[11]

Finally, a pro-Roma protest was organized in Miercurea Ciuc (in Hungarian, Csíkszereda), seat of Harghita County, and some fifty to sixty people marched on the city streets with banners inscribed in Romanian, with messages such as "Is ethnic cleansing the first step toward territorial autonomy?,"[12] "Harghita above everything, above justice and human rights!?," and "Prevent spreading of interethnic conflicts!," in addition to a number of other calls for nonviolence. Even if some of the banners were bilingual (Romanian/Hungarian), conscious spelling mistakes in the Hungarian texts attracted criticism and amusement from local Hungarians (Mihály 2009).

As the demonstrators lined up for the march, a handful of men wearing black masks also gathered, holding insulting banners in Hungarian and chanting anti-Roma slogans. They were quickly apprehended and fined by the gendarmes who were present to protect the demonstrators. It turned out that the masked men were members of the "Sixty-Four Counties Youth Movement" (in Hungarian, Hatvannégy Vármegye Ifjúsági Mozgalom), a far-right youth organization nurturing nostalgia for Greater Hungary and promoting revisionist ideology.

Some Hungarian locals complained that these youngsters were just worsening the situation by confirming that Szeklers are by definition intolerant. Meanwhile, Hunor Kelemen, a leading politician of the DAHR and the ethnic Hungarian candidate for the presidential elections, commented on these events, stating that any demonstration such as that organized by Romani CRISS and carrying such banners in the region can only be seen as a provocation: "Organizers should protest in Bucharest in front of the Government instead, rather than taking these fifty–sixty people to this city. They would do better to persuade their co-ethnics to follow social norms, since Szeklers are law-abiding citizens," he concluded (quoted in Mihály 2009). A group of villagers from the settlements involved in the conflict attended the demonstration as bystanders (both Roma and Szeklers), including a local councilor from Sânmartin. They came to town to see "what intentions the Roma demonstrators have," while one Roma leader from Sâncrăieni declared to the Hungarian language newspaper *Krónika* that they also consider themselves Hungarian so there is no "ethnic conflict" and everybody just wants peace in the village (*Krónika* 2009). This particular double allegiance of the local Hungarian-speaking Roma in Szeklerland would need more in-depth analysis. Here, I just would like to note that being Hungarian and "*cigány*" are not mutually exclusive social and ethnic categories, so the *Romungre* can chose to identify as Hungarians, as they usually do, for example during the national censuses or other interactions with the officialdom.

While the initially declared intention of the demonstration was to protest against human rights violations and to stop the violence against Roma in the region, the majority of the local inhabitants clearly perceived the march as an anti-Hungarian event in spite of the original intentions as a pro-Roma demonstration. Some of the participants in the protest also realized that their message was "lost in translation." The Roma sociologist Nicolae Gheorghe and Gergő Pulay, a young anthropologist from Hungary working in Romania, were both present at the demonstration in Miercurea Ciuc and immediately after the event coauthored and released a brief and insightful report (Gheorghe and Pulay 2009), arguing that the local understandings of the events should not be neglected but brought out into open discussion. They identified two narratives. The "ethnic cleansing" discourse conflated the image of contemporary Hungary, where actions against the Roma, underpinned by rising anti-Roma sentiment, were taking place, with the local villages where Szekler Hungarians live, turning them symbolically to "nests of racism and violence" against Roma. The other narrative was a more general opposition between "peasants versus nomads"; these oppositions were clearly embedded in the region, generally perceived as marginal and economically underdeveloped. These discourses framed the general contradiction between the universalistic messages "against violence" and calling for "human rights" and their understanding in the local context as demonstrations of "strangers versus locals" or even as "Romanians versus Hungarians." Gheorghe and Pulay called for an alternative discourse of *shared responsibility* and advocated for a dialogue with local forms of knowledge.[13]

The idea of *shared responsibility* became the catalyst and headline for a meeting convened later that summer in Târgu Mureș (in Hungarian, Marosvásárhely), the seat of Mureș County, on 17 and 18 August. Two local human rights activists, a Romanian and a Hungarian,[14] jointly hosted the workshop; Nicolae Gheorghe and several Roma activists from Romania and Hungary organized and attended the workshop. The main aim was to further the understanding of the emergence of ethnic conflicts in the region, and more broadly in Romania and Hungary, and also to prevent the spread of such events. András Bíró, a journalist from Hungary with a long personal history in human rights advocacy and community development, was among the participants, as well as a number of university professors from Budapest and Cluj-Napoca; the RIRNM was represented by Stefánia Toma and myself.[15] Representatives of Romani CRISS did not attend the meeting, but the reports of this organization, in addition to other documents, were shared in advance and discussed.

After a long day of discussions, all participants agreed to sign a common position paper, which was published in the Romanian press in Romanian and Hungarian. The position paper laid out a vision for social peace and anti-discrimination, but it also proposed to complement the antiracist fight with new ways of engagement and shared responsibilities that would encompass a whole range of actors, political stakeholders, civil society organizations (including Roma associations), state authorities, and actors responsible for implementing public policies for Roma inclusion. A subgroup of participants agreed to develop a joint research project that would look into the local conditions of the villages involved in the conflicts, follow up on the social consequences of the events that led to the conflict, and organize public discussions with local authorities. This plan was later enacted with the support of the Open Society Institute (see Magyari et al. 2010).

The initiative contributed to creating a more balanced approach and opened dialogue between different stakeholders of various backgrounds, as none of these actors would have been able to act on their own with the same effect. While advocacy groups, epitomized by Romani CRISS in the description above, performing their "watchdog" role are fast in reacting to situations by sending unequivocal public messages, identifying targets for legal action, or formulating demands for public apology, individuals working for state institutions are relatively slower in their reactions.

However, not all tensions or conflicts play out in this competitive way. In the next section, I turn to discuss some events related to issues of definition, in which academics usually feel at home and, as I will show, where there was more space for cooperation.

Țigan versus Roma: The Debate around Ethnonyms

After a long day of discussions during the "shared responsibility" meeting, on a warm August evening, we sat down with some of the participants in a beer garden in Târgu Mureş. Nicolae Gheorghe was leading the discussion, switching between three languages depending on whom he was address- ing.[16] After a vivid exchange in Romani with the delegation of Roma from Hungary about the sources of "*Gadjo* power" (in Romani, *zor le gadjenge*)[16] he turned toward me and teasingly said in Romanian, "So at least we finally agreed today that while I would like the Gypsies from Szeklerland (in Roma- nian, *ţiganii din Secuime*) to declare themselves Roma, László wants them just as much to say clearly that they are Hungarians."

We both burst into laughter. I certainly did not want anybody at that mo- ment living in those villages to claim any other identity than the one they claimed in their everyday interactions, a point that I had tried to make during earlier discussions. Even if Gheorghe was more strategic in suggesting con- textual identity claims as a form of ethnic mobilization, the claim that simply vocal allegiance to the term "Roma" would be empowering enough sounded like a self-ironic caricature. Little did I know that in a few months' time, issues related to "definitions" and "ethnonyms" would become the main Roma-related topic in the media.

As I have shown, there are Gypsy groups (like the *magyarcigányok* dis- cussed above) who do not necessarily identify themselves as Roma. Mem- bers of these groups can opt for being or "becoming" Roma, joining a political identity that is organized at the higher levels, but often the expe- rience of this political identity is rather limited or even lacking in the local context. Gheorghe was a leading promoter of this political identity at the national and international levels, but, at the same time, he was reflecting on its political dynamism, being well aware of the limitations of its appeal in certain contexts. I was familiar with Gheorghe's arguments about the insti- tutional context of social constructions of Romani identity (Gheorghe 1992; 1997) and it was also well known that in his practical social projects around the idea of *pakiv* (in Romani, loyalty/honesty/reliability) he insisted on con- necting identity building and economic activities as forms of exercising both trust and self-reliance within Roma communities (see also Tanaka 2015). At the moment of our exchange, we shared the understanding of the *Romungre* in Szeklerland as a group with locally embedded socioeconomic relations and a particular identity formation.

Starting in 2009, the conservative newspaper *Jurnalul Naţional* pub- lished a series of articles culminating in 2010 in a campaign for a referen- dum demanding that the ethnic group known in different European states as Gypsies or *Zigeuner* should be officially named *ţigan* in Romania, and that the "Rom" or "Roma" terms should be taken out of use. Similar initiatives existed previously, as since the 1990s there were political and public cam- paigns attempting to "revert" the ethnonym Roma to *ţigan*. The initiators of this campaign argued that the confusion between "Romanian" and "Roma" should be avoided, and that the "correct" name should therefore be used; this "confusion" was even more disturbing in the wake of the westward migration of an increasing number of Romanian Roma.[17] In September 2010, a legislative initiative supporting the name change was submitted by Silviu Prigoană, a member of Parliament. The initiative passed by check of the parliamentary commission for equality of opportunities, but it was rejected by the commission for human rights and national minorities–related issues.[18] The Romanian government requested an opinion from the Romanian Academy. The Section of Philology and Literature of the Romanian Academy issued a letter in late October 2010, which argued, "Having in mind the situation of groups which belong to the Gypsy ethnicity (in Romanian, *etniei țigănești*) in Europe and in the Romanian area, our Section considers that the term *țigan* represents the correct name for this transnational population."[19] After obtaining this "scientific reassurance," the proponents of the law persevered with their proposal, in spite of the growing concern and open protests from Roma NGOs, human rights activists, and other political actors. It would be misleading to imagine that this letter by the Romanian Academy represents the position of all researchers of that institution, let alone of all scholars doing Roma-related research in Romania. However, the symbolic and political consequences of this letter should not be downplayed: it was used strategically by political actors in order to grant legitimacy to the conservative turn seeking to introduce in public administration the stigmatizing ethnic label for Roma.

Late in 2010, in the middle of this period of intense political debate and confrontation, I received a phone call from Nicolae Gheorghe. He proposed that the RIRNM should convene a workshop with researchers and activists, and debate the issues related to the ethnic terminology. He suggested that such a workshop could be well in line with the profile of our institute and after scientific debate we could come up with a position that might differ from the one expressed by the Romanian Academy. I agreed with his proposal, and following a discussion with my colleagues and the director of the institute I started to organize this meeting.

The event finally took place on 18 January 2011, with the participation of a large number of activists and social researchers from different disciplines. In the meantime, an unexpected event happened in Cluj-Napoca on 17 December 2010; the office of the mayor decided to evict fifty-six Roma families, demolishing their settlement in a coveted central part of the city (Coastei Street). The evicted families were offered shelter at the margins of the city's administrative area, in the vicinity of the municipal landfill. This action brought Cluj into the headlines of the national media, and with the effective help of a group of local civil activists and academics, a campaign was initiated that also attracted the attention of international human rights and advocacy groups (Amnesty International, European Roma Rights Centre, among others). The issue of the eviction and of its consequences has generated a continuous discussion in the past years (see Vincze 2013).

In the process of preparing and organizing the workshop on ethnic terminology, I received many suggestions from Nicolae Gheorghe, including on whom to invite. It became increasingly clear to me that he had a rather well-defined strategy for how we should disseminate the results of the workshop on the international scene most effectively. Finally, a large number of invitations were sent out with the expectation that many would attend the meeting. On the morning of the workshop, Nicolae Gheorghe showed up wearing a large hat and a red scarf, with a broom under his arm. He used the broom as a walking stick but also clipped documents on it while sitting among the participants. By using the broom, his main purpose was to popularize the work of a particular Roma group who makes brooms, in a public performance of ethnicity (figure 3.1). This became even clearer when the next day Gheorghe attended a demonstration organized as a protest against the Mayor of Cluj who had evicted the Roma. He symbolically attached a Romani flag on the top of his broom (see cover image of this volume), holding it up in the air for everyone to see (*Transindex* 2009).[20]

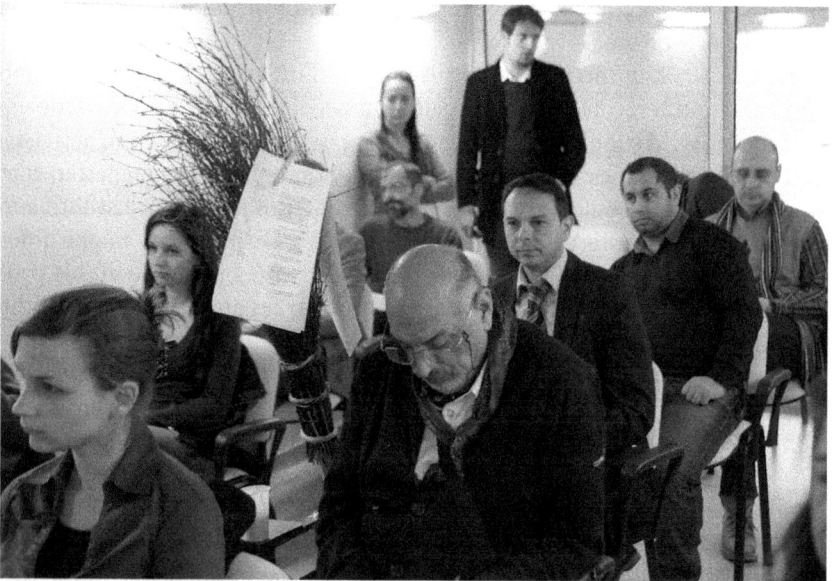

Figure 3.1. Nicolae Gheorghe during the event organized by the RIRNM in January 2011. Photo courtesy of Albert Zsolt Jakab.

The workshop consisted of a number of presentations by RIRMN researchers and other invited academics and activists, as well as a long and
intense debate on issues connected to identity, self-determination, political
correctness, and human rights. Gheorghe was often provocative, and challenged his younger colleagues active in the Romani movement to be more
creative and open to discussions. He challenged them in particular, as he
later explained to me, because some of them nurtured political ambitions
and they were in the process of building up a large coalition of NGOs that
had electoral ambitions during the forthcoming local elections, and he
feared they lacked the necessary determination.[21]

The tensions surrounding the meeting contributed to a lively debate, resulting in the conclusion that we needed to reject the position that claims
that there is a single "correct" term for the name of an ethnic group. Rather,
we should look into the classification process itself and be aware of the social and political processes at work in the right of ethnic self-determination, maintaining that the rights of ethnic communities should prevail. The
conclusion seemed not to fully satisfy all the participants. A minority of
Roma activists prepared a position paper, which listed additional historical
and philological arguments in support of retaining the term "Roma" as the
proper ethnonym. We all agreed that a report would be prepared about the
results of the workshop and posted on the institute's website, and circulated
among the workshop participants and the general public. I made a summary
of the proceedings, which was quickly translated into English and widely distributed. A volume—*Rom sau țigan. Dilemele unui etnonim în spațiul românesc*
("Rom or Gypsy: Dilemmas of an ethnonym in the Romanian space")—was
later edited on these issues (Horváth and Nastasă 2012).[22] At the book launch,
activists criticized the editors, claiming that such a volume should have made
a clear case for the term "Roma." Moreover, one activist started an email
campaign claiming that the RIRNM was playing a duplicitous game, and that
we had made a case for the term "Gypsy" by publishing in the same period
an ethnographic working paper titled "We are Gypsies, not Roma!" (Marin
2010). This title reflects how some local Roma groups identify themselves as
țigani (Gypsies) and distance themselves from the term "Roma."

The topic slowly seemed to fade from interest, but in press outlets we
kept emphasizing the importance of avoiding stigmatization and maintaining respect for the self-ascription of ethnic groups.[23] Finally, in April 2011,
the legislative initiative for making the term *țigan* the official name for the
ethnic group was rejected by the Senate. At the RIRMN, we put together
an archive of the whole debate, gathering, with the help of volunteers, hundreds of sources from the press and other publicly accessible sources. While
I had hoped that it would be the final moment of this narrative, in early 2015,

a new petition appeared for the same purpose, to obtain the necessary number of signatures for a referendum on the *țigan*/Roma terminology, and another member of Parliament (Bogdan Diaconu) announced his support for
this cause.[24] Clearly, the debate about this issue is far from being settled in
the Romanian public sphere; some politicians will continue to rely on antigypsyism as a political vehicle.

Conclusion

Concluding the reflection on these cases, I argue that Roma activism should
not be interpreted independently from the processes and exchanges in which
it is entangled. Activism, by its very nature, is embedded in these entangle-
ments. The dynamics of racism and antigypsyism (in Romanian, *antițigan-
ism*; in Hungarian, *cigányellenesség*) is a persistent element of this scene.
Strong emotional reactions from activists and researchers are evoked when
threats of violence occur, be it physical—as in the first case discussed—or
symbolic, through the manipulation of symbolic categories and terms—as
in the second case. The two cases are different in many respects. The first is
an example of a localized conflict and the subsequent intervention of state
institutions and external actors, such as Romani CRISS. In this case, a watchdog NGO addressed and denounced issues related to the ineffectiveness
of the state to protect the rights of its citizens in case of physical threat by
their neighbors. Yet the local understanding shared by the authorities and
the majority of the local population turned these activist undertakings into
an unwelcome intrusion. Conflicting regional, social, and ethnic categories
pop up time and again, so ethnic ascriptions, other social identities, and
belonging cannot be seen as politically neutral. Positions are both actively
self-assumed and externally attributed (Barth 1969). Neglecting local perceptions of activism has a potential for misguided action. The example of the
Miercurea Ciuc protest illustrates that defining human rights without tuning
them to local understandings might easily be interpreted as a nationalist or
anti-Hungarian intrusion in the region, or both, shifting the nature of the
original conflict.

The second case—the nation-wide debated issue of the definitional struggles around the ethnonym Rom/*țigan*—demonstrates how different actors are
orienting themselves between institutions like the Romanian government,
the section of the Romanian Academy conferring pseudoscientific legitimacy
to political actions, the Parliament, NGOs, academics, and the RIRNM. Activism, as exemplified by the intervention of the late Nicolae Gheorghe, can
be described as skillful navigation between different organizations and actors
in order to forge alliances, achieve balance, and reach one's goals.

There are some implications for the position of researchers and their relationship with activist roles. As I tried to show in the ethnographic description, every person involved in these events is politically engaged and needs to take a particular position: no one can stay "neutral." Certainly, there are more marginal and more central positions in processes associated with activism. From the beginning, I perceived myself at the margins, where I remained throughout these events; this proved to be a rather comfortable position for me as a researcher. However, a marginal role is still political, but not necessarily activist. Other people had a more central role in these stories, and Nicolae Gheorghe was such a person. Undeniably, he had an important role in shaping these discussions, but it would be misleading to say that he was the one who defined these situations. The main force leading these events was the logic of the dialogue, the discourse created throughout the encounters. Definitions of the situation emerged from the conversations into which I tried to offer a glimpse, and as I intentionally positioned myself at the margin, I sought to document all sides of the arguments and present the outcome. While doing this, I tried continuously to negotiate my role as researcher as a distinct position, not in terms of absolute neutrality but in relations to my and others' personal engagement.

In order to bring back the state into the discussion about activism, we need to remember that many of the actors who are present in the ethnography have been involved in these events due to their official roles or employment in some government body either directly maintained by the state (local administrations and institutions) or closely related to the state sector. In contemporary Romania, academics are often in this position, working in state educational institutions, or even—as in the case of my workplace—directly linked to governmental structures. This approach widens the field of "activism," since we can see that there is no necessary opposition between professional research and the performance of roles that can be interpreted as activism.

This chapter could be read as a fragment of institutional history, an attempt to summarize, in some detail, some of the activities in the field of Romani studies carried out within the Romanian Institute for Research on National Minorities in its early period. The idea of this institute emerged as part of a broader process of institutionalizing the system of minority protection (naturally oriented toward activism and advocacy) and knowledge production on ethnic minorities in Romania. The context of these exchanges between research and activism was shaped, on the one hand, by powerful external agencies, and, on the other hand, by ongoing social processes on the ground. Entering into these dialogues, the parties benefited from the exchanges without blurring or merging the roles of activist and researcher. While many researchers are also involved in activism, those whose positions do not overlap and are engaged in either activism or research should certainly continue to engage in dialogue. They should seek to reach common goals while trying to improve the situation—by influencing state institutions to be more effective, for example, and by providing a more complete and nuanced analysis of the ongoing processes. We can walk different paths toward these goals while keeping up the dialogue that defines our roles as researchers and/or activists.

László Fosztó is a social anthropologist working at the Romanian Institute for Research on National Minorities in Cluj-Napoca, Romania. His academic interests include studies of ethnicity and nationalism, ritual, religious revival, and social mobilization among the Roma. More recently, he has been working on mobility, migration, remittances, and informal economy. He was appointed secretary of the European Academic Network on Romani Studies (http://romanistudies.eu/) from 2011 to 2015, and he continues to serve the Romani studies community as voluntary moderator for the Network.

Notes

I owe thanks to the editors of this volume, Sam Beck and Ana Ivasiuc, for their patience and support, as well as for their comment on the first draft. I am grateful to Stefánia Toma, who participated in many of the events discussed here, read my description with a critical eye, and pointed out some shortcomings. She also organized a seminar at the RIRNM in mid-March 2016 where I could present this paper and discuss it with colleagues. Ana Chirițoiu and Gergő Pulay also read this chapter in draft and offered insightful comments; I am grateful to them. During the writing I worked as part of the Romanian team in the MigRom research project, which is cofunded by the European Union's Seventh Framework Programme for research, technological development, and demonstration under grant agreement number 319901.

1. Source: "About the Institute," Romanian Institute for Research on National Minorities website, accessed 20 January 2016, http://ispmn.gov.ro/page/despre-institut.
2. Viorel Achim's (2004) general history of the Romanian Roma includes chapters on Roma leadership and organizations. Petre Matei (2010; 2011) describes the "Gypsy assemblies" that were organized in 1919 following the Union of Transylvania to Romania; in addition, he gives a chronology of the Roma-related events (Matei 2016). There are pioneering studies by Sam Beck (1984;1990; 1993) and Nicolae Gheorghe (1991; 1997) on the more recent history of the Roma, public policies, and activism. István Haller (2009) offers a glimpse on the history of ethnic conflicts.
3. For exceptions, see Paloma Gay y Blasco's (2002) work on Spain and my publications (Fosztó 2009; 2010) on Romania.

4. Together with Viorel Anăstăsoaie I published an overview (Fosztó and Anastasoaie 2001) and continued to keep an interest in the development of Romani activism in the domestic context, while also developing an international outlook (see Fosztó 2003a; 2003b; 2009; 2010).

5. Szeklers are a particular group of Hungarians who live in Covasna, Harghita, and Mureş counties. Historically, they have enjoyed special status and their distinct ethnic/collective identity persists today.

6. For a detailed discussion of the events and the interpretation of the conflict see Toma 2012.

7. The social historian István Imreh (1983) published several volumes about these local laws, which were effective until the late nineteenth century; for similar self-governing village communities among Romanians, see Stahl 1980.

8. In that period, Romania was in the middle of the presidential electoral campaign, and the DAHR had its own candidate.

9. Certain Romanian words are considered to have roots in the ancient Dacian language, so pronouncing them properly might be perceived as a test for being a "proper Romanian."

10. A Roma activist woman whom I met in Bucharest months later told me about her experience in trying to work in the region: she felt that not only language barriers were in place, but that the local ethnic Hungarians were refusing cooperation: in one of the villages, when the Szeklers noticed her presence in the village, they quickly notified the person in charge of the church bells, who started to sound the bells as an alarm, as when a house is burning in the village.

11. Most of the Roma in the region speak Hungarian as their mother tongue. The advocates of Romani CRISS used translation in their interactions with them. The name list consists almost exclusively of Hungarian names.

12. The idea of "ethnic cleansing" connected to "autonomy" emerged earlier on the main email list of the Roma activists in Romania (RomLink); the situation was also associated with the threatening vision of an emerging "new Kosovo" in Transylvania, where the local majority will expel internal minorities.

13. These ideas are developed in more detail in Gheorghe and Pulay 2013: 88–94, the intellectual testament of the late Nicolae Gheorghe.

14. Namely the ethnic Romanian Smaranda Enache, and the ethnic Hungarian Maria Koreck.

15. The list of participants (twenty-three in total) included Roma activists from both Romania and Hungary, as well as academics.

16. Romani, Romanian, and English, which was used between Hungarians from Hungary and the ethnic Romanians.

17. *Gadjo* means non-Roma in Romani.

18. For the collection of the contributions to this debate and the campaign, see "Ţigan în loc de rom: Romi, ţigani sau BMW-uri?" [Gypsy instead of Roma: Roma, Gypsies or BMWs?], Jurnalul.ro, accessed 10 February 2016, http://jurnalul.ro/campaniile-jurnalul/tigan-in-loc-de-rom/.

19. Pl-x nr. 37/2011- Propunere legislativă privind terminologia oficială utilizată pentru etnia ţiganilor, inițiator Prigoană Vasile-Silviu [Legal proposal for adopting the official terminology for the Gypsy ethnic group initiative by Prigoană Vasile-Silviu], published 1 September 2010 and accessed 10 February 2016, http://www.cdep.ro/pls/proiecte/upl_pck.proiect?cam=2&idp=11279.

20. Official Letter on 20 October 2010 by Academician Haiduc Ionel President of the Romanian Academy to the Romanian Government regarding the legal initiative for the official use of the term "țigan," accessed 10 February 2016, http://www.transin dex.ro/images/__leo/cikkek/cikkek_41518.pdf.

21. See also the press article: "Méltó élethez való joguk tiszteletben tartásáért tüntettek a patarétiek" [People from Pat Rât demand respect for their right to live in dignity], transindexed 19 January 2011 and accessed 20 January 2016, http://itthon.transin dex.ro/?cikk=13438.

22. Alianța Civică Democrată a Romilor (ACDR) (The Civic Democratic Alliance of the Roma).

23. In Horváth and Nastasă 2012, there is a single note on the workshop in January 2011 (footnote 3, page 320).

24. Gy. A., "Tananyag ne 'niggerezzen.' És mi a helyzet a Román Akadémia 'cigá-nyozásával'?" [Curriculum should not use terms like "nigger": What about the Romanian Academy calling the Roma "țigani"?], Transindex, 2 February 2011, accessed 20 January 2016, http://itthon.transindex.ro/?cikk=13542.

25. "Înlocuirea denumirii de rrom cu țigan, sau cu altă denumire care să facă referire la originile lor" [Replace the Roma name with Gypsy or another name referring to their origins], Petitieonline, accessed 20 January 2016, http://www.petitieonline .com/inlocuirea_denumirii_de_rrom_cu_tiganstop_discriminarii_romanilor.

References

Achim, Viorel. 2004. *Roma in the History of Romania*. Budapest: Central European University Press.

Anăstăsoaie, Viorel-Marian, and Daniela Tarnovschi. 2001. *Proiecte pentru romii din România, 1990–2000* [Projects for the Roma of Romania, 1990–2000]. Cluj-Napoca: Fundația CRDE.

Bakk-Dávid, Tímea. 2009. "Látlelet egy roma-magyar konfliktus hátteréről" [Report on the background of a conflict between Roma and Hungarians]. *Transindex,* 18 June. Accessed 20 January 2016. http://itthon.transindex.ro/?cikk=9695.

Barth, Fredrik, ed. 1969. *Ethnic Groups and Boundaries: The Social Organization of Culture Difference.* Oslo: Universitetsforlaget.

Beck, Sam. 1984. "Ethnicity, Class and Public Policy: Tiganii/Gypsies in Socialist Romania." In *Papers for the V. Congress of Southeast European Studies, Belgrade,* edited by Kot Shangriladze and Erica Townsend, 19–38. Columbus, OH: Slavica Publishers.

———. 1990. "Opposition and Dissent: The Romanian Opposition's Symbolic Use of Space in June 1990." *Mario Einaudi Center for International Studies* 90 (9): 3.

———. 1993. "Racism and the Formation of a Romani Ethnic Leader." In *Perilous States: Conversations on Culture, Politics and Nation,* edited by George E. Marcus, 165–86. Chicago: University of Chicago Press.

Fosztó, László. 2003a. "Diaspora and Nationalism: An Anthropological Approach to the International Romani Movement." *REGIO* (English issue): 102–20.

———. 2003b. "The Tyrant, the Terrorists and Disruptive Elements: Aliens in the Romanian Revolution of December 1989." In *Breaking the Wall: Representing Anthropology and Anthropological Representations in Post-Communist Eastern Europe,* edited by Viorel-Marian Anăstăsoaie, Csilla Könczei, Enikő Magyari-Vincze, and Ovidiu Pecican, 71–84. Cluj-Napoca: EFES.

———. 2006. "Mono-Ethnic Churches, the 'Undertaker Parish,' and Rural Civility in Postsocialist Romania." In *"Civil Religion" Group, The Postsocialist Religious Question: Faith and Power in Central Asia and East-Central Europe,* edited by Chris Hann, 269–92. Münster: LIT Verlag.

———. 2009. *Ritual Revitalisation after Socialism: Community, Personhood, and Conversion among Roma in a Transylvanian Village.* Halle Studies in the Anthropology of Eurasia. Berlin: LIT Verlag.

———. 2010. "Mobilising 'Culture' and 'Religion': Ritual Practices and Social Relations among Two Minority Groups in Rural Transylvania." *Sociologie Românească* 8 (1): 132–46.

Fosztó, László, and Marian V. Anăstăsoaie. 2001. "Romania: Representations, Public Policies and Political Projects." In *Between Past and Future: The Roma of Central and Eastern Europe,* edited by Will Guy, 351–69. Hatfield: University of Hertfordshire Press.

Gay y Blasco, Paloma. 2002. "Gypsy/Roma Diasporas: A Comparative Perspective." *Social Anthropology* 10 (2): 173–88.

Gheorghe, Nicolae. 1991. "Roma-Gypsy Ethnicity in Eastern Europe." *Social Research* 58 (4): 844–79.

———. 1997. "The Social Construction of Romani Identity." In *Gypsy Politics and Traveller Identity,* edited by Thomas Acton, 153–71. Hatfield: University of Hertfordshire Press.

Gheorghe, Nicolae, and Gergő Pulay. 2009. "Raport de analiză a violenţelor împotriva romilor din Ungaria şi România" [Analysis report of anti-Roma violence in Hungary and Romania]. Bucharest: unpublished manuscript in the possession of the author.

———. 2013. "Choices to be Made and Prices to be Paid: Potential Roles and Consequences in Roma Activism and Policy-Making." In *From Victimhood to Citizenship: The Path of Roma Integration; A Debate,* edited by Will Guy, 41–100. Budapest: Kiadó.

Guy, Will, ed. 2013. *From Victimhood to Citizenship: The Path of Roma Integration; A Debate.* Budapest: Kiadó.

Haller, István. 2009. "Conflicte nesoluţionate de aproape 20 de ani" [Conflicts remained unsolved for nearly twenty years]. *Sfera Politicii* 138: 34–37. Accessed 10 April 2017. http://www.sferapoliticii.ro/sfera/138/art04-haller.html.

Heyman, Josiah M. 2010. "Activism in Anthropology: Exploring the Present through Eric R. Wolf's Vietnam-Era Work." *Dialectical Anthropology* 34 (2): 287–93.

Horváth, István, and Lucian Nastasă, eds. 2012. *Rom sau Ţigan: Dilemele unui etnonim în spaţiul românesc* [Roma or Gypsy: Ethnonym dilemmas in Romanian space]. Cluj-Napoca: Editura Institutului pentru Studierea Problemelor Minorităţilor Naţionale.

Imreh, István. 1983. *A Törvényhozó Székely Falu* [The law-making Szekler villages]. Cluj-Napoca: Kriterion.

Krónika. 2009. "Romatüntetés vármegyésekkel" [Roma demonstration with activists from the counties], 31 July. Accessed 20 January 2016. http://www.kronika.ro/erdelyi-hirek/romatuntetes_varmegyesekkel.

Magyari, Nándor, László Fosztó, Mária Koreck, and Stefánia Toma. 2010. "Kettős kisebbségben és konfliktuális helyzetben, a székelyföldi romák." [Roma in Szeklerland in dual minority status and conflict situation]. Unpublished research report, Open Society Institute, June.

Marin, Timeea E. 2010. "'We Are Gypsies, Not Roma!' Ethnic Identity Constructions and Ethnic Stereotypes. An Example from a Gypsy Community in Central Romania." Working Papers in Romanian Minority Studies no. 36. Romanian Institute for Research on National Minorities. Accessed 10 April 2017. http://www.ispmn.gov .ro/node/we-are-gypsies-not-roma-ethnic-identity-constructions-and-ethnic-ste reotypes--an-example-from-a-gypsy-community-in-central-romania.

Matei, Petre. 2010. "Adunările țiganilor din Transilvania din anul 1919 (I)" [Gatherings of the Gypsies of Transylvania in 1919 (1)]. *Revista Istorică* 21 (5–6): 467–87.

———. 2011. "Adunările țiganilor din Transilvania din anul 1919 (II)" [Gatherings of the Gypsies of Transylvania in 1919 (2)]. *Revista Istorică* 22 (1–3): 135–52.

———. 2016. "Romi." In *Cronologia Minorităților Naționale Din România.* Vol. 3: *Italieni, Romi, Slovaci Și Cehi, Ucraineni,* edited by Attila Gidó, 23–186. Cluj-Napoca: Editura Institutului pentru Studierea Problemelor Minorităților Naționale.

Mihály, László. 2009. "Tüntetés értük, de nélkülük. Nem csatlakoztak az alcsíki cigányok a tegnapi romafelvonuláshoz" [Protest for them but without them. The Gypsies from Harghita have not joined the Roma demonstrations yesterday]. *Hargita Népe,* 31 July 2009.

Parászka, Boróka. 2009. "Nesztek nektek csabakirályfizás." Posted 27 January 2018 and accessed 23 February 2018. https://althir.org/paraszka-boroka-nesze-nektek-csa bakiralyfizas-2009-11145739.html.

Pulay, Gergő. 2014. "Staging Ethnicity: Cultural Politics and Musical Practices of Roma Performers in Budapest." *Acta Ethnographica Hungarica* 59 (1): 3–24. doi: 10.1556/ AEthn.59.2014.1.2.

Romani CRISS. 2009a. "Conflict interetnic în localitatea Sânmartin, județul Harghita" [Interethnic conflict in Sânmartin, Harghita County]. Bucharest: unpublished report in the possession of the author.

———. 2009b. "Raport de caz Comuna Sâncraieni, Județul Harghita: Conflict interetnic" [Case report: Sâncrăieni, County Harghita. Interethnic conflict]. Bucharest: unpublished report in the possession author.

Rostas, Iulius. 2009. "The Romani Movement in Romania: Institutionalization and (De) mobilization." In *Romani Politics in Contemporary Europe,* edited by Nando Sigona and Nidhi Trehan, 159–85. New York: Palgrave Macmillan.

S.M.L. 2009. "Feljelentés Borboly Csabától" [Denunciation from Csaba Borboly]. *Új Magyar Szó,* 29 July 2009.

Safta, Paula. 2009. "Mai multe ONG-uri lansează '11 porunci pentru maghiari': Ungurii, rugați să nu se comporte ca hunii" [Several NGOs launched "11 commandments for Magyars": Hungarians are requested to not behave like the Huns]. *Antena 3,* 23 July 2009. Accessed 20 January 2016. http://www.antena3.ro/actualitate/mai-multe-ong-uri-lanseaza-11-porunci-pentru-maghiari-ungurii-rugati-sa-nu-se-comporte-ca-hunii-76447.html.

Sarău, Gheorghe. 2013. "Istoricul studiului limbii rromani și al școlarizării rromilor în România (1990–2012)" [The History of the study of Romani language and of Roma education in Romania (1990–2012)]. Romanian Institute for Research on National Minorities. Accessed 10 April 2017. http://ispmn.gov.ro/node/istoricul-studiului-limbii-rromani-i-al-colarizrii-rromilor-n-romnia-19902012.

Sipos, Zoltán. 2009a. "Mi áll a székelyföldi roma-magyar konfliktus hátterében?" [What is in the background of the Roma-Hungarian conflict in the Szeklerland?]. *Transindex*, 11 August 2009. Accessed 10 January 2016. http://itthon.transindex.ro/?cikk=9990.

———. 2009b. "Befolyásolta a magyarországi közbeszéd a székelyföldi roma-magyar konfliktust?" [Does the public discourse in Hungary influence the Roma-Hungarian conflict?]. *Transindex*, 12 August 2009. Accessed 10 January 2016. http://itthon.transindex.ro/?cikk=9993.

Stahl, Henri. 1980. *Traditional Romanian Village Communities: The Transition from the Communal to the Capitalist Mode of Production in the Danube Region.* Cambridge: Cambridge University Press.

Tanaka, Jennifer. 2015. "The Centrality of Economic Development in the Vision of Romani Nation-Building." *Roma Rights: Journal of the European Roma Rights Centre* (1): 41–42.

Taussig, Michael. 1991. *The Nervous System.* London: Routledge.

Toma, Stefánia. 2012. "Segregation and Ethnic Conflicts in Romania: Getting Beyond the 'Last Drop' Model." In *The Gypsy "Menace": Populism and the New Anti-Gypsy Politics,* edited by Michael Stewart, 191–213. London: Hurst.

Transindex. 2009. "Méltó élethez való joguk tiszteletben tartásáért tüntettek a patarétiek." [People from Pata Rât are demonstrating for their right to decent life], 19 January. Accessed 20 January 2016. http://itthon.transindex.ro/?cikk=13438.

Trouillot, Michel-Rolph. 2001. "The Anthropology of the State in the Age of Globalization." *Current Anthropology* 42 (1): 125–38.

van Baar, Huub. 2009. "Scaling the Romany Grassroots: Europeanization and Transnational Networking." In *Roma-/Zigeunerkulturen in neuen Perspektiven: Romani/ Gypsy Cultures in New Perspectives,* edited by Fabian Jacobs and Johannes Ries, 217–41. Leipzig: Leipziger Universitätsverlag.

———. 2017. "Boundary Practices of Citizenship: Europe's Roma at the Nexus of Securitization and Development." In *Within and Beyond Citizenship: Lived Experiences of Political Membership,* edited by Roberto G. Gonzales and Nando Sigona. London: Routledge.

Vincze, Enikő, ed. 2013. "Spatialization and Racialization of Social Exclusion: The Social and Cultural Formation of 'Gypsy Ghettos' in Romania in a European Context." Special issue, *Studia Sociologia* 58 (2). Accessed 10 April 2017. http://www.studia.ubbcluj.ro/download/pdf/816.pdf.

PART II

❋ ❋ ❋

RENEWING EPISTEMOLOGIES

CHAPTER 4

✿ ✿ ✿

PARADIGM SHIFT AND ROMANI STUDIES
Research "on" or "for" and "with" the Roma

Andrew Ryder

The concept of community participation in research—certainly as equal partners—has been, and remains, contested by some. Is the knowledge generated "tainted" by activism and engagement or can it be critical and objective? This chapter explores the debates around community-led research, drawing on the specific case study example of European Roma, Gypsy, and Traveller research networks and methodological approaches. It seeks to determine how well the academic community is responding to acute exclusion experienced by Roma, Gypsy, and Traveller communities and identifies the challenges in the coproduction of research knowledge and how inclusive approaches to research might be developed in future.

According to Blaikie (2007), research can be "on," "for," or "with" the researched. A common accusation is that there has been a long tradition of research "on" Roma communities (Ryder 2015). From the eighteenth century, academic interest in Roma communities grew apace. However, academia has at times been more of a foe than friend, adopting hierarchical research approaches but also forms of scientific, racial, and cultural racism, which gave credence and support to policies of genocide and assimilation.

Romani Studies encompasses fields such as sociology, anthropology, linguistics, and political science, and can be termed an interdisciplinary subject. This area of study centers on a number of diverse and heterogeneous communities that come under the labels of Roma/Gypsy and Traveller. One of the key challenges in the study of these groups is that, in their nomadic journeys and early centuries of settlement in Europe, no first-hand account was given from within these communities to offer us insights into their experiences and perceptions. Added to this is the fact that these communities have suffered profound and multiple exclusions, with few attaining higher levels of education. In addition, acute forms of exclusion and bonding social capital has in some communities created a strict form of boundary maintenance, making these communities highly mistrustful of outsiders, including academics (Rostas and Ryder 2012). Only in recent times have a small but relatively significant number of Roma started to achieve status within academia and produce "insider" accounts.

A dearth of insider accounts and hierarchical research approaches that have tended to project the mores and values of various external observers onto the Roma have impeded the development of insightful research. A prominent scholar at the outset of academic study on the Roma, Heinrich Grellmann (1783), put forward the theory of the Indian origins of this group through linguistic study, but his interpretation of these communities as deviant and untrustworthy betrayed the enlightenment principles of the times. In the nineteenth century, the study of Romani communities received further stimulus in the writings of George Borrow (1851), which reflected the romantic notions held by those who were repulsed by the brutality of the industrial age and who yearned for an earlier/imagined rural idyll, to which the nomadic Romani communities—with their perceived symbiotic relationship with nature and the countryside—appeared to espouse. There were others who followed in the wake of Borrow, including the founders of the Gypsy Lore Society; they helped formalize this area of study, but paraded through their journal, established in 1882, an array of misleading and deeply problematic stereotypes about Romani communities, bolstering a series of ingrained societal prejudices about these groups (Acton 1974).

Among the detrimental perceptions that emanated from the "Gypsylorists" was that these communities were in a state of cultural decline and that there were in fact few "real Romanies" left. It was proclaimed by the Gypsylorists that those who claimed to be Romanies were a mixed and diluted breed of people, who had lost much of the culture and tradition of their forebears. The longevity of this perception was reflected in the infamous episode where the then U.K. home secretary Jack Straw proclaimed in an interview,

> There are relatively few real Romany gypsies [sic] left, who seem to mind their own business and don't cause trouble to other people, and then there are a lot more people who masquerade as travellers or gypsies [sic], who trade on the sentiment of people, but who seem to think because they label themselves as trav-

ellers [*sic*] that therefore they've got a licence to commit crimes and act in an unlawful way that other people don't have. (in Burell 1999)

Such episodes illustrate the harm caused by weak and biased research shaping mainstream cultural and political perceptions of Roma communities, but also inherent dangers posed when observers are in effect disconnected from the communities they purport to understand. This is a central topic of discussion in this chapter.

From the 1960s, work within and around the orbit of Romani studies took on the mantle of a more academic approach through the work of Thomas Acton (1974), Judith Okely (1983), Jean-Pierre Liégeois (1987), Michael Stewart (1997), and Ian Hancock (2002), among others. From the 1970s, Western and Eastern policy makers were becoming increasingly interested in the research of Roma experts, elevating the status of Romani studies, commissioning research, and appointing experts from the academic community. However, another driving force that has brought the Roma issue to the fore is the ethnogenesis of Roma communities from the late 1960s. Yet, Roma mobilization and advocacy has often felt like the poor relation in the triad of policy-making, research, and advocacy; there is a feeling among activists that their value and contribution is not always appreciated by political and academic elites. This has been a factor in recent tensions within Romani studies.

A number of fault lines exist between researchers that have been long standing but have grown deeper and more bitter as the ranks of researchers in this field have swollen and opportunities for patronage have grown; however, they also reflect the weakness of dominant paradigms. A core area of dispute has focused on the relationship between the researcher and the researched. Some researchers have sought to champion emancipatory agendas with publications seeking to prompt policy change, allying with Roma social movements. This tension and emergence of a critical cadre of Romani scholars has been described as the "Roma Awakening," with activist-scholars asserting that the present academic order is too hierarchical and self-interested (Ryder et al. 2014). In contrast, other academics have accused these activist scholars of losing objectivity and producing unscientific, devalued knowledge by compromising academic honesty for the sake of campaign objectives. In the opinion of these critics, the best way to help the Roma is to furnish policy makers with expert and scholarly advice. This tension may reflect what Kuhn (1962) described as a paradigm shift, where the anomalies of an established and dominant paradigm are exposed through critique on the seeming inability to meet present challenges. On occasion, and in the absence of credible responses, a crisis of confidence can appear in the now vulnerable paradigm (revolutionary phase); if unable to adapt, the old paradigm is consequently replaced with a new conceptual world view, which is sovereign in its assumptions at least until the cycle repeats itself.

Institutional Debates

A number of institutional developments reflect the growth of, and increased interest in, Romani studies. In 2011, with support from the Council of Europe and European Union, a European Academic Network on Romani Studies (EANRS) was established to foster cooperation between researchers, policy makers, and other stakeholders (EANRS 2011). However, something of a furor broke out upon the election of a scientific committee, to which the EANRS failed to elect any members of the Roma community. This led to the resignation of Professor Thomas Acton. Later, other academics (Enikő Vincze and Jean-Pierre Liégeois) also resigned.[1]

A further furor ensued in 2014 when the scientific committee opposed the proposed establishment of a European Roma institute. For a number of years prior to the formation of the EANRS, there had been proposals to establish an institute for Romani studies. This idea was revived when the billionaire philanthropist George Soros expressed interest. The idea also found some favor within the Council of Europe and European Union and among a younger generation of professionalized Roma advocacy workers and emerging Roma scholars, influenced by activist scholarship and frustrated with the perceived monopolization of knowledge production on the Roma by academics imbued with the principles of scientism. In April 2014, José Barroso, the then president of the European Commission, raised the idea of an institute publicly (Barroso 2014). A consultation process was initiated within the Council of Europe on the European Roma Institute for Arts and Culture (ERIAC), which articulated the vision some of its supporters held: the institute would have a focus on cultural matters and promote debate and research in this area. The paper outlined a proposal for an academy called *Barvalipe* (in Romani, pride), which would serve as the governing body of the ERIAC and consist of twenty public intellectuals of Roma origin, who would invite ten non-Roma experts to join them. The academy would elect the ERIAC board from among its members. The scientific committee of the EANRS was highly critical and issued a statement:

> We believe that the academic rigour of research and training in Romani studies, their reputation, their appeal to early career and aspiring researchers, and their ability to flourish in an environment that promotes genuine intellectual freedom and creativity are best protected within established and recognised higher education institutions that are subject to the standard procedures of student and staff

selection and promotion, peer-review scrutiny of research and research ethics, and quality assurance of curriculum design and delivery. The academic engagement with Roma culture belongs within universities. It deserves to maintain the same reputation as other serious academic disciplines. Only on that basis is it possible to produce knowledge that can inform policy and public attitudes in a reliable and transparent manner. (EANRS 2014)

Critics denounced the statement, claiming it was elitist and represented an attempt by an academic cabal to monopolize knowledge production. The statement of the scientific committee can be viewed as an example of cultural reproduction of the type Bourdieu described, namely the domination of academic elites who sacralize the institutions and practices on which their authority rests (Wacquant 1993), creating a form of "misrecognition," where such a situation is made to appear natural and necessary despite the obvious flaws and contradictions. In debates, some critics of the ERIAC claimed that it represented an attempt by a group of Roma intellectuals to fast-track their career progression and attain positions and influence based on their ethnicity rather than expert ability. Conversely, the supporters of the ERIAC claimed that a *Gadjé* academic establishment were frightened of losing their influence, which had been based on misleading assertions of expertise and objective scholarship. Thus, a deep fracture appeared to have opened up between lead academic voices committed to scientific notions of research, which exalted objectivity and the role of academic expert, and those wedded to more critical forms of research, which promote emancipatory agendas and activism.

However, it should not be assumed that the ranks of academia with an interest in Roma issues are divided into diametrically opposed factions wedded to diverging paradigms: there is in fact overlapping support for the EANRS and ERIAC and the viewpoints they espouse. However, such has been the ferocity of the debate that observers with more nuanced or intermediate perspectives between the two poles of debate at times may have been intimidated from making active contributions to the discussion or simply not heard in the midst of a series of bitter exchanges. A point of difference between the ERIAC and EANRS might be the focus the ERIAC stresses on direct support and empowerment to Roma communities, raising their esteem and enabling them to challenge stereotypes (Soros and Jagland 2015), but the EANRS commitment in its mission statement to social inclusion and interculturalism should in theory endorse such actions, too (EANRS 2011). ERIAC, it should be noted, was to have a focus on arts and would work with a range of community and service-based groups, while the EANRS sought to focus on academic researchers informing the work of policy makers.

A Factional Conversation[2]

It was an evening flight from New York to Brussels. Margaux had given a special lecture at the United Nations to a gathering of officials interested in Roma issues. It had been a hard year at the Belgian university where she worked as a professor, not made easier by the role she had taken on in the EANRS. In the last few months in particular, there had been a series of bitter arguments, played out over the EANRS online forum, in which she seemed to spend a lot of time having to read or respond to increasingly fractious emails. This dissension had culminated in a call for the scientific committee to resign. So Margaux was looking forward to watching a few films on the long flight home, over a well-deserved bottle of wine. Margaux was directed to her seat by one of the flight attendants; being a rather large-sized lady, she had informed the airline and expected to be placed in the front-row seats of economy class, which provided extra leg room. Margaux was startled to see Hilda sitting in the row; Hilda gave an equally bemused look of surprise to see Margaux.

Margaux and Hilda had known each other for many years, ever since they started their doctoral studies on Roma and Traveller/Voyageur communities in Belgium, but they were not friends. Far from it. From the outset there had been a tension in their relations: Hilda had aligned her research with an activist agenda and based much of her research on a Roma campaign group she was closely allied with. Margaux had avoided such activism, questioning how representative these activist Roma and Travellers really were of the communities they purported to represent. Margaux had conducted ethnographic research for her doctoral studies but for most of her working life she had spent her time developing insights into policy and conducting research commissioned by the government and the EU, and was a professor at a prestigious university in Brussels.

Hilda's continued activism may have been one of the factors that kept her at the margins of commissioned research: she tended to be rather uncompromising in the ideals she expected from research, and these standards could deter prospective funders and research consortia from funding or approaching her. Some feared that "objectivity" and "neutrality" might be compromised by Hilda's avowed activist research. She was also demotivated in searching for funding because of the continual struggles with administrators at the university about the time she devoted to research when grants were secured. Although Hilda had attained the position of professor, it was at one of the new universities in Belgium, where work pressures and job insecurity were acute. Hilda had often found it difficult to juggle teaching and research commitments, frequently working for many more days than what she had been contracted; this tended to bring her into increasing conflict with university administrators. Hilda had been in New York to examine a Ph.D. student who was from the Roma community. She had leapt at the opportunity, feeling developments like this were indicative of a seismic shift in Romani studies, which would increasingly threaten the dominance of a small academic elite.

A history of tension between Margaux and Hilda, centered on their different approaches to research and working on/with Roma communities, had prompted a number of squabbles and jousts over the years, which had been played out in seminars, reviews, and the like, and would have made their encounter on the plane awkward at the best of times. However, these tensions had been inflamed recently by the fact that Hilda had been among the signatories calling for Margaux to resign from the scientific committee of the EANRS. Margaux felt that she had no choice but to sit where the flight attendant was directing her, but was full of dread at the thought of spending an eight-hour journey in the company of Hilda. She determined on a strategy of having a polite conversation, then making the excuse of having work to do and then sleeping.

After a period of polite conversation, which lasted for ten minutes and a long pause, Margaux abruptly veered from her plan and plunged into a discussion of academic matters.

Margaux: You do know I was very disappointed by the letter you signed calling for the EANRS scientific committee to resign. I think the committee had good reason to express doubt about this European Roma Institute, this ERIAC. For a start, why should a billionaire philanthropist from the U.S.A. march into Europe with a big idea and have everyone dance to his tune? More worryingly though, who will be the leaders of the ERIAC? It appears as if an elite band of Roma will form the leadership, and they will have attained these positions by virtue of their ethnicity, and not their expertise.

Hilda: I'm sorry you were upset by the letter, but tensions were running high. The scientific committee should have involved the membership more in its statement, and this has been part of the problem. The committee has behaved as if it has an authoritative mandate to make all the decisions without sufficiently involving the membership. The Roma members have been growing increasingly angry; initially, none were elected to the committee and only got a small foothold when you later agreed for associate members like Ph.D. students to have a vote, since most Roma scholars are at this early stage of their academic career.

Margaux: But the EANRS is not some nongovernmental organization or identity project where the Roma must be automatically expected to lead.

The leadership must be based on merit and expertise; otherwise its views and outlooks will be discarded as mere activist propaganda.

Hilda: Can you imagine a feminist academic group being led by men? Try and imagine how galling it is for the Roma members to have a largely *Gadjé* leadership. Things would not have been so bad, though, if all the members had been more involved in developing policy positions so that the scientific committee at least represented the collective views of the membership.

Margaux: There you go again with your activist agenda! The EANRS is not an NGO, but an academic association. We need to base our work on academic principles; decisions need to be informed by scholarly expertise, not by a twisted sense of political correctness and whipping up majorities through emotive appeals to emancipate the Roma!

Hilda: The term "expert" is hegemonically loaded! Experts assume that lay people, including ordinary members of an ethnic group, are not themselves expert witnesses and that their opinions have less value. But how valid and informed are the views of an academic elite that professes to be the guardian of academic objectivity, yet too often dances to the tune of its paymasters and produces weak and tepid research that changes nothing?

Margaux: I really must take exception . . .

To be continued

Scientism versus Critical Research

The tensions summarized and revealed in the historic overview of Romani studies and the factionalized conversation between two protagonists reflect debates and tensions within the wider realm of academia between what can be termed scientism, on the one hand, and critical research, on the other. Smith (2003) observed that, according to Descartes, knowledge was based on a form of dualism, the knowing subject and the known object, an enlightenment philosophy labeled by some as scientism. Scientism glorifies "objectivity," and thus the tenets of this approach stipulate that research should be detached from the researched; identifying too closely with those being researched may lead to the researcher going "native," no longer being an objective observer and instead succumbing to bias.

Conversely, embodied knowledge is a research approach grounded in the reality of everyday life. Debates have raged as to the legitimacy of traditional notions of hierarchies of knowledge, which place the expert as the filter and shaper of what is perceived as knowledge and wisdom at the summit of the hierarchy. Critics argue this is an elitist stance that reduces the value and recognition of grounded and localized knowledge (Weiler 2009). Critics of scientism assert it places too high a value on "pure" science and is based on epistemologies that are inherently antifeminist (Sorrell 2002) and majoritarian. Such critics opine that positivist thinking is deeply conservative, adopting quasi-scientific methods and conceptions of detachment, and that the pursuit of objective truth is delusional (Mies 1983). Hence, feminist and critical researchers believe, in what has been termed standpoint theory, that research should be situated in the concerns of marginalized people (Harding 1991). More inclusive approaches to research can be achieved through participatory and egalitarian forms of research, where community members are involved in the design, data collection, and analysis of research (Maguire 1987).

For the critical researcher, what scientism labels as the "truth" is both contested and politicized. For Foucault (1991), power permeates everything and is diffused in discourse, knowledge, and "regimes of truth": types of knowledge and discourse that are given the status of truth by those in power, which includes those who portray themselves as the "all-knowing experts." For Gramsci (1971), the arbitration of what is accepted as the truth and what norms and behaviors are part of the controlling framework of hegemony can constitute a site of both power and control, but also of resistance; hence, there is the possibility to contest and subvert power (Gaventa 2003). In what has been termed counterhegemonic action, not only are the intellectual elite capable of developing critical consciousness, but also those at the margins, whom Gramsci described as "organic intellectuals." Gramsci's theory is evident within Freire's (1971) conception of critical pedagogy and participatory action research. These approaches take as a starting point the experiences of those at the margins, but seek to expand their understanding of those experiences and link them with deeper perceptions, which connect immediate marginalization with wider structural factors, but also prompt a desire for transformative action (see Mirga-Kruszelnicka, this volume).

The Impact of Policy and Economy on Research

The diverging and polarized schools of thought embodied in scientism and critical research can and do enjoy an interdependent relationship that at times can be mutually beneficial, rather than always being in constant struggle and opposition to each other. Both approaches are shaped by the policy and economic landscape within which they operate; however, as will be elaborated, the current state of affairs may not be conducive to either approach. This point is developed with reference to the case of Romani studies.

At a European level, there is growing recognition of the size and level of exclusion being suffered by the Roma, Europe's largest ethnic minority, as reflected in a range of initiatives by a number of supra-European bodies. One of the most significant is the European Union Framework for National Roma Integration Strategies (NRIS). The Framework was launched in 2011 and involves member states devising NRIS. The framework is not highly prescriptive, being based on the Open Method of Coordination (OMC): the rationale is that EU members will examine their policies critically, thus leading to the exchange of good practice, and that peer pressure will spur on some to "do better" (Meyer 2010). This can be described as a deliberative framework, and the European Commission has stressed the importance of ongoing dialogue and partnerships between governments and Roma groups in the Roma Framework; indeed "empowerment," "participation," and "interculturalism" are popular buzzwords at the center of European policy formulation. In 2009, the Roma Platform, a periodic gathering of the European Commission, policy makers, and civil society, devised the "Ten Basic Principles of Roma Inclusion," which are guiding principles for policy-making, emphasizing the importance of partnership, dialogue, and interculturalism.

Despite the rhetoric of empowerment and inclusion, the results of the EU Roma Framework have been sporadic. Evaluation reports by the Decade of Roma Inclusion Secretariat Foundation (2012; 2013; 2014), a Soros-supported international NGO, reveal a range of countries have failed to adequately prioritize the Roma issue, or consult Roma and work in partnership, or both. Often, mere lip service has been paid to notions of empowerment and partnership; hiding behind this facade there remains a policy agenda that is either paternalistic or assimilatory. Critics argue that this is due in part to a securitization agenda in which policy makers perceive Roma as a threat to be managed and controlled (van Baar 2011); this is perhaps of particular relevance with regard to the Roma who have migrated from central eastern Europe to the West. Some argue that the Roma Framework is merely an attempt to stem this flow of migrants. Others perceive the Roma Framework as an assimilatory tool where paternalistic development approaches normalize neoliberal and assimilative policy agendas and "responsibilization," which individualizes and pathologizes the victims rather than the structural agents of exclusion (van Baar 2011). Such a critique applies the thoughts of theorists such as Foucault (1998), who theorized forms of control through the concept of governmentality (van Baar 2011). Another impediment to the realization of effective inclusion agendas has been austerity, accentuated across Europe through a fiscal compact, which is leading to cuts in services and is clearly not conducive to the development of tailored and targeted policies to alleviate exclusion (Ryder et al. 2014).

A danger of postdevelopment theory is that the concept of progress may be lost and an unquestioning exaltation of ethnic cultures can promote static and narrow versions of identity. Research has a crucial role to play in identifying cultural adaptations within groups and understanding the importance of community aspirations, but also in highlighting the discrepancies between avowed policies, and agendas and outputs. Furthermore, given the fact that the EU Roma Framework is based on the OMC, which stresses the value of deliberation, comparison, and even shaming as levers and tools for change, research again could play a fundamental role in this process.

Thus, effective research should not only be directed at institutional processes but should also have an inward dimension, "opening up" within the group issues; this could reveal internal group practices that might be oppressive (McCabe et al. 2013). The critical researcher may have difficult choices to make in this respect, but should be ethical in the sense that choices and decisions made should be carefully balanced on the basis of human rights and fairness. In the field of Roma studies this has been reflected in recent times by researchers who have sought to navigate the pulls and tensions of cultural conservatism and the pitfalls of being misinterpreted. Such difficult, even contentious, research has brought to the surface problems of domestic violence and hypermasculinity within some Gypsy, Roma, and Traveller communities (Cemlyn et al. 2009). Such research promotes the ideal of interculturalism, which supports review and negotiation in the cultural realm, but such research should be a two-way process prompting change in majoritarian society by critiquing not only traditional conceptions of ethnicity, but also its links to wider societal drivers behind oppressions, such as sexism and homophobia.

Funding and resources for research to evaluate the situation of the Roma and the impact of policies are available; one of the biggest funders is the European Union. However, the bureaucracy and complexity of EU funding streams for research is notorious (Armingeon 2007), which invariably means that established universities or research agencies are the best placed to compete for funds. The advantage enjoyed by the research establishment can crowd out more innovative research design by emerging researchers, and often means that community organizations are impeded from bidding for research funds and/or are consigned to more tokenistic roles within research consortia led by universities. Reflecting upon the process of inclusive research being subverted, Brydon-Miller et al. (2003) note that, increasingly, participation has become a required component of evaluation assessment, appraisals, and research, but there is a danger that this approach is being undermined, tokenized and co-opted to reinforce existing power relations

(Gaventa and Cornwall 2001). Furthermore, genuinely participatory and innovative research approaches may be deemed to not meet the approval of scientific committees responsible for the evaluation of grant applications, committees which tend to be monopolized by more established and potentially scientistic-oriented researchers. Although the evaluation process is enveloped in what appears to be a scrupulous process of review and assessment, it is an open secret that those applicants who are most likely to succeed are those who have proficiently played the "game" in the academic field of power, pouring the majority of their time and energy into securing entry into elite academic institutions, circles, and journals (Sparkes 2007). Another impediment to inclusive research on Roma communities is that commissioned research by powerful institutions, with little or no community involvement, has in fact tended to uphold longstanding stereotypes on Roma communities (Acton 2006; see also Ivasiuc, this volume).

For Pohl et al. (2010), coproduction of knowledge between academic and nonacademic communities is essential to ensure research that promotes more sustainable development paths. Thus, a key challenge in this quest is addressing power relations between the researcher and those being researched and reorienting relations on a more equitable basis than that afforded by traditional research hierarchies based on scientism. The critical researcher seeks to use research as a tool to promote transformative change; relationships with those being researched are of paramount importance. Such researchers contend that empathy with the researched—in the tradition of feminist and critical research—can foster more equal relations between the researcher and the researched. For researchers influenced by the teachings of Paolo Freire, such participatory relationships and alliances enable forms of critical pedagogy where Roma communities can draw connections between their immediate experiences and the structural factors that shape their exclusion. This research, it has been argued, facilitates the development of critical consciousness and mobilizes communities into forms of transformative action (Ledwith and Springett 2010).

So there is a case for more inclusive forms of research to be promoted. But why should researchers who adhere to a more positivist approach support such change? One might presume that, as the most likely beneficiaries of existing funding regimes, they might be rather wedded to the status quo. Here an appeal needs to be made to the rather platonic notion of the deliberative academy. Bourdieu (1991) described such a deliberative academy as a "working dissensus," an arena that affords critical acknowledgement of compatibilities and incompatibilities—in other words, a space where academics from diverging intellectual traditions can at least agree to participate in constructive dialogue. It has been in the best interests of various approaches in Romani studies for engaged dialogue and critique to highlight the weakness of a particular theory, but in turn prompt further inquiry that strengthens a particular theory, or opens a new line of investigation, or both. We thus need our adversaries and counterapproaches to research. In addition, often in forwarding argument, many researchers draw on the works of rivals or those advocating a diverging approach to research, hence mixed methods of research and argument construction are already in practice, which is another indicator of the symbiotic relationship between a range of research perspectives. To make a more general point with reference to the distinction drawn between pure and applied science, Roll-Hansen (2009: 20) notes that "theory provides practice with new concepts and theories, and practice presents theory with unexpected facts. Some of the most important achievements, both in basic and applied research, have their origin in settings which include both."

Within Romani studies, obsessing about organizational arrangements—whether we need a European Academic Network on Romani Studies or a European Roma Institute—may be misplaced. The author of this contribution would argue that the two bodies, in the spirit of academic dissensus, could coexist and spur each other on in a form of healthy competition. Although institutional and organizational structures such as the EANRS and ERIAC are valuable in articulating collective aspirations, they are meaningless or devalued if communication and internal forms of democracy are weak. This, indeed, may be a real flaw in both the EANRS and ERIAC concepts, which needs to be addressed. A common failing has been the disconnection between pan-European structures and communities, a failing that has been evident in the realm of Romani issues also (Ryder et al. 2014). While institutions and bodies like the ERIAC and EANRS have a valuable role to play in providing platforms and counternarratives, there is always the danger that financial reliance on funders might dull and mute critical voices. Alongside such bodies, and indeed in the vanguard of the Roma social movement, there is a need for broad coalitions of groups to come together at the national and international level. Here, research could play a valuable role, shaping dialogue and frames in the formation of a dynamic social movement.

Another impediment to the vision of inclusive research is the fact that universities have become like corporations with formulas, incentives, and targets guided by the principles of "new managerialism" (Miller 2010). Academia can in fact be viewed as a field of power dominated by an audit and managerial culture that exalts and promotes the "competitive academic," adept at self-promotion, voluminous publication in top academic journals, and the acquisition of grants (Strathern 2000; Sparkes 2007). It has been said that the contemporary university has changed from a platonic academy to a commercial mall (Wood 2010). In this marketplace, other academics become competitors—less inclined to acknowledge and respect the views and aspirations of their competitors, but also less likely to forge links with the researched. In part, such distancing will be prompted by time and resource factors, as the "managed" academic and researcher race to complete the task within the agreed budget and time frame, but such distancing will also be prompted by the desire to win the contract. Inclusive research that gives those being researched real voice is more likely to challenge the status quo and the perceived wisdom of power, and thus may find it harder to win the tender. On this point, a case needs to be made for the reform of research funding regimes, creating a culture that better nurtures innovation but also ensures a range of stakeholders are actively involved in the research process.

Margaux and Hilda—Continued

After a series of sharp and bitter exchanges, one of the flight attendants had to intervene and warn the two women that their heated exchange was disturbing other passengers. This jolted Margaux and Hilda into a more restrained form of discussion, which over the course of an hour touched on the points discussed above, while easing tensions.

Hilda: I do acknowledge that over the years you have somehow been sitting on my shoulder: whenever I write something, I am asking myself how you might respond and what the best strategy might be to weaken your critique and make my argument stronger. For that I have to be grateful.

Margaux: Strangely, the same is true for me. We have to realize that different approaches in academia, and indeed divergence and dissension, are the hot furnace of knowledge production testing and tempering our work. Academics in Romani studies, as in any other field, are never likely to agree, and I would not want them to, but we need to ensure that there is a respectful, open, and deliberative arena for debate.

Hilda: In that respect, we as academic elders should do more to set an example and standard of behavior that the younger generation of researchers can follow. But we should also be alert to some of the real dangers that are impeding research from attaining the achievements many of us desire. Who reads or is aware of our research? Does our research prompt real action by policy makers or communities, or both? Whatever our approaches, we need to find ways to more widely disseminate research, and for campaigns and lobbyists to use that material more effectively in change agendas. For my part, I feel that can best be achieved through participatory research, which is grounded in the realities of life at the grassroots, but which also gives communities voice and inspires. Most of all, policy makers need to take greater note of research, and instead of just turning up at the launch of a report and making a nice speech, they need to make a greater effort to feed research into policy formulation.[3]

Margaux: I can agree with you on the very last point, but there is another huge obstacle to achieving an environment where research makes a real difference, and that comes down to what is happening in our universities. Forty years ago, when I first entered academia, university life as a lecturer gave you sufficient time to develop first-rate teaching and support to students, but also sufficient time to conduct research. Now we work under commodified regimes like factory workers—every hour and every minute has to be accounted for, and the time given for research projects is not enough. Some may perceive me as being part of a "Gypsy industry," but I often have to work over seventy hours a week and on weekends to fulfill my commitments, and often work beyond the days I am contracted in research to do the best I can to write insightful research.

Hilda: Idem ici. I often feel I am on a treadmill and despair at how this audit and corporate university culture might shape future generations of researchers. In our obsessing with institutional structures and networks, be it the European Academic Network on Romani Studies or the European Roma Institute, we might merely be building sand castles and falling into the trap of politicians by dreaming up top-down initiatives that fail to address the real issues or genuinely connect with communities . . . Maybe we should think about ordering a bottle of wine.

Margaux: Excellent idea. I only disagree with you on the question of the number.

The final part of the discussion between our two protagonists may be more indicative of a fairy tale, for rarely do longstanding academic protagonists "bury the hatchet," discard long-standing grievances, and give due recognition to their opponents. For a fleeting period, Margaux and Hilda reached some form of rapprochement. Although they continued to disagree over the coming months on what, in their opinion, were the best organizational structures for Romani studies, they were for a brief period of time more restrained and guarded in the public pronouncement of their views on the institutional debates within Romani studies. But the cease-fire was to be short-lived: they eventually returned to the war of attrition that existed prior to their shared flight, with their intellectual tussles waged through barbed exchanges in email forums and acidic grant and article reviews. The sincerity of their disagreements should not be questioned, and the value of disagreement in generating new assumptions should not be discounted either. However, some—rightly or wrongly—recoiled from the intensity of their clashes. These clashes and disagreements may have been to the detriment of knowledge production by obscuring and personalizing the nature of their intellectual jousts. There was, in fact, a danger that their reputations and the impact of their important and valuable work were undermined by the manner in which they conducted their disputes. Thus, in debates and controversies, the views of Hilda and Margaux were at times discounted or sidelined; the tragedy of this state of affairs was that their knowledge and expertise, when properly applied, still had much to offer Romani studies.

Conclusion

To enumerate the points made in this chapter, academics should appreciate the value of disagreement, being the engine of knowledge production. As noted earlier, such intellectual contests are part of what Kuhn (1962) called "paradigm change": at the sharpest point of conflict between the old and new conceptual worldview, the two sides are incommensurate, each by virtue of their rules and frames judges the alternative and finds it lacking and at cross-purposes, a model revolution. It may be that we are witnessing within Romani studies something of a model revolution leading to a paradigm shift that will nurture more collaborative and participatory relationships with those being researched, while bringing to the fore Roma intellectuals.

The materialization of this shift in research approaches may be evident in a historic motion proposed by Professors Thomas Acton and Yaron Matras at the Gypsy Lore Society (GLS) board meeting in 2016. The motion acknowledges that like other institutions, the GLS and its publications have not been immune over the past century to "attitudes that may be interpreted as overtly patronizing, disenfranchising, or otherwise biased toward the people whose culture was at the centre of the society's attention" (GLS motion, 13 September 2016). The motion concludes with the GLS noting that research with Roma communities should not cause harm and remains committed to promoting knowledge of and engagement with Romani communities.

Yet ultimately the emergence of more inclusive research and progress in the material conditions of Roma communities will be dependent on a paradigm shift at the macro level. Over the last century, fundamental and revolutionary shifts in worldviews took place, for instance when Keynesian economic approaches usurped more laissez-faire outlooks in the wake of the Wall Street crash. In turn, the oil crisis of the mid-1970s gave rise to the Washington Consensus with a neoliberal agenda of deregulation and minimal social intervention and welfare. The financial crisis of 2008 led to challenges being made to dominant paradigms, but the critics of neoliberalism were confounded by the rise of even more rampant forms of neoconservatism and capital accumulation under the guise of austerity politics. It is in this context that Roma economic and social exclusion and increased scapegoating has to be viewed. A Romani social movement is needed that includes members of the research community and places the predicament of the Roma in the wider structural and cultural context of the crisis of capital by offering a counterhegemonic discourse. Inclusive research will have a valuable role to play, reaching out and discussing issues beyond the academy by involving and mobilizing those at the margins in the research process and in the development of a critical consciousness (Beck and Maida 2013).

Andrew Ryder is an associate professor at the Corvinus University Budapest and an associate fellow at the Third Sector Research Centre at the University of Birmingham. Prior to this he was a policy officer respectively to the Irish Traveller Movement in Britain and the Gypsy and Traveller Law Reform Coalition, and researcher for the All-Party Parliamentary Group for Gypsies, Roma, and Travellers. Ryder recently authored *Sites of Resistance: Gypsies, Roma and Travellers in School, Community and the Academy* (Institute of Education UCL/Trentham Press, 2017).

Notes

1. There was great frustration from the network's associate members, who were debarred from participation in the initial election, which was reserved for members holding a doctorate. Initially the scientific committee had no Roma representation. Roma involvement in the coordination of the EANRS did eventually increase through the election of Roma Ph.D. students to two newly created posts for associate members on the scientific committee. This organizational adaption was prompted by the protests over non-Roma representation on the scientific committee, from Roma and non-Roma scholars/activists who signed a letter of concern addressed to the body.
2. The conversation is not based on real characters, but can be viewed as a piece of "faction," as it is based on viewpoints held by differing poles of opinion within Romani studies. Faction is a form of writing that treats real people or events as if they were fictional or uses real people or events as essential elements in an otherwise fictional rendition.
3. On the issue of the tensions between research and policy formulation, see Margaret Greenfields's chapter in this volume.

References

Acton, Thomas. 1974. *Gypsy Politics and Social Change: The Development of Ethnic Ideology and Pressure Politics among British Gypsies from Victorian Reformism to Romany Nationalism.* London: Kegan Paul.
———. 2006. "Romani Politics, Scholarship and the Discourse of Nation-Building: Romani Studies in 2003." In *Gypsies and the Problem of Identities: Contextual, Constructed and Contested,* edited by Adrian Marsh and Elin Strand, 27–38. London: I.B. Tauris.
Armingeon, Klaus. 2007. "Two Perspectives on EU Research Funding: The Present is Lacklustre, the Future is Potentially Shining." *European Political Science* 6: 315–21.
Barroso, José. 2014. "Speech by President Barroso at the European Roma Summit." 4 April 2014. Accessed 26 August 2016. http://europa.eu/rapid/press-release_SPEECH-14-288_en.htm.
Beck, Sam, and Carl Maida, eds. 2013. *Toward Engaged Anthropology.* New York: Berghahn Books.
Blaikie, Norman. 2007. *Approaches to Social Enquiry: Advancing Knowledge.* Malden, MA: Polity Press.
Borrow, George. 1851. *Lavengro.* London: John Murray.
Bourdieu, Pierre. 1991. "Epilogue: On the Possibility of a Field of World Sociology." In *Social Theory for a Changing Society,* edited by Pierre Bourdieu and James S. Coleman. Boulder, CO: Westview Press.
Brydon-Miller, Mary, Patricia Maguire, and Alison McIntyre, eds. 2003. *Traveling Companions: Feminism, Teaching, and Action Research.* Westport, CT: Greenwood Publishing Group.
Cemlyn, Sarah, Margaret Greenfields, Sally Burnett, Zoe Matthews, and Chris Whitwell. 2009. *Inequalities Experienced by Gypsy and Traveller Communities: A Review.* Research Report 12. Equality and Human Rights Commission. Accessed 26 August 2016. https://www.equalityhumanrights.com/sites/default/files/research-report-12-inequalities-experienced-by-gypsy-and-traveller-communities.pdf.
Decade of Roma Inclusion Secretariat Foundation. 2012. *Monitoring Report: Progress within the EU Framework for National Roma Integration Strategies.* Budapest: Decade of Roma Inclusion Secretariat Foundation. Accessed 7 May 2018. https://cps.ceu.edu/roma-civil-monitor-civil-society-monitoring-reports.
———. 2013. *Monitoring Report: Progress within the EU Framework for National Roma Integration Strategies.* Budapest: Decade of Roma Inclusion Secretariat Foundation. Accessed 7 May 2018. https://cps.ceu.edu/roma-civil-monitor-civil-society-monitoring-reports.
———. 2014. *Monitoring Report: Progress within the EU Framework for National Roma Integration Strategies.* Budapest: Decade of Roma Inclusion Secretariat Foundation.
EANRS (European Academic Network for Romani Studies). 2011. "A European Union / Council of Europe Joint Programme (2011–2015)." Accessed 26 August 2016. romanistudies.eu.
———. 2014. "Statement of the Scientific Committee of the European Academic Network on Romani Studies (RAN) on the Council of Europe's proposal for a European Roma Institute." News release. 30 April 2014. Accessed 26 August 2016. http://romanistudies.eu/wp-content/uploads/2015/02/RAN_paper_on_ERI_30April2014.pdf

Foucault, Michel. 1991. *Discipline and Punish: The Birth of the Prison.* Translated by Alan Sheridan. London: Penguin.

———. 1998. *The History of Sexuality.* Translated by Robert Hurley. London: Penguin.

Freire, Paulo. 1971. *Pedagogy of the Oppressed.* New York: Herder and Herder.

Gaventa, Jonathan. 2003. *Power after Lukes: An Overview of Theories of Power since Lukes and Their Application to Development.* Brighton: Institute of Development Studies.

Gaventa, Jonathan, and Andrea Cornwall. 2001. "Power and Knowledge." In *Handbook of Action Research: Participative Inquiry and Practice,* edited by Peter Reason and Hilary Bradbury, 70–80. London: Sage.

Gramsci, Antonio. 1971. *Selections from the Prison Notebooks of Antonio Gramsci.* New York: International Publishers.

Grellmann, Heinrich. 1783. *Die Zigeuner: Ein historischer Versuch über die Lebensart und Verfassung, Sitten und Schicksale dieses Volks in Europa, nebst ihrem Ursprunge.* Dessau: Verlagskasse.

Hancock, Ian. 2002. *We Are The Romani People.* Hatfield: University of Hertfordshire Press.

Harding, Sandra. 1991. *Whose Science? Whose Knowledge? Thinking from Women's Lives.* Ithaca, NY: Cornell University Press.

Kuhn, Thomas. 1962. *The Structure of Scientific Revolutions.* Chicago, IL: University of Chicago Press.

Ledwith, Margaret, and Jane Springett. 2010. *Participatory Practice: Community-Based Action for Transformative Change.* Bristol: Policy Press.

Liégeois, Jean-Pierre. 1987. *School Provision for Gypsy and Traveller Children: A Synthesis Report.* Luxembourg: Office for Official Publications of the European Communities.

Maguire, Patricia. 1987. *Doing Participatory Research: A Feminist Approach.* Amherst, MA: The Center for International Education, University of Massachusetts.

McCabe, Angus, Alison Gilchrist, Asif Afridi, Kevin Harris, and Paul Kyprianou. 2013. *Making the Links: Poverty, Ethnicity and Social Networks.* Report. Joseph Rowntree Foundation. Accessed 26 August 2016. https://www.jrf.org.uk/sites/default/files/jrf/migrated/files/poverty-ethnicity-social-networks-full_0.pdf.

Meyer, Henning. 2010. "The Open Method of Coordination (OMC): A Governance Mechanism for the G20?" *Social Europe,* 1 December 2010. Accessed 26 August 2016. https://www.socialeurope.eu/2010/12/the-open-method-of-coordination-omc-a-governance-mechanism-for-the-g20/.

Miller, Brian. 2010. "Skills for Sale: What is Being Commodified in Higher Education?" *Journal of Further and Higher Education* 34 (2): 199–206.

Okely, Judith. 1983. *The Traveller-Gypsies.* Cambridge: Cambridge University Press.

Pohl, Christian, Stephan Rist, Anne Zimmermann, Patricia Fry, Ghana S. Gurung, Flurina Schneider, Chinwe Ifejika Speranza, Boniface Kiteme, Sébastian Boillat, Elvira Serrano, Getrude Hirsch Hadorn, and Urs Wiesmann. 2010. "Researchers' Roles in Knowledge Co-production." *Science and Public Policy* 37 (4): 267–81.

Roll-Hansen, Nils. 2009. *Why the Distinction between Basic (Theoretical) and Applied (Practical) Research is Important in the Politics of Science?* Technical Report 04/09. London: Contingency and Dissent in Science Project, Centre for Philosophy of Natural and Social Science, and London School of Economics and Political Science. Accessed 26 August 2016. http://www.lse.ac.uk/cpnss/research/concluded researchprojects/contingencydissentinscience/dp/dproll-hansenonline0409.pdf.

Rostas, Iulius, and Andrew Ryder. 2012. "EU Framework for National Roma Integration Strategies: Insights into Empowerment and Inclusive Policy Development." In *Gypsies and Travellers: Accommodation, Empowerment and Inclusion in British Society*, edited by Joanna Richardson and Andrew Ryder, 187–206. Bristol: Policy Press.

Ryder, Andrew. 2015. "Co-producing Knowledge with Below the Radar Communities: Factionalism, Commodification or Partnership? A Gypsy, Roma and Traveller Case Study." Third Sector Research Centre Working Paper, Discussion Paper G. Accessed 26 August 2016. http://www.birmingham.ac.uk/generic/tsrc/documents/tsrc/discussion-papers/2015/gtr-discussion-paper-g-ryder-28janfinal.pdf.

Ryder, Andrew, Sarah Cemlyn, and Thomas Acton, eds. 2014. *Hearing the Voice of Gypsies, Roma and Travellers: Inclusive Community Development*. Bristol: Policy Press.

Smith, Arthur D. 2003. *Routledge Philosophy Guidebook to Husserl and the Cartesian Meditations*. London: Routledge.

Soros, George, and Thorbjørn Jagland. 2015. "Why We Are Setting Up a European Roma Institute." Open Society Foundations website, 27 March 2015. Accessed 26 August 2016. http://www.opensocietyfoundations.org/voices/why-we-are-setting-european-roma-institute.

Sorrell, Tom. 2002. *Philosophy and the Infatuation with Science*. London: Routledge.

Sparkes, Andrew. 2007. "Embodiment, Academics, and the Audit Culture: A Story Seeking Consideration." *Qualitative Research* 7 (4): 521–50.

Stewart, Michael. 1997. *The Time of the Gypsies*. Boulder, CO: Westview Press.

Strathern, Marilyn, ed. 2000. *Audit Cultures: Anthropological Studies in Accountability, Ethics and the Academy*. London: Routledge.

Wacquant, Loïc. 1993. "Bourdieu: A Case Study in Scientific Consecration." *Sociology* 47 (1): 15–29.

Weiler, Hans N. 2009. "Whose Knowledge Matters? Development and the Politics of Knowledge." In *Entwicklung als Beruf,* edited by Theodor Hanf, Hans N. Weiler, and Helga Dickow, 485–96. Baden-Baden: Nomos.

van Baar, Huub. 2011. *The European Roma: Minority Representation, Memory and the Limits of Transnational Governmentality*. Amsterdam: F&N.

CHAPTER 5

❀ ❀ ❀

TRANSGRESSING BORDERS
Challenging Racist and Sexist Epistemology

Angéla Kóczé

> *What does it mean to have to create oneself from scratch,*
> *in environments where one is not supposed to exist?*
> —Alexander G. Weheliye

Feminist critical race theorist Kimberlé Williams Crenshaw (1991) offers an intersectional framework for women of color to explain their multiple oppressions. She demonstrates how injustice and social inequality interplay in a multidimensional system. Intersectionality theory explains that various oppressions within society, such as racism, sexism, classism, and many other forms of oppression, intersect and interrelate, creating a system of multidimensional domination. It is never just about racism, classism, or sexism; it is always the combination of several oppressions that create the intersectional obstacles for Romani women in academia. This paper is an attempt to demonstrate how Romani feminists are shaping and maintaining the content of critical Romani studies by transgressing the constructed binary between activism and scholarship. Through candid confessions, Romani women scholars are exposing the intersecting dynamics between racism and sexism. Their claims challenge the academic epistemology to accommodate a new kind of knowledge production, where different knowledge sources and locations are connected and recognized.

The presence of Romani women in knowledge production evokes the question that was formulated by Alexander G. Weheliye (2016) in his public lecture, "Black Life": "What does it mean to have to create oneself from scratch in environments where one is not supposed to exist?"[1] What does it mean to be a Romani woman in academia, where we are not supposed to exist as scholars? Undoubtedly, we have to create ourselves from scratch in environments that usually construe Roma/Romani women as subjects of research and never imagine them as scholars who inhabit a space where knowledge is produced or published in academic journals, and certainly not as theorizers of the forces that condition Romani lives. To be a Romani woman scholar is beyond the imagination of many scholars, who imagine Roma exclusively as activists and/or research subjects.

Critical Scholarship

Craig Calhoun (2008: xxiv) persuasively argues that activist social science is a very productive research paradigm: it "may inform both activism and social science by pursuing critical knowledge." He underscores that critique is a crucial part of social science; it is therefore important to understand how research could be different, and why existing theoretical frameworks do not explain the actual possibilities of lived experience. He explains this in the following way:

> Critical theory is not just criticism of other theories, it is an orientation to the world that combines the effort to understand why it is as it is (the more conventional domain of science) and how it could be otherwise (the more conventional domain of action). Precisely because of attention to possibilities of change, critical social science is often focused on the ways in which power, privilege, and self-interest as well as ideology and limited vision reinforce actually existing patterns in social life and limits on potentially positive change.[2] (Calhoun 2008: xxv).

Michael Burawoy's (2005) ideas resonate with Calhoun's stance on activist scholarship; he passionately writes about the growing gap between the sociological ethos and the world we research. He challenges sociology to engage with the public in multiple ways (see also Beck and Maida 2013; 2015). Civil society and NGO activism, besides their ambivalences (Kóczé and Trehan 2009) and internal hierarchy, are still important terrains to understand and engage with contradictions, as well as to reflect on their ambiguous politics; as Burawoy (2005: 25) argues, it is "the best possible terrain for the defence of humanity—defence that would be aided by the cultivation of a critically disposed public sociology." For many Romani feminists, civil society and NGO activism, despite their systemic contradictions pointed out in earlier work (Kóczé 2009; 2011; Kóczé and Trehan 2009), are still more accessible environments than academia. Most Romani feminists are still located in (or come from) NGO activism, from where they seek to create a politics of possibility by connecting political/social activism and academic scholarship.

So, in short, activist scholarship is engaged with the public. It is a legitimate form of academic scholarship that sometimes lacks recognition from hierarchical academia, which privileges intellectual work to the detriment of active engagement. Andrew Ryder's chapter in this volume explores the debates around community-led research, engaging with the current debate in Romani studies, and comes to the conclusion that academics should appreciate the value of disagreement, as well as the use of different theory and methodology as instruments to create new knowledge and understandings. This message resonates with the seminal work of Sam Beck and Carl A. Maida (2013: 1–13), who suggest a more responsible role for anthropologists working with people, communities, and movements—that is, to engage with them in a way that they might benefit from the study. This "engaged anthropology" encourages collaboration with the people who are the objects of their studies, to create social change (Beck and Maida 2013: 13). This approach requires a change in methodology, and use of a different theoretical approach, even of developing an attitude that moves away from traditional anthropological observation, already largely contested since the seventies (Asad 1973; Huizer and Mannheim 1979; Harrison 1991a; 1991b; Scheper-Hughes 1995; Bennett 1996). In this chapter, taking stock of previous critical writings on knowledge production, I intend to bring to the fore the racialized and gendered lived experiences of Romani women in the academia, in order to highlight mechanisms of oppressive hierarchization, and argue for an epistemic change within Romani studies.

Romani scholars' gendered and racialized lived experience, as well as their social and political activism, provides a unique basis for theorizing the intersection of gender, race, and class. Instead of being discouraged, Romani activist-scholars should be supported by scholars who pursue critical knowledge and seek nonhierarchical and reflexive partnership. The way forward in Romani studies is to critically reflect on the hierarchical nature of academic knowledge production. This entails critical dialogue among Roma and non-Roma scholars, activist-scholars, activists, policy makers and those who implement policies, as well as those who have opportunities to create new knowledge-making avenues and horizons that were hitherto structurally and epistemologically denied to Roma. These changes will help us liberate our imagination and see Roma as equal partners in knowledge production, instead of Roma being objectified as the other and used as informants solely to enhance knowledge produced by non-Roma in hierarchical, nonegalitarian ways, and to advance their careers. Too often, Roma still feature as an ethnographic spectacle, instead of Roma activist-scholarship being recognized as an important contribution in its own right, by which academics may work with Roma communities in determining their own futures. Although the move toward Roma activist-scholarship will be contested, I believe that it will gradually decolonize Romani studies, as well as challenge the structural conditions of intersectional racism and sexism, which constantly (re)produce and perpetuate existing racial and gender hierarchies and inequalities.

Challenging Racist and Sexist Epistemology

When the women's movement in the 1960s and '70s fundamentally challenged positivist epistemology and methods of social science, Romani studies was still dominated by non-Romani scholars and experts, and their hegemonic voices (in a Gramscian sense) were coined "Gypsylorists" or "Gypsyologists" by Roma and non-Roma scholars (Okely 1983; Mayall 2004). The most comprehensive definition of "Gypsylorists" is provided by David Mayall (2004) in his seminal work. He defines nineteenth-century "Gypsylorists" as those "who were particularly keen to show that their work and publications were an objective and scientific enterprise, and so would stand alongside any serious investigation, and were not just the indulgent pastime of amateurs. These miscellaneous writers, past and present, are frequently seen, by others and by themselves, as well, as Gypsy 'experts'" (Mayall 2004: 24).

One of the central critiques raised by Romani feminist scholars is about the non-Romani male domination of the genealogy of knowledge production (Brooks 2012; Kóczé 2011; Matache 2016a). One primary feminist assumption is that "truth" is perceived and explained depending on the specific subject position of the teller (Haraway 1988). Feminism also takes the stance from the 1960's slogan that the "personal is political," therefore any knowledge is political, regardless where it was produced (Harding 1986). There is no knowledge that can be purely objective outside the social context in which it was produced, or that can be detached from the positionality of the scholar who produced it (Naples and Gurr 2014). Feminist scholars—mainly women of color—expose, deconstruct, and critique sexism and gender bias in academic discourse.

For instance, Black feminist scholars Patricia Hill Collins, bell hooks, Audre Lorde, Angela Y. Davis, Kimberlé W. Crenshaw, and many others provided inspiration and intellectual guidelines for Romani women scholars to think about gender, race, class, sexual identity, and other forms of oppressions as intersecting categories. Collins (1990) underscores that Black feminists need to challenge the very definition, as well as the content, of intellectual discourse constructed about Blacks, which is embedded in racial and sexist bias. This resonates with the scholarly endeavors of Romani women scholars, who, influenced by Black feminist theory, interrogate sexist and racist academic discourse. The well-established knowledge by feminist scholars,[3] claiming that theories, epistemologies, and even scientific facts are produced from specific standpoints and interests, is still being contested in academia. Romani feminists, working from this understanding, critique some of the Romani studies scholars for continuing to believe in objectivity, as well for being reluctant to reflect on their own power position in the knowledge-making process (Kóczé 2018). For instance, Margareta Matache (2016a), the first Romani instructor at Harvard University, critically reflects on "Gypsy and Romani Studies" in the first part of her blog series, originally published in the *Huffington Post*:

> The work of early scholars served to reproduce the widespread racism and negative imagery circulating in the public that demonized Romani people and nurtured their exclusion. Gypsy scholarship not only contributed to racializing and dehumanizing Romani identities,[4] it also reinforced the hierarchy, established through the means of policy and law, between white Europeans and Roma, and further solidified the social and political construction of whiteness/gadjeness, its hidden powers and value.

Ethel C. Brooks, the first tenured Romani woman scholar, critically points out that the "Gypsylorists," instead of exposing the racialization of Roma and the mechanism of structural racism, attribute the oppression of Roma to their culture. She poignantly explains: "In their [Gypsylorists] judgement, tautologically, our 'culture' explains our oppression, and our 'salvation' would preserve their superiority over our historically and socially determined practices and situations" (Brooks 2012: 4). Both of these Romani women scholars are bravely challenging the epistemology of Romani studies and the discourse of "Gypsylorists," which has had a long-lasting, hegemonic effect on contemporary structures of thought—crucially, even among some Roma, who internalized these representations (Acton 2016).

Gypsyologists/Gypsylorists' logic can be explained by using Max Horkheimer's delineation of the difference between traditional, positivist, and critical theories. Horkheimer (1972), in his essay *Traditional and Critical Theory,* argues that traditional theory is typically encountered in natural sciences, and pervaded other academic fields. Positivism claims "independent, 'supra-social,' detached knowledge" (Horkheimer 1972: 196). He argues that despite its assumed "neutrality," knowledge is derived from its very specific social context. He claims that the positivist scholar's knowledge is "incorporated into the apparatus of society; his [sic] achievements are a factor in the conversation and continuous renewal of the existing state of affairs, no matter what fine names he gives to what he [sic] does" (Horkheimer 1972: 196). The positivist approach brings a wide variety of facts into conceptual frameworks, in "a way as they fit into theory as currently accepted" (ibid.), but keeps the status quo and the foundation of the existing state of affairs, no matter which and how many facts are introduced. In some ways, this reflects a pragmatic version of the institutionalization of biases (gender, racial, and others), combined with the sense of "objectivity" and neutrality that pervades Gypsyologists' writings (Acton 2016; Mayall 2004). Thomas A. Acton's (2016) seminal work on *Scientific Racism, Popular Racism and the Discourse of the Gypsy Lore Society* analyzes the legacy of institutional racism based on the corporeal distinction between white superior men and inferior Romani others, something that I will discuss in the next section.

Race Is a Practical Question

Feminist and critical race theory question and challenge the status quo that benefits from the positivist traditional forms of knowledge production, which usually disadvantages women and racialized groups, and this is a reflection that has not yet pervaded Romani studies thoroughly. As long as we do not use gender and race as analytical categories, the effects of sexism and racism remain invisible. Particularly, Romani and pro-Romani feminists, who deal with racism and sexism in a practical way in their political activism, seek to talk about race and racialization in theoretical terms too (Kóczé 2018; Vincze 2014). Although the concept of race, as a social marker of difference, pervades all forms of social relations, in contemporary Europe (particularly in central and eastern Europe) the effect of race and the process of racialization are not sufficiently acknowledged by social studies or, as Balibar (1991) points out, there is a "racism without race," which shifts the focus from "race" to "culture," and builds hierarchies in which some cultures would be superior to others. The fact that Romani studies prefer to use "ethnicity" over "race/racialized minority" thus obscures systemic institutional racism, including in the knowledge production stemming from Romani studies itself (Kóczé 2018). For instance, in her second blog post, Margareta Matache (2016b) writes about the hegemonic approach in Romani studies that still emphasizes the exoticism or marginality of Roma, instead of exposing "systemic racism and cultural domination." She also critically pins down the hegemonic approach that fixes and essentializes the marginality of Roma in Romani studies (see also Ivasiuc, this volume). I concur with Matache: focusing only on Roma marginality, without a broader process of race-making and "othering" in various spheres of society, conceals the scales and manifestations of racial discourses and practices, as well as hiding, or disguising, racialized gendered hierarchical domination in European societies. The gendered racialization of Roma is a process of "othering" that has profoundly shaped and continues to shape the history, politics, economic structure, and culture of European societies. Consequently, the study of race, racism, and theory of gendered racialization requires a significant shift in Romani studies.

Mathias Möschel (2014) eloquently explains the sociopolitical and historical development after World War II, which did not support critical race theory in European academic discourse. According to Möschel (2007: 70), "The basic ideological concept that racism consists of one 'dominant' group, mostly the 'white' majority, targeting other groups as being (biologically) inferior and then consolidating this ideology into legal, social and political rules, is common to both Europe and the United States." For Du Bois, race and racialization is not just theoretical, but also a practical question, one that happens in everyday life; it is a lived experience. As the first Black sociologist, W.E.B. Du Bois obtained his second bachelor's degree from Harvard University before traveling to Berlin. According to his biography, Germany was the first place in his life where his blackness was not the most important and relevant thing about him (Levering-Lewis 1993). The white Germans perceived him as a "young American," Harvard-educated bourgeois. It was a liberating period in his young life because race did not define him and was not an obstacle to interacting with people. His description of this experience was that he became more human (Levering-Lewis 1993). Kwame Anthony Appiah (2014) explores the impressive life of Du Bois and discusses his German experience. In that period, Germany was not free from racial prejudice, but targeted a different racialized group: the Jews. Du Bois had to learn how to interact with people in a place where his race did not matter. He came to realize that it is possible to relate to racism and racial prejudice in a different way (Appiah 2014).

Race is a practical issue to me, too. I had to come to the United States to clarify my understanding of European racism against the Roma and my place within the feminist paradigm where "the personal is political." One segment of my racialized experience in an academic context is similar to what W.E.B. Du Bois experienced in Germany between 1892 and 1894 as a Black scholar from the United States. I had a very similar revelation being a Romnja European Fulbright visiting scholar, and afterwards a visiting professor at Wake Forest University, North Carolina. In the United States, my Roma identity is invisible; I am not racialized; being Roma is unimportant, while my gender is more significant. As a professor in Hungary, working in an academic context assumed to be liberal and progressive, the first and most important markers about me are my Roma identity and female body. This defines people's perception about me and my interaction with white academic colleagues. In the U.S. academic context, there is no need, nor urgency, to constantly prove my intellectual capacity, because I am perceived as a European intellectual. However, in Europe, where I am noted as a Romani woman (even in Romani studies circles), there is a need to overcome the racial prejudice that is silently imposed on my inferiorized female body. It is a challenge for anyone, even with stellar academic skills, to perform under such a debilitating gaze. As Du Bois did in Germany, in the United States I have had the time and space to reflect on my racialized European existence as I contemplate and reflect on the lived experiences of my Black students in post–Jim Crow North Carolina.

Like Du Bois, I had to travel several thousand miles to gain trust and respect, and to experience liberation from academic gender and racial profiling.[5] To put this into perspective, I am not the only Romani woman in our European academic world who has experienced lack of trust and respect. Patricia Caro, a Romani feminist from Spain, whom I interviewed for my research, explained that non-Roma teachers (*Gadjé*) never supported her in pursuing an academic degree: "When I was growing up . . . I decided that I wanted to develop my intellectual capacities, though my *Gadjé* teachers told me that studying at university is not for Calis."[6] Caro also talked about a later, positive encounter with a professor who taught at the university: "It was the first time that a professor believed in my abilities and established a human relationship with me."

This experience can be pertinently related to what Sylvia Wynter (2003), critical race and cultural theorist, discusses, when she analyzes the hierarchization of black, brown, and other bodies that are perceived as "less than human," deviating from the deeply gendered and sexualized, normative white heterosexual and able bodies. The racialization of Roma and the ongoing construction—through sociopolitical relations, social and cultural discourses, everyday practices, and economic exploitation and dispossession—of a visible racial identity in popular culture are the manifestations of excluding racialized bodies from the category of "human" (Wynter 2003). According to Wynter, racialization, as a sociopolitical mechanism, systematically classifies people within a hierarchical relationship that identifies social groups as human, subhuman, and nonhuman.

Mills's (1997) theoretical elaboration on the "racial contract" exposes the devastating effect of unacknowledged racial presumptions that influence social relations. Mills (1997: 3) suggests that the "racial contract," as a manifestation of white supremacy, is itself an invisible, even hidden, social contract, "a particular power structure of formal or informal rule, socioeconomic privilege, and norms for the differential distribution of material wealth and opportunities, benefits and burdens, rights and duties." He criticizes and provokes mainstream philosophy for the omission of unnamed theoretical architecture, for justifying an entire history of European atrocity and violence against nonwhites and racially identified "others" more generally, such as the Jews and the Roma, from David Hume's and Immanuel

Kant's claims that Blacks had inferior cognitive power. Mills's "racial contract" classifies people into the system of domination by which white people historically ruled over and dominated nonwhite people. Similarly to feminist theory, which revealed how orthodox political philosophy is saturated by white male bias, Mills's explication of the "racial contract" exposes the racial foundation of Western political philosophy, challenging the assumption that mainstream theory is itself raceless, and problematizing thereby the racialized social relations at the very core of the knowledge production apparatus—academia. The current colorblind approach in European academic discourse occludes the structural racial violence against Roma embedded in a hidden "racial contract."

Rethinking and Reviewing the Conceptual Language

B., a Romani Ph.D. candidate in communication studies, deplored the lack of understanding of racialization and racial hierarchy in her academic program. She explained that "our [mainly Romani female scholars'] interest in critical race theory or postcolonial theory emerges from the inability of classical Romani studies to deal adequately with the perspectives of Roma, as well as the complexities of race as a lived experience and the effect of racialization. Race, racialization and racial identity remain unmarked in most of the studies on Roma." B. also explained, "When I am using critical race or postcolonial theory to explain the racialization and subordination of Roma, then I am ridiculed by my white academic colleagues. It seems that it's illegitimate to use a different theoretical framework, other than what they are using."

Romani and non-Romani feminist scholars in central and eastern Europe (CEE) are in the process of rethinking and reviewing the conceptual language that has been used by scholars on Roma. They opted to highlight the importance of using the social-political construction of race as a conceptual and analytical category (Vincze 2014; Kóczé 2018). Similarly to critical race theorists suggesting that race is not a transcending category that stands above gender, class, and other axes of inequality, they demonstrate that these categories co-constitute and recreate the subject position of the racialized person. Romani feminists (Izsák 2009; Kóczé 2009; Brooks 2012) were among the first in CEE to introduce and adopt intersectional theory (Crenshaw 1991) to challenge the normative hierarchical, gendered, and racialized structures.

The large body of Roma-related studies conceptualizes Roma as ethnicity, hence downplaying the shifting historical and social configuration of the racialization of Roma in relation to the nonracialized "white" majority.

The racialized lived experience of Roma is sustained by invisible, unmarked, and unreflexive hegemonic white supremacy, where Roma suffer the consequences of racism in most of the countries in which they live in substantial numbers and where, through their physical features, occupations, and other characteristics, they are recognized by the population as a whole as "Gypsies." As activist scholars, Romani or otherwise, we must lead the charge to theorize these phenomena and liberate scholarship and popular culture accordingly. The emerging critical Romani studies that is envisioned by a fragile minority of Romani and non-Roma scholars must critique the academic discourse that privileges the theory of ethnicity as the only or primary paradigm that frames Roma lived social experiences. Omi and Winant (2015: 21) convincingly show that theoretical trajectories of ethnicity-based theories are "an approach to race that affords primacy to cultural variables," which limit the reality experienced by Roma in public and in the academy. They also explain how ethnicity theory cannot capture racial conflict and that it becomes an ally of "colorblindness" politics that has created a new "post-racial" and "common sense" reality: "In a colorblind society, it is claimed, racial inequality, racial politics, and race consciousness itself would be greatly diminished in importance, and indeed relegated to the benighted past when discrimination and prejudiced ruled" (Omi and Winant 2015: 22). Omi and Winant (2015: 22–23) critique the construction of ethnicity as a cultural phenomenon and assert that theories of ethnicity "undermine the significance of corporeal markers of identity" that deny the historically accumulated and enduring injustices of people of color.

Silence and Invisibility

Judith Okely, one of the most reflexive feminist scholars in Romani studies, distinctly writes about her gendered lessons in academia. She asserts that feminist knowledge involves unsettling forms of power that are not equally open to all, in particular the power to produce authoritative knowledge (Okely 2007: 228). Richelle D. Schrock (2013: 52) points out that women's writing in ethnography has historically been undervalued, mainly because of the form they use and the nature of the content that includes personal reflections and narratives.

I interviewed several Romani women in academia, who complained about forms of condescending treatment and attitudes of "presumed incompetence" by their white colleagues; they recall situations similar to the experiences of Black women, Latinas, and Native Americans, who are still underrepresented in U.S. academia (Gutiérrez y Muhs et al. 2012). The experiences of women of color resonate with those of a Romani female professor of linguistics:

> I think Romani women historically have been invisible, underestimated and not acknowledged for their contributions and their knowledge. The historical representation of Romani women shapes our existence in academia. . . . When I have been looked down on, I always wished I had more racially diverse colleagues, with whom I could share even these kinds of concerns. (L.SZ.)

A junior scholar who started her Ph.D. in her late thirties explained,

> I have never been invited to any Roma-related research, even though there are not many Roma in academia. I participated only for one day in research about education of Roma, when I was nagging the research coordinator to involve me at least as a pollster. . . . I cannot gain research experience without participating in various Roma-related research projects. (C.)

Anna Mirga-Kruszelnicka, a young Romani scholar, reflects on her "impossible subject position":

> I found myself in a situation where my ethnic background began to bear relevance in the way I was treated in academia. Numerous times my objectivity was questioned: it was argued that not only am I Roma, but I am also an activist, so surely my "activist agenda" obscures my academic findings.

Her scholarly subject position was questioned in virtue of her Romani and activist background. Her "impossible subject position" provides a reason to dismiss, silence, and invisibilize her. In anthropology, decades ago, there was a similar argument: anthropologists could not be objective if they studied their own culture and society because their familiarity would render them uncritical; anthropologists were confined to researching unfamiliar cultures. This kind of limitation prevented anthropological research in Europe and in the United States, except for the study of indigenous populations. This way of thinking also created limitations on "native" versus "real" anthropologists, similar to what Roma scholars face. According to Kirin Narayan (1993: 672), this kind of polarization derives from the colonial setting "in which natives were genuine natives (whether they liked it or not) and the observer's objectivity in the scientific study of Other societies posed no problem." With changing times, this asymmetrical power relationship has somewhat changed; however, not so for Roma scholars, whose abilities to describe lived Romani racialized experience, and theorize their condition, are continuously questioned.

Grada Kilomba (2010), a feminist postcolonial scholar, spoke about the transformation enacted by Black women when they converted silence into language and action. In her book, *Plantation Memories,* she talks about the unspeakable larger phenomenon described as a contestation of silence by Black scholars in a white academic world.[7] It should not be surprising that Romani scholars experience such positions of marginality that evoke pain and feelings of stigmatization in a predominantly white world. Kilomba (2008) theorizes the academic space as an oppressive institution regarding the representation of Black people:

> This is a white space where Black people have been denied the privilege to speak. Historically, this is a space where we have been voiceless and where white scholars have developed theoretical discourses which officially constructed us as the inferior "Other"—placing Africans in complete subordination to the white subject. Here, we were made inferior, our bodies described, classified, dehumanized, primitivized, brutalized and even killed. We are therefore, in a space which has a very problematic relationship to Blackness. Here, we were made the objects, but we have rarely been the subjects.

On one of her Facebook posts, one well-educated Romani woman critiqued the academic sphere as a place that silences, infantilizes, and patronizes Roma: "Non-Romani voices are still lauded as more legitimate when talking about Romani issues. We are still minimized in a way that implies some kind of parent-child relationship, that we simply cannot speak up for ourselves or recognize the injustices done to us daily because we are not mature enough as a people" (Q., Facebook post, June 2016). Aimé Césaire (2001) identified this language as a colonial technique of infantilizing and silencing the colonized.[8] In the twenty-first century, Roma increasingly have broken through the barriers to higher education and are entering academia, but Romani women have to confront additional barriers of white patriarchal privilege.

Activist Knowledge Production

Romani women, political activism, and feminist intellectual thought are deeply connected and embedded in the restructuration of economic, social, and political structures produced by market capitalism in central and eastern Europe. This ambiguous transformation in CEE, after 1989, created some space for activism and encouraged activists to transform silence into voice and action (Kóczé 2018). The knowledge that is produced by Romani and pro-Romani feminist scholars is essential to understanding the intersection of gendered and racialized oppressions under market capitalism in CEE. Most of them are deeply connected with social activism and academia. Subsequently, they are often disqualified as scholars and their work classified as "activist knowledge" by non-Roma, mainly male, scholars, who deem this kind of knowledge irrelevant and tainted by subjectivity. When I interviewed Anna Mirga-Kruszelnicka, she explained the condescension she felt in an academic context: "I felt put down and patronized by older non-Roma scholars who often acted as a 'know-it-all' authority, while I was 'just an activist pretending to be an academic.' I felt like I have to prove my academic merits and should work harder to prove my value as an early career scholar."

Black feminist and sociologist Patricia Hill Collins (1990: 202–3) succinctly explains: "What to believe and why something is true are not benign academic issues. Instead, these concerns tap the fundamental question of which versions of truth will prevail and shape thought and action." Regarding Roma-related academic discourses, one of the main questions is which version is the most dominant in social and political discourse. Who has greater credentials in the academic community? Who has the power to delegitimize knowledge experiences or views that are produced from a different position and epistemological perspective? I argue, in accordance with feminist theorists, that it always depends on the prevailing power and the validation of the privileged scholars in the academic community. The precarious scholars, such as the small number of rising Romani scholars, structurally depend on the validation of established, privileged scholars, who are considered the source of information about Roma (Hancock 2010).

Thomas Kuhn's (1962) classic *Structure of Scientific Revolution*'s central argument is that "truths" are formulated and validated within a specific paradigm. However, he also emphasizes that revolutionary breakthroughs in science often derive from growing recognition of contradictions and irresolvable internal conflicts within these paradigms, which are resolved by a process of change with the introduction of new ideas. Any science, including social science, is validated in a historical process that is always open-ended, incomplete, and in constant change.

Concerning academic validation, it is important to differentiate between epistemic authority and epistemic privilege: they are connected, but not the same. Marianne Janack (1997: 133) noted that "epistemic authority is conferred . . . as a result of other people's judgment of our sincerity, reliability, trustworthiness, and 'objectivity'; certain people are in a better position to 'see' the world than are other people." In contrast, epistemic privilege is socially more complex and tied to opportunities that are structured by gender, race, class, sexuality, citizenship, social network—even institutional belonging—and so on. Subsequently, this is also related to political power and control in a very specific historical moment. Those Roma scholars who can speak to the center either speak the validated language of academia, or speak via another scholar who has power in a mainstream academic context. Epistemic privilege is a flexible, temporal, and spatial position, conditioned by those who possess material and symbolic power over knowledge production. In regard to knowledge-making about Roma, historically, the epistemic authority is claimed by non-Roma scholars and "Roma experts" or policy makers (Hancock 2010). Currently, the involvement of some Romani scholars in the establishment of the European Roma Institute for Arts and Culture (ERIAC), or in the new academic program "Roma in European Societies" at the Central European University, offers a historical opportunity for Romani scholars to possess epistemic privilege.

Postcolonial feminist theorists also refer to the geopolitical structures of dominance and control, which provide more epistemic privilege for those who are located in a dominant (central) geography (Mohanty 2003). In the Roma-related knowledge-making process, it is native-English-speaking, Western-trained Roma and non-Roma scholars who maintain language and knowledge hierarchies and asymmetrical power relations. A significant number of Roma intellectuals from central and southeastern Europe have limited access to English resources and their work and efforts remain marginal or invisible.

The politics of location, standpoint, and positionality play an important role in knowledge-making. Sandra Harding (1986) argues that subordinated groups may offer stronger objectivity due to increased motivation for the subordinated to understand the perspective of those who are in power positions. This stronger objectivity and motivation to understand leads to the shift that occurs when subordinated groups, in this case Romani intellectuals within the new cultural institute and academic department, gain some epistemic privilege to influence cultural representation and academic discourse on Roma. It does not mean than this will be a perfect representation of Roma in the European academic canon; however, it will ensure that Roma lived and racialized bodily experiences will be gradually recognized and integrated. It might give an opportunity for social political activism to offer scholars political consciousness that can be transformed and theorized into academic knowledge. Activist scholarship provides us with a unique opportunity to learn from errors and to recognize the highly contextual, political, and conditional nature of knowledge production within social science.

Much of the important work done by the first generation of Romani feminists in mainstream academia remains invisible to the public because, instead of writing journal articles, they are more engaged in supporting the forthcoming young generation of Romani scholars. "We are taking all the emotional burdens which are attached to the token academic position that prevent our academic productivity," explained B., one of the rising Romani feminist scholars. There is an emerging young generation of Romani scholars who would simply not exist without the pioneering work of Romani feminist mentorship and their invisible labor in creating new structures and lineages in higher education.[9] These types of work remain the unacknowledged labor of intellectual and professional mentoring in academia. Nevertheless, it is crucial to work with the emerging generation, as well as to offer a theorization for social and political activism, especially in underrepresented fields of academic inquiry, which can be shaped and developed by critical scholarship and activism (that, in itself, is also a form of knowledge), such as critical Romani studies.

Angéla Kóczé is an assistant professor of Romani studies at Central European University, Budapest. She has published several peer-reviewed academic articles and book chapters with various international presses, including Palgrave Macmillan, Ashgate, and Central European University Press, as well as several thematic policy papers related to social inclusion, gender equality, social justice, and civil society. She is currently preparing a monograph, *Gender, Race, and Class: Romani Women's Political Activism and Social Struggles in the Post-Socialist Countries in Europe*. In 2013, the Woodrow Wilson International Center for Scholars in Washington, D.C., honored Kóczé with the Ion Rațiu Democracy Award for her interdisciplinary participatory research on the situation of the Roma.

Notes

1. ICI Berlin Institute for Cultural Inquiry, "Alexander G. Weheliye: Black Life," YouTube, posted 17 May 2016, accessed 10 February 2017, https://www.youtube.com/watch?v=X0I6xGqMHns.
2. Craig Calhoun (1995) elaborated his vision about critical theory in detail in *Critical Social Theory: Culture, History and the Challenge of Difference*.
3. In the mid-1970s and early 1980s, several feminist theorists began developing alternatives to the traditional methods of scientific research. The result was a new theory, now recognized as standpoint theory, developed by Sandra Harding and many others, such as Dorothy Smith, Donna Haraway, Patricia Hill Collins, Nancy Hartsock, and Hilary Rose. Standpoint theory caused heated debate and radically altered the way research is conducted.
4. Matache refers to Ken Lee's (2000) article "Orientalism and Gypsylorism."
5. There is a body of social science research that indicates racism and sexism in academia mainly targets women of color (Gutiérrez y Muhs et al. 2012).
6. Romani group in Spain, generally known as Gitanos.
7. See Kilomba 2008 for an excerpt, "Africans in Academia: Diversity in Adversity."
8. Originally published as *Discours sur le colonialisme* by Editions Présence Africaine, 1955.

9. For example, in 1996, I founded the Romaversitas Foundation in Hungary, which still provides mentorship and scholarship for Romani university students. In 2001, as International Policy Fellow, supported by Open Society Institute, Budapest, I introduced this higher education mentoring program in several central and southeastern European countries.

References

Acton, Thomas. 2016. "Scientific Racism, Popular Racism and the Discourse of the Gypsy Lore Society." *Ethnic and Racial Studies* 39 (7): 1187–204. doi:10.1080/014 19870.2015.1105988.

Appiah, Kwame A. 2014. *Lines of Descent: W.E.B. Du Bois and the Emergence of Identity.* Cambridge, MA: Harvard University Press.

Asad, Talal. 1973. *Anthropology and the Colonial Encounter.* London: Ithaca Press; Atlantic Highlands: Humanities Press.

Balibar, Etienne. 1991. "Is There a Neo-Racism?" In *Race, Nation, Class: Ambiguous Identities,* edited by Etienne Balibar and Immanuel M. Wallerstein, 17–28. London: Verso.

Beck, Sam, and Carl Maida, eds. 2013. *Toward Engaged Anthropology.* New York: Berghahn Books.

———, eds. 2015. *Public Anthropology in a Borderless World.* New York: Berghahn Books.

Bennett, John W. 1996. "Applied and Action Anthropology: Ideological and Conceptual Aspects." *Current Anthropology* 37 (1): S23–S53.

Brooks, Ethel C. 2012. "The Possibilities of Romani Feminism." *Signs* 38 (1): 1–11. doi:10.1086/665947.

Burawoy, Michael. 2005. "For Public Sociology." *American Sociological Review* 70 (1): 4–28. doi:10.1177/000312240507000102.

Calhoun, Craig. 1995. *Critical Social Theory: Culture, History, and the Challenge of Difference.* Cambridge: Wiley-Blackwell.

———. 2008. "Foreword." In *Engaging Contradictions: Theory, Politics, and Methods of Activist Scholarship,* edited by Charles R. Hale, xii–xxvi. Berkeley, CA: University of California Press.

Césaire, Aimé. 2001. *Discourse on Colonialism.* Translated by Joan Pinkham. New York: New York University Press.

Collins, Patricia H. 1990. *Black Feminist Thought: Knowledge, Consciousness, and the Politics of Empowerment.* Boston: Unwin Hyman.

Crenshaw, Kimberlé. 1991. "Mapping the Margins: Intersectionality, Identity Politics, and Violence against Women of Color." *Stanford Law Review* 43 (6): 1241–99. doi:10.2307/1229039.

Gutiérrez y Muhs, Gabriella, Yolanda Flores Niemann, Carmen G. González, and Angela P. Harris, eds. 2012. *Presumed Incompetent: The Intersections of Race and Class for Women in Academia.* Boulder, CO: University Press of Colorado.

Hancock, Ian. 2010. *Danger! Educated Gypsy: Selected Essays.* Hatfield: University of Hertfordshire Press.

Haraway, Donna. 1988. "Situated Knowledges: The Science Question in Feminism and the Privilege of Partial Perspective." *Feminist Studies* 14 (3): 575–99.

Harding, Sandra. 1986. *The Science Question in Feminism.* Ithaca, NY: Cornell University Press.

Harrison, Faye, ed. 1991a. *Decolonizing Anthropology: Moving Further toward an Anthropology for Liberation.* Washington, DC: American Anthropological Association.

———. 1991b. "Anthropology as an Agent of Transformation: Introductory Comments and Queries." In *Decolonizing Anthropology: Moving Further toward an Anthropology for Liberation,* edited by Faye Harrison, 1–11. Washington, DC: American Anthropological Association.

Horkheimer, Max. 1972. *Critical Theory: Selected Essays.* Translated by Matthew J. O'Connell and others. New York: Seabury Press.

Huizer, Gerrit, and Bruce Mannheim. 1979. *The Politics of Anthropology.* Berlin: De Gruyter Mouton.

Izsák, Rita. 2009. "The European Romani Women's Movement: The Struggle for Human Rights." *Development* 52 (2): 200–7. doi:10.1057/dev.2009.9.

Janack, Marianne. 1997. "Standpoint Epistemology without the 'Standpoint'? An Examination of Epistemic Privilege and Epistemic Authority." *Hypatia* 12: 125–39.

Kilomba, Grada. 2008. "Africans in Academia: Diversity in Adversity." Excerpt from *Plantation Memories.* Accessed 10 February 2017. https://edoc.hu-berlin.de/bitstream/handle/18452/3759/299.pdf?sequence=1.

———. 2010. *Plantation Memories: Episodes of Everyday Racism.* Münster: Unrast.

Kóczé, Angéla. 2009. "The Limits of Rights-Based Discourse in Romani Women's Activism: The Gender Dimension in Romani Politics." In *Romani Politics in Contemporary Europe,* edited by Nando Sigona and Nidhi Trehan, 133–55. New York: Palgrave Macmillan.

———. 2011. "Gender, Ethnicity and Class: Romani Women's Political Activism and Social Struggles." Ph.D. dissertation, Central European University.

———. 2018, forthcoming. *Gender, Race, and Class: Romani Women's Political Activism and Social Struggles in the Post-Socialist Countries in Europe.* Budapest: Central European University Press.

Kóczé, Angéla, and Nidhi Trehan. 2009. "Racism, (Neo-) Colonialism and Social Justice: The Struggle for the Soul of the Romani Movement in Post-Socialist Europe." In *Racism Postcolonialism Europe,* edited by Graham Huggan and Ian Law, 50–76. Liverpool: Liverpool University Press.

Kuhn, Thomas. 1962. *The Structure of Scientific Revolutions.* Chicago, IL: University of Chicago Press.

Lee, Ken. 2000. "Orientalism and Gypsylorism." *Social Analysis: The International Journal of Social and Cultural Practice* 44 (2): 129–56.

Levering-Lewis, David. 1993. *W.E.B. Du Bois: Biography of a Race, 1868–1919.* New York: Henry Holt and Company.

Matache, Margareta. 2016a. "Word, Image and Thought: Creating the Romani Other." FXB Center for Health & Human Rights, Harvard University. Originally published in the *Huffington Post,* 3 October 2016. Accessed 10 February 2017. https://fxb.harvard.edu/word-image-and-thought-creating-the-romani-other/.

———. 2016b. "The Legacy of Gypsy Studies in Modern Romani Scholarship." FXB Center for Health & Human Rights, Harvard University. Originally published in the *Huffington Post,* 10 November 2016. Accessed 10 February 2017. https://fxb.harvard.edu/the-legacy-of-gypsy-studies-in-modern-romani-scholarship.

Mayall, David. 2004. *Gypsy Identities 1500–2000: From Egipcyans to Moon-men to the Ethnic Romany.* London: Routledge.

Mills, Charles W. 1997. *The Racial Contract.* Ithaca, NY: Cornell University Press.

Mohanty, Chandra T. 2003. "'Under Western Eyes' Revisited: Feminist Solidarity through Anticapitalist Struggles." *Signs* 28 (2): 499–535.

Möschel, Mathias. 2007. "Color Blindness or Total Blindness? The Absence of Critical Race Theory in Europe." *Rutgers Race and the Law Review* 9 (1): 57–128.

———. 2014. *Law, Lawyers and Race: Critical Race Theory from the United States to Europe.* London: Routledge.

Naples, Nancy A., and Barbara Gurr. 2014. "Feminist Empiricism and Standpoint Theory: Approaches to Understanding the Social World." In *Feminist Research Practice: A Primer,* edited by Sharlene Nagy Hesse-Biber and Patricia Lina Leavy, 14–41. Thousand Oaks, CA: Sage.

Narayan, Kirin. 1993. "How Native Is a 'Native' Anthropologist?" *American Anthropologist* 95 (3): 671–86.

Okely, Judith. 1983. *The Traveller-Gypsies.* Cambridge: Cambridge University Press.

———. 1992. "Anthropology and Autobiography: Participatory Experience and Embodied Knowledge." In *Anthropology and Autobiography,* edited by Judith Okely and Helen Callaway, 1–28. London: Routledge.

———. 2007. "Gendered Lessons in Ivory Towers." In *Identity and Networks: Gender and Ethnicity in a Cross-Cultural Context,* edited by Deborah Fahy Bryceson, Judith Okely, and Jonathan Webber, 228–46. Oxford: Berghahn Books.

Omi, Michael, and Howard Winant. 2015. *Racial Formation in the United States.* New York: Routledge.

Scheper-Hughes, Nancy. 1995. "The Primacy of the Ethical: Propositions for a Militant Anthropology." *Current Anthropology* 36 (3): 409–40.

Schrock, Richelle D. 2013. "The Methodological Imperatives of Feminist Ethnography." *Journal of Feminist Scholarship* 5 (December): 48–60.

Vincze, Enikő. 2014. "The Racialization of Roma in the 'New' Europe and the Political Potential of Romani Women." *European Journal of Women's Studies* 21 (4): 435–42. doi:10.1177/1350506814548963.

Weheliye, Alexander G. 2016. "Black Life." ICI Berlin: Institute for Cultural Inquiry. 22 March 2016. Accessed 10 April 2017. https://www.ici-berlin.org/events/alexander-g-weheliye/.

Wynter, Silvia. 2003. "Unsettling the Coloniality of Being/Power/Truth/Freedom: Towards the Human, after Man, its Overrepresentation. An Argument." *The New Centennial Review* 3 (3): 257–337. doi:10.1353/ncr.2004.0015.

CHAPTER 6

❀ ❀ ❀

ALTER-NARRATIVES
Seeing Ordinary Agency

Ana Ivasiuc

> *Nothing has ever humiliated me more than*
> *to be seen as a victim, even in the worst moments.*
> —Saimir Mile[1]

A while ago, I was involved in the organization of a conference panel within an anthropology conference on Modes of Appropriation and Social Resistance; the aim of the panel was to uncover the ways in which Roma resist, appropriate, and sidetrack development and policy interventions. The clearly stated focus of the panel was the agency of ordinary Roma, exploring the question of what Roma groups actively *do* to deviate, alter, resist, or challenge the policy and development interventions targeting them. The panel enjoyed wide interest from established scholars and young researchers alike—many of whom were involved in various forms of activism—and announced a very promising encounter. Nevertheless, most of the presentations and discussions during the three-sessions-long panel were primarily devoted to what the Roma suffer: the multiple ways in which they are subjected to racism and discrimination, the mechanisms which relegate them to the margins of society, and the intricate workings of the inequality-producing neoliberal order. With striking naturalness, the emphasis on agency deliquesced in familiar narratives: from subjects, the Roma quickly became direct objects of non-Roma agency as victims of oppression. The panel provided a valuable opportunity for observant participation (Fassin and Rechtman 2009: 11).[2] This discreet but persistent slippage back into familiar discourses of oppression pointed to a certain unease of the participants to move away from victimization narratives and to consider the Roma as actively engaged in strategies and tactics of resistance, beyond external support from activist organizations. Notwithstanding the repeated attempts at bringing it back in the spotlight, the agency of the Roma remained, in most of the accounts and in the following discussions, nearly invisible. To my sense, our panel failed at eliciting a different framing, prompting reflection on the mechanisms that preclude the emergence, in engaged scholarship and activism, of "alter-narratives": alternative framings that explicitly build on forms of agency, away from familiar narratives of subordination and suffering.

A great deal of research adopting militant perspectives with regard to Roma populations emphasizes their subordination, discrimination, marginalization, and exclusion, mostly drawing on the language of human rights, and from the logic of denunciation. Such framings embody the "anti-politics" moment (Hage 2015) of Romani activism and engaged scholarship: a denunciation of the unjust social order producing suffering subjects. These efforts are certainly necessary, as they offer a valuable critique of social mechanisms producing subordination, marginalization, and exclusion. Yet, more often than not, such studies tend to frame the Roma mainly as passive victims, rather than active shapers of tactics and strategies of resistance and escape. In this chapter, I examine the discursive workings and production mechanisms of the narrative built around the subordination of the Roma. I focus on policy-oriented studies and "gray literature" issued by international development organizations, national activist organizations, and researchers engaged in advocacy, which disproportionately emphasize the domination of the Roma by mainstream societies, to the point that forms of agency of Roma groups are effaced from public debate.

The chapter articulates three moves. First, I deconstruct the discourses that focus exclusively on the subordination of the Roma and posit them as a surreptitious form of Orientalism (Said 1979). In the second section, I analyze the mechanisms through which these strands of knowledge are generated and perpetuated, by contextualizing them and locating their production in the wider international development apparatus. I argue that a necessary shift in perspective can open up a path toward understanding how an "alter-politics" (Hage 2015), seen as political alternatives to an unjust social order, may be formulated by mobilizing ethnographically informed alter-narratives attentive to the forms of agency that the Roma enact within the development encounter. In my chapter, I show the ambiguities and limits of current forms of activist involvement within gray literature produced for advocacy and policy purposes, and explore a possible renewal of the epistemology underpinning this kind of literature.

Essentially Trapped: The Victimhood Discourse as a Form of Orientalism

The choice to focus on development and policy documents—generally subsumed under what is known as "gray literature" as opposed to peer-reviewed literature produced within academic institutions—is underpinned by the observation that, often, the knowledge produced through gray literature slips into academic research. The opposite is less true: rarely does one find, in policy reports, references to ethnographies on the Roma focusing on their agency in the context of policy interventions. The one-sided permeability of this boundary is not innocent, nor inconsequential, and prompts reflection on the kinds of selections operated in and through gray literature. In this section, I approach critically the predominant discourse generated by international and nongovernmental (pro-)Roma organizations in Eastern Europe, commissioned by either national governments or international agencies.[3] Usually linked to the advocacy goals of NGOs, to the funding agendas of international donors, or to the policy aims of bodies such as the EU, this gray literature takes the form of research reports and studies for policy and intervention purposes. Although some authors draw clear distinctions between political activism stemming from (pro-)Roma organizations (Kovats 2001) or expert literature (Surdu 2015) as opposed to peer-reviewed scholarship, in practice a number of academics are simultaneously involved in activism and consultancy, and their commitments blur the boundaries between the narratives generated by these different settings of knowledge production (Matras 2015). I intend to show that activist engagement through the production of gray literature is ambiguous: even though it stems from a will to denounce injustice, improve the living conditions of Roma communities, and thus operate political openings, it tends, at the same time, to affect a closure by precluding the examination of forms of agency of the Roma.

The discourse I wish to scrutinize here underlines the victim status of Roma, overemphasizing poverty, discrimination, and suffering, and thereby constructing a subject needy of policy and development interventions (Timmer 2010; Schneeweis 2015). The narrative on the victimhood of Roma is riddled with vocabularies of entrapment: "vicious circles" (Spolu and CEGA 2000), "dependency traps" (UNDP 2002) and "poverty cycles" (Ringold et al. 2005) immobilize the Roma in a static and rigid position without escape. The impossibility to escape poverty even over future generations is demonstrated by means of expert statistics (as in Bodewig and Sethi 2005). The most pervasive feature of these narratives is to be found in the multiple deficits that continuously produce the inferior difference of the Roma: they lack education, jobs, proper housing, identity papers, knowledge, and capital—

financial, of course, but also social and cultural. These lacks are defined in relation to the unquestioned norms of mainstream society, thereby natural- ized as legitimate rule-maker. If the Roma do not comply with these rules, it is deplored that they lack "awareness" regarding the importance of various aspects of mainstream societies, such as schooling, or voting, or having iden- tity papers—in short, of not doing what everyone else does.

This activist narrative solidifies a depoliticized, ahistorical account of the relationship between the Roma and various institutions of mainstream so- cieties, negating their uneasy, conflict-ridden dynamics with, for instance, mainstream schooling (Toninato 2014).[4] Without crucial historical and eth- nographic insights on the complex and ambiguous relation between Roma groups and mainstream institutions, framing the withdrawal or refusal to participate in education as mere "lack of awareness" or "lack of interest" risks contributing to miscomprehension and the solidification of antigypsyist prej- udice. The focus on what the Roma are "lacking" removes the critical edge of academic writings, too, when this narrative crosses boundaries, leading to perplexing, tautological, and unwittingly victim-blaming statements such as the following: "lacking many prerequisites for effective participation, Romani individuals and communities alike retract from engagement with the majority public, and thus enhance public perceptions of Romanies' self- exclusion, entrenching stereotypes about the 'Gypsy' further and feeding the prejudice against the 'Roma problem'" (Agarin 2014). Inadvertently, prejudice against the Roma is here legitimized by the idea that the Roma lack "prerequisites for effective participation," pointing to their own "failure" to engage in dialogue with mainstream societies. Yet, the rules underlying "ef- fective participation" are those decided by the majority, and often remain unquestioned even in well-intentioned scholarship.

By popularizing a view of Roma groups as essentially excluded, deprived, and unable to challenge their status quo, the victimhood discourse legiti- mizes, normalizes, and perpetuates the necessity of interventions as a "civi- lizing project" (Powell 2011) that enable the Roma to "include" themselves in mainstream societies. The logic of these interventions focuses on "edu- cating" them and "raising their awareness" as to the importance of aspects deemed key in mainstream societies. Interventions aimed at education or insertion in the wage labor system have been criticized for pathologizing the Roma as defective and for failing to take into account resistance to ed- ucational (or, generally, state) institutions, experienced by some Roma as oppressive or assimilationist (Hancock 2000; Timmer 2010; Powell 2011; Trubeta 2013; Engebrigtsen 2014; Matras et al. 2015). By uncritically taking for granted mainstream institutions as the only way of being in the world, Roma agency opposing, resisting, and implicitly critiquing non-Roma ways is made invisible. These accounts and the obsessive mantra of Roma inclusion through education and wage labor remain thus unreflexive and largely ethnocentric, constructing the Roma as the deficient other in relation to an unquestioned—therefore posited as superior—majority norm.

Persistently defining the Roma by their supposed deficits naturalizes their subordination, as well as the material, social, and intellectual deprivation of the group, constructed as passive victims unable to successfully mobilize resources for self-initiated life trajectories that are disconnected from familiar forms of political activism. Conceptions of "imperfect" (Sigona and Monasta 2006) or "partial citizenship" (Casa Nova 2012: 122) prolong the "dreadful secondariness" (Said 1989: 207) of the Roma. In other contexts, such narratives, grounded in an exclusive focus on issues of domination and poverty, have been termed "miserabilist" (Grignon and Passeron 1989; Olivier de Sardan 2005: 47), leading to impoverished and sterile representations.

Notwithstanding their benevolent aim to advocate for the Roma toward the improvement of their lot, many authors contribute to a discourse that fails to suggest a way out of either the intellectual or the political conundrums inherent in this perspective: the Roma remain "permanent victims of outside society" (Matras 2013: 220). These pauper representations disregard the agency of Roma, their diversity, and their diverging interests, thus authorizing the reading of the victimhood discourse as a form of Orientalism. Flagrantly, these accounts obfuscate the internal politics and the mechanisms of domination both among the Roma and among the non-Roma internally, in a move that "sanitize[s] the internal politics of the dominated" (Ortner 1995: 179), dividing the world into simplistic, binary categories.[5]

Despite criticism (Lee 2000; Saul 2007; van Baar 2011), forms of Orientalism not only subsist in our days, but lurk behind engaged scholarship. They constitute a prime example of a political opening—embodied in the will to denounce injustice—turning into a discursive closure (Rose 1999: 192). Such discourses escape criticism and establish themselves as the pervasive narrative on Roma because activism and the benevolent stance enacted by institutions purporting to work for the inclusion of the Roma take the higher moral ground in a self-legitimizing move. The danger of (re)producing simplifications in the construction of the Roma amplifies when the researcher assumes an engaged position: being a pro-Roma activist seems to constrain the researcher to adopt exclusively perspectives, themes, and motives subsumed under the topic of domination (Blum Le Coat and Catarino 2003: 17). The victimhood paradigm is "a worldview with considerable political force" (Said 1989: 211) and remains relatively unchallenged within the Romani movement, with notable exceptions, mostly from Romani scholars (Kóczé 2009; Kóczé and Trehan 2009; Rostas 2009). It is only in recent years that prominent figures such as Nicolae Gheorghe came to question the foundations of the Romani movement in what he coined the "eternal Roma victimhood" (Gheorghe and Pulay 2013: 46; see also Chirițoiu, this volume, and Mirga-Kruszelnicka, this volume).

While policy-oriented research emphasizes the lacks and inabilities of the Roma, naturalizing them as entrapped victims, activist research has a tendency to overemphasize the agency of the oppressor and to reduce it to a mere racist common denominator. In these representations, there is again no space for the agency of the Roma. Far from being a mere inconsequential intellectual endeavor to represent the Roma, this view shapes policy practices in crucial ways: the Roma, like "the poor," emerge discursively as a group to be managed through paternalistic interventions, but also through policing (Das and Randeria 2015: 4). As Romani activist Saimir Mile (2014: 52) perceptively remarked, the victim and the criminal are two sides of the same representational coin. In debates around the marginality of the Roma, two simplistic tropes alternate and superpose each other without leaving the space for alter-narratives: the Roma either *cannot* (as victims) or *do not want to* "integrate" (as deviants).

The ritualistic injunctions to "involve the Roma" at every step of policy-making or intervention reflect the profound inability of the authors of such narratives to imagine them as *already* active subjects. Perhaps it is less about "involving" the Roma as if they were passive outsiders, than it is about *seeing* how they are already involved in active tactics of resistance, sidetracking, and appropriation of policy and development interventions. What the Roma do in these contexts—in short, their ordinary agency—is a crucial but unexplored source of knowledge on where and why most policy and development interventions do not bear the expected results, despite their promoters' good intentions.

The Locus of Production of the Victimhood Discourse: The Development Apparatus

The confinement of the Roma to the victim position is a "metonymic prison" (Appadurai 1988: 40); such ideas "periodically come into compelling configurations, configurations which, once formed, resist modification or critique" (ibid.). The consolidation of certain ideas occurs due to their capacity to summarize (thereby simplifying) complexity, to transcend variation, but also to provide nutrients for wider discursive needs (Appadurai 1988: 45–46). The wider discursive needs to which the victimhood discourse responds can be found in the development apparatus mobilized to normalize the Roma precisely because of their "lacks."[6]

Recent ethnographies of development organizations and their practices have revealed contradictions and impasses in the production of knowledge from within the development apparatus (Mosse 2011), and stem from a long stream of critical writings regarding the development paradigm (Hobart 1993; Escobar 1995; Ferguson 1994; 1997; Cooper and Packard 1997; Strathern and Stewart 2001; Edelman and Haugerud 2005; Mosse 2005; Murray Li 2007; Gardner and Lewis 2015). Such critiques, however, have been hitherto rarely mobilized to understand the current mechanisms aimed at implementing development policies and projects for Roma groups (with the exceptions of van Baar 2011; Kóczé 2011; Ivasiuc 2014). Ethnographies of Roma development work, or of Romani organizations, are even rarer (with the notable recent exception of Synková 2017).

In this section, I mobilize as observant participation my past experiences in a Romanian Roma NGO, in which I have coordinated and produced research for advocacy and intervention purposes over the course of six years.[7] I problematize the conditions of production of the victimhood discourse from within the development apparatus by analyzing how it is generated at the intersection between development and activism, in a context of unequal power relations on several levels. This particular intersection seals the knowledge produced on the Roma in a position of unquestioned authority as expert knowledge from development workers in close contact with Roma communities, and as activist engagement on moral grounds. Beyond discourse analysis, I also engage with the dimension of *practice* within development, showing how practices are intertwined with discourses that are simultaneously produced and consumed by its institutional nodes.

Theoretically, I draw upon Tania Murray Li's understanding of "governmental assemblage" as "the field of knowledge, practices, and devices from which particular programs of intervention are derived . . . assembled under a dominant governmental ethos or rationality" (Murray Li 2016: 83). In her analysis of the production of differentiated subjects of colonial and postcolonial rule, Murray Li mobilizes a Foucauldian reading of the role of expert knowledge in neoliberal governmentalities concerned with "fixing"—understood both as tethering and as repairing—indigenous populations as nonmarket subjects. For Murray Li (2007), two key processes frame development practice within particular rationalities: problematization—as the construction of problems to be solved—and "rendering technical"—by advancing technical solutions from a position of expertise. As she puts it,

The identification of a problem is intimately linked to the availability of a solution. They coemerge within a governmental assemblage in which certain sorts of diagnoses, prescriptions, and techniques are available to the expert who is properly trained. Conversely, the practice of "rendering technical" confirms expertise and constitutes the boundary between those who are positioned as trustees, with the capacity to diagnose deficiencies in others, and those who are subject to expert direction. It is a boundary that has to be maintained and that can be challenged. (Murray Li 2007: 7)

In the same vein, the problematization of the Roma as deficient, passive victims may be seen through the conceptual lens of developmental rationalities drawing on the expert knowledge critiqued above. In the same move, this knowledge constitutes itself as a regime of truth, and generates technical interventions aimed at maintaining the boundary between the development expert and the deficient subjects of development.

The development machinery operating in Roma communities is riddled with unequal power relations, structural constraints, and a dose of cynicism: some authors refer to "the Gypsy industry," critiquing its self-interested dynamics and lack of reflexivity regarding power relations (Cossée 2000; Trehan 2001; 2009; Rorke and Wilkens 2006; Kóczé and Trehan 2009; Rostas 2009). The development apparatus intersects and interacts with many of the institutional nodes within Romani activism: many Roma NGOs compete to access development funding, while their activist agendas are often surreptitiously molded by neoliberal policies and themes imposed by donors (Trehan 2009: 56; Acton, Rostas, and Ryder 2014: 184). Moreover, in order to ensure institutional survival, organizations tend to prioritize their work around accessing available grants and securing jobs for their employees (Trehan 2001 and 2009; Rostas 2009; Acton, Rostas, and Ryder 2014). I do not want to suggest that these organizations have no agency in relation to their donors. During my activity as research coordinator in the NGO, I have been able to observe numerous instances in which organizations developed various strategies aimed at influencing donors' and policy makers' agendas, from lobby and advocacy efforts, negotiations between organizations and donors, to certain forms of creative implementation and reporting. However, organizations remain in a highly dependent position and are constrained to submit to the rules designed by donors in order to access funds and ensure their own survival.

Organizations are enmeshed in power relations also with their beneficiaries. The unequal power relations between activists from professionalized Roma NGOs and the "grassroots" beneficiaries of development projects is compounded by the disconnection between the two (Trehan 2009: 64; Gheorghe and Pulay 2013: 42 and 86). As project funding depends on how convincingly activists are able to convey the urgency of the need for intervention and the dire straits in which the "target group" finds itself, funding seekers are actively engaged in framing the Roma in ways deemed able to move the donors toward granting funds, even if this requires ignoring the views of ordinary Roma as to *their own* priorities or visions of "development." This does not escape ordinary Roma: they often criticize Roma organizations for "making money on their backs" while failing to bring benefits to communities.

Within project proposal forms, there is no space for nuanced representations or conceptual complexity; the target groups need to be constructed as passive victims, completely unable to challenge their own fate unless the funds required are mobilized in support: showing that Roma communities have some kind of agency might suggest that they could manage their problems by themselves, and such a view risks diverting funds toward subjects deemed less empowered. Conforming to the language of the donor and using certain buzzwords and privileged narratives are part of the tactics of maximizing the chances to access funding. Thus, the discourse produced by organizations in their advocacy efforts toward policy makers is also simultaneously a *practice* of accessing funds.

Besides limiting the areas to which funding is devoted and the kind of narratives mobilized in project proposals, the way in which the development apparatus functions also limits the length of fieldwork-based research. Most applied research produced by organizations is based on short periods of fieldwork, mainly consisting of group discussions or interviews with key informants; typically, these are "community leaders" taken to be representatives and spokespersons of their communities (see, for instance, Szalai and Zentai 2014: 24–25). But the power relations between these often-contested leaders and the rest of the community are complex, questioning their role as unambiguous democratic representatives. Often, they are motivated by their own interest as development brokers in wider client-patron networks (Ivasiuc 2014; see also Fosztó and Anăstăsoaie 2001). These dynamics tend to remain invisible when research is limited to interviews with "community leaders." This manner of carrying out research limits the range of possible insights, generating more often than not superficial knowledge that often reiterates commonplaces. For NGOs, obtaining funding for research from development donors is a consequence of formulating the research questions along already established modes of representation of the Roma as victims, and research is subordinated to the more concrete goal of implementing interventions aimed at solving the problems "identified" by research. As a consequence of the subordination of research to development and policy goals, this kind of research tends to produce the ready-made answers that are necessary to justify the intervention for which funds are simultaneously requested (see also Marushiakova and Popov 2011; Matras et al. 2015), leading to tautological mechanisms of reciprocal legitimation between research and intervention that have been wittingly described as "policy-based—or decision-based—evidence making" (Boden and Epstein 2006). Policy questions are defined by those in power (Shore and Wright 1997), limiting the focus of research to issues they deem necessary or relevant. Thus, the conditions of knowledge production within gray literature are inextricably linked to power and to the closures that power effects (Hobart 1993; Murray Li 2007).

Research produced from within the development machinery invariably positions itself at a pessimistic standpoint, in which things either do not change as fast as they should, do not change at all, or regress. During my involvement in various research partnerships and teams, I noticed that whenever quantitative data were mistakenly interpreted in a gloomy way, they remained unquestioned by researchers. For example, in one of the policy reports on which I was working together with other colleagues, the analysis of the evolution of the highest level of education attained by Roma in comparison to their parents concluded that the level of education of the cohort in question did not change, and in some cases even regressed in comparison to the previous generation. The text included the table with quantitative results, in which some of the figures were in bold letters, as to show the correspondence between the higher or equal level of education of the parent and that of the offspring. However, the bold letters were not the ones showing the trend: to the contrary, the data showed a considerable increase of the level of education of the younger generation compared to their parents. In another instance, a research proposal draft stated that over two-thirds of Roma children drop out of school, when in fact it was misquoting the original source. The latter stated that out of all children dropping out of school, over two-thirds are Roma; indeed, the two statements give a very different view about the extent of the school dropout issue among Roma children.

Conversely, when seemingly "optimistic" data surfaced, they were subjected to multiple verifications, on grounds that "it looked too good to be true." In other cases, such trends were simply ignored and left out of the analysis as anomalies. For instance, in a cross-tabulation showing the percentage of Roma employed with legal contracts by gender, the researcher extensively commented on the dramatic underrepresentation of men (only a quarter of working Roma men had labor contracts), but left completely out of the analysis the fact that three-quarters of Roma women *had* legal working contracts—an unexpected fact that surprised the entire team when pointed out, but which nearly passed unnoticed. Correcting pessimistic conclusions mistakenly drawn from the data required not only demonstrating the inaccuracy of the numbers (imputable perhaps to "bad science" or inattentiveness), but, more importantly, unsettling the thought formations that allowed otherwise good researchers to fall into the trap of a pessimistic bias. The knowledge production mechanisms within organizations demand in-depth ethnographic research capable of revealing how selections are constantly operated on the basis of the relevance of the data for implementing future projects, feeding already framed advocacy and policy agendas, or maximizing the chances of accessing funds by matching the donors' perspectives. The miserabilist narrative and the development apparatus fuse into a Foucauldian power-knowledge regime built on hegemonic universals of human rights and development that often function in much more ambiguous ways than is generally assumed (Cooper and Packard 1997; Rostas 2009; see also van Baar, this volume). The victimhood discourse can thus be read as a case of "rearranging reality" (Ferguson 1994: 177) to suit premade, unimaginative, and ethnocentric packages of policies and interventions produced by the development apparatus.

The researcher-cum-activist takes sides on moral grounds, "no less problematic because they generally remain unquestioned" (Fassin 2012a: 3) in virtue of the activist engagement and its "self-evident nobility" (Schneeweis 2015: 236). Thus, the victimhood discourse acquires solid moral and expert legitimacy, instituting itself as a self-replicating hegemony through the workings of the development apparatus and the ways in which knowledge produced in this framework is bent to respond to wider discursive, but also practical, needs. Yet, many engaged researchers who produce gray literature seek to impact policy-making and development interventions to the benefit of the Roma. Given the complicity of the development apparatus with power—the structural constraints of NGOs and their reliance on narratives of inadequacy and disempowerment to access funds—is it possible to envisage a way out of the victimhood narrative, and renew the epistemological tenets of gray literature? In short, (how) is it possible, precisely from within the "anti-politics machine" of development (Ferguson 1994), to maintain political relevance and open up new spaces for a less ambivalent activism?

Alter-Narratives of Ordinary Agency

In this section, I want to propose a way out of the "skilled vision" (Grasseni 2007) that the pessimistic bias seems to have imprinted on applied research on the Roma. I argue for the necessity of a third space between academia and activism, which would enable research to "become a . . . reflexive project of resistance" (Routledge 1996: 411), opened to alter-narratives and to what Appadurai (2013: 3) called "the politics of possibility": the capacity to aspire toward desired futures, thus opening horizons instead of closing them. Part of this project of bringing "the ethics of possibility" in focus is an epistemological and methodological move to render the agency of ordinary Roma visible in gray literature harnessed to policy and advocacy goals. Here, I take agency to mean, in a broad way, intentionalized and culturally constructed forms of action embedded in particular, context-specific dynamics of power (Ortner 2006: 134–37).

Increasingly, anthropologists attend to the implications of focusing on "the suffering subject" (Thin 2005; Fassin and Rechtman 2009; Robbins 2013) in terms of obscuring alternative possibilities equally "out there." In a recent article, Sherry Ortner (2016: 49) calls the focus of anthropology on suffering, exploitation, pervasive inequality and power "dark anthropology": scholarship which, roughly starting in the nineties, emphasizes "the harsh and brutal dimensions of human experience, and the structural and historical conditions that produce them." She explains the emergence of this strand of anthropology partly as a dialectical move away from the apolitical culturalist school of Clifford Geertz and his followers, and partly by the actual deterioration of life conditions under neoliberal policies. She then charts the emergence of an "anthropology of the good," focusing among other "optimistic themes" on happiness, morality, empathy, and care, and sees it as an equally dialectical move away from "dark anthropology": "what is the point," she asks, "of opposing neoliberalism if we cannot imagine better ways of living and better futures?" (Ortner 2016: 60). This is a call that other scholars have embraced too: in a plea to free thought from the pervasive trope of neoliberalism's inescapable grip on everything, Isabelle Stengers and Philippe Pignarre (2005) defamiliarize this narrative by showing how it functions like a paralyzing sorcery spell.[8] As with sorcery, the authors maintain, it is always possible to think of practices of disenchantment, and break the spell even while searching for alternatives. Their call for thinking about such alternatives is underscored by the observation that the logic of denunciation is not sufficient in itself to break the power of domination, exploitation, and inequality, and by the belief that "another world is possible."

A reflection on alternatives, or what I call alter-narratives, reinstates research as a practice of the imagination (Appadurai 2000: 8), sharpening our senses to discern, in what ordinary Roma do in their ordinary lives, spaces from which order can be contested, destabilized, and rearranged. The focus on the formal part of the Romani movement (as in Acton and Klímová 2001; Vermeersch 2005; Rövid 2012; van Baar 2013) tends to preclude researching possible forms of an everyday alter-politics framed and enacted by people whose political agency remains below the radar for macro accounts, but which can be revealed through long-term immersive ethnographic research. It is this micropolitics of the everyday, which is not only a "less dramatic notion of politics" (van Baar 2011: 236) but also an alter-politics altogether, which I would like to explore. The cognitive move I propose is not only a change of lens toward the micro level of daily interactions, but also a transformation of perspective disconnected from the moralist critique of the actors producing subordination and open to *other* ways of being political (Beck and Maida 2015). Thus, I suggest how, through a focus on the agency of ordinary Roma, in-depth anthropological research might contribute to the project of an alter-politics which challenges the miserabilist discourse and suggests productive paths for research and novel ways to engage in activism. This project of a critical and transformative applied anthropology suggests, beyond the mere opposition to structures of domination and oppression, to be "always on the lookout for minor and invisible spaces or realities that are lurking in the world around us." For Ghassan Hage (2015),

> if I am an anthropologist working on a racist social formation, I should take it for granted that part of my work is to elucidate the working of racist relations of power, their history and the various ways they lodge themselves in all kinds of subtle and not so subtle ways within a given culture. But, if I am to be a critical anthropologist . . . I must also think outside such racist relations to see what exists outside them as a radically other form of sociality that might initially exist only in symptomatic form. I have to train my ethnographic gaze to see certain social forms that hint metonymically at the existence of minor, less obvious realities in which people are equally enmeshed.

While abundant in academic ethnographies of Roma groups, this sort of critical investigation with a focus on their agency is rare in gray research on the Roma explicitly produced for purposes of policy advice and advocacy (Solimene 2013; Ivasiuc 2014; Pulay 2014). In this section, I wish to put forward an example of resisting agency that I have examined in the context of a World Bank–funded development intervention aimed at "empowering" Roma communities in Romania. I am specifically proposing this vignette to emphasize that the sort of occurrences it exemplifies is perfectly visible to NGOs implementing Roma inclusion interventions, and, by extension, to many (pro-)Roma activists; in fact, many of the development projects carried out in Roma communities are replete with examples in which the Roma deploy forms of agency that often counter and unsettle the logic of these interventions. Such examples are often effaced from project reports and gray literature, and the agency of Roma is invisibilized.

The context of the project and its technical elements have been detailed elsewhere (Ivasiuc 2014); I will only summarize here the main tenets of the intervention. The project methodology involved working with voluntary "initiative groups" formed of individuals who were supposed, at the end of the intervention, to be "empowered" enough as to take initiative in advocating for concrete improvements in their communities, and thus influence the local agenda for the benefit of the Roma. These groups were "mentored" by a facilitator, whose role was to provide them with empowering tools during community meetings, increase their capacities to act at local level, and, through a learning-by-doing process, enhance their trust in their own abilities in order to empower them to become "real partners" in a dialogue with the local authorities. Clearly, the way in which the initiative groups—and, by extension, Roma communities—were constructed in the rationality of the project corresponded to the image of a powerless, deficient, and passive victim, incapable of its own agency. The scenario that was expected was one in which the groups—from a position of inferiority in which they were supposedly unable to negotiate in their own way for their own benefit—were "taught" how to be empowered.

Yet, in one of the communities, unexpectedly, this scenario played out differently. The initiative group, with its core comprised of the school mediator, the local expert, and a Roma counselor, tried at a very early stage to bargain with the facilitator by framing in transactional terms, and from a position of equality, their participation in community meetings: "we will come to the meetings," they said, "but only if this project will do something to repair our community road." Certainly, the improvement of the road was for the common good, as the project required, and it was a "need" identified by the initiative group; so far, the process could meet the methodological criteria of the intervention. However, instead of formulating its request from within the project's logic of "learning" from a position of disempowerment, the group did not follow the scenario supposed to be played out within the project, using instead the bargaining logic from a position of equality. Sensitive to the unexpected alteration of his role, the facilitator reported back to the implementing organization, framing the request of the initiative group as an attempt of "blackmail." The group had acted in ways fully contradicting the idea that they were powerless and incapable, thus destabilizing the facilitator, unable to recognize that the group's strategy was, in fact, exhibiting unmistakably the very capacities of negotiation that the project aimed at developing. Rather than playing out the mentor–mentee relationship following the project's script, the group had proven itself already empowered to negotiate, and repositioned itself in egalitarian terms in relation to the project team. This example illustrates a sense of refusal to participate in the development make-believe, in which a supposedly altruistic logic brings superior expertise to bestow benefits on a supposedly helpless, passive, and disempowered group.

These forms of micropolitics, in which Roma groups challenge existing power relations, including with their supposed "benefactors," and manage to alter them to their advantage in a piecemeal way, are an invitation for scholarship engaged in policy and advocacy consultancy to shift its focus from perceiving and portraying the Roma as powerless and passive victims to considering the complexity and inventiveness of their strategies. Such a perspective has certainly less to offer to certain strands of advocacy that fare more lucratively on the victimhood discourse. Yet, it has the merit of recentering reflection on the ways the Roma actually engage with non-Roma right at the heart of the development encounter, and of prompting an exploration of the Roma's strategies to improve their own position from within their own logic.

One needs to be always watchful for the risk of romanticization or ethnocentrism creeping up into conceptualizations of resistance and agency. By representing the Roma as "resistors" in oversimplified ways and without embedding their agency in the wider power relations in which they are enmeshed, one may unwittingly effect the flattening of internal politics on both sides, as well as a thinning of the underlying assumptions and logics at play (Abu Lughod 1990; Ortner 1995; 2006). The danger of rendering strategies of resistance and agency as exaltations of a putative human "resilience," creativeness, and freedom demands particular vigilance, a requirement that can be attended to by thick ethnographic contextualization.

Conclusion: Ethnography as a Form of Activism

In this chapter, I have deconstructed the victimhood discourse on the Roma as a form of Orientalism that confines the Roma to a perpetual state of inadequacy and secondariness, and renders them primary targets for development interventions aimed at educating and molding them to fit mainstream ways of life. I have also explored the locus of the production of the victimhood discourse by revealing how development practices and mechanisms reproduce this perspective while feeding on representations of powerlessness and exclusion: the victimhood discourse and current development practices substantiate and legitimate each other in a powerful governmental assemblage.

The reduction of Roma groups to their domination in mainstream society is an essentialization exerted within unequal power structures, legitimized through the authority invested in expert knowledge, and coproduced by the constraints imposed by the development apparatus. The narratives produced by engaged scholars escape criticism not only thanks to their scientific "expertise," but also by virtue of the moral stance in which humanitarian activism is grounded (Fassin 2012b). Criticism of these forms of activism may thus be perceived as reactionary and conservative. Such unsophisticated interpretations of criticism of engaged activism lock the debate in an intellectual and political stalemate and preclude not only an honest intellectual debate in academia, but prevent creative renewals of activism itself.

I have concluded by proposing a shift in the way researchers producing gray literature can engage with Roma groups by focusing more extensively on their agency in the contexts relevant to their research. I have exemplified what a microlens on the agency of Roma groups can reveal about the ways in which they shape and negotiate relations of power at the very heart of the development apparatus, eluding and transforming relations of subordination into egalitarian participation on their own terms. I have argued that the focus on such forms of agency is likely to open up new productive frames for (pro-)Roma activism. Ethnography's focus on agency makes it a method uniquely able to portray the complexity of the processes in which Roma are enmeshed in the development encounter, demonstrating a respect for their wholeness as human agents, for their world-making (or, as in Stewart 1997, remaking) abilities, and for their ability to challenge power relations. This, I argue, the victimhood discourse does not and cannot do.

As accessing funding will most likely remain dependent on the convincing use of a rhetoric of victimhood, the trope of "empowering" Roma and the moral and expert legitimacy of organizations to intervene on behalf of less than able, passive victims, a simple cognitive move toward the agency of ordinary Roma might be an illusory prescription. But academics doing applied research for (pro-)Roma NGOs or consultancy work for international organizations should consider carefully the consequences of the discourses they produce, beyond their evident utility in accessing funds. It is part of the intellectual endeavor to be alert to the emergence of particular regimes of truth that may obscure other perspectives and undermine the project of continuously opening new frames for understanding the world, and for challenging power. Within research, there are productive ways of being engaged in pro-Roma activism, beyond and, in fact, in opposition to the victimhood paradigm (see also Mirga-Kruszelnicka, this volume). Research based on in-depth, long-term, and immersive ethnography, with its attention to other ways of being, has affinity with a necessary micro-alter-politics toward a renewal of forms of activism through gray research.

Ana Ivasiuc is an anthropologist affiliated with the Centre for Conflict Studies at the Philipps University in Marburg, Germany. Through her past activity as a research coordinator within a Romani NGO in Romania, she has conducted research at the confluence between Romani activism and academia. After obtaining her Ph.D. in 2014 from the National School of Political Science and Public Administration in Bucharest, she joined a Roma-related postdoctoral research project at Justus Liebig University in Giessen. She is the winner of the 2017 Herder–Council for European Studies Fellowship.

Notes

I am indebted to Sam Beck, Gergő Pulay, Ana Chirițoiu, and Danielle V. Schoon for their very useful comments on earlier versions of this chapter, and to the anonymous reviewers' constructive criticisms that have helped me improve the argument.

1. Mile 2014: 56, originally in French, my translation. Saimir Mile is a Roma activist, president of the French-based association La Voix des Rroms (Voice of the Roma).
2. An inversion of "participant observation," this term signifies that the observation is conducted from the point of view of an active participant, instead of from the classical position of the anthropologist primarily as observer.
3. In Western Europe, Williams (1989) identified two contrasting approaches of knowledge production on the Roma discernible from the sixties, warning against their pitfalls. While the culturalist approach posited that Romani culture is at risk of disappearing under the oppression perpetrated by an omnipotent mainstream society, the social marginality approach highlighted their status of outsiders and spun a web of narratives around their social failure. This latter approach is currently predominant in literature on European Roma produced by the institutions of the European Union, the World Bank, the United Nations Development Program, but also (pro-)Roma organizations engaged in the Romani movement. I distinguish between Roma organizations, usually "operationalized" among activists as having a Roma leadership and at least half of employees of Roma background (see also Mirga-Kruszelnicka, this volume), and pro-Roma organizations, which are engaged in projects for Roma but are led by non-Roma and with a majority of non-Roma employees. For conciseness, I will thus refer to (pro-)Roma organizations to mean both.
4. By this, I do not want to suggest that *all* the Roma seek autonomy from schooling, and in fact Roma in central and eastern Europe increasingly reach levels of education superior to the ones attained by their parents. The heterogeneity of Roma groups subtends a great variation in terms of aspirations, attitudes, and behavior toward mainstream schooling.
5. Against this oversimplification, Romani feminism is one of the increasingly resounding voices contesting the binary opposition between Roma victims and non-Roma oppressors, by rendering visible gender hierarchies within Roma communities, but also by criticizing, in line with earlier feminist observations, antiracist strategies as based on male experiences of racism, and antisexist politics rooted in the concerns of non-Roma women (Kóczé 2008).
6. What I call here "development apparatus" refers to the complex machinery of project and policy implementation for the benefit of Roma groups, in which a multiplicity of actors is involved, from EU-level policy makers, public and private funding bodies, national or international development organizations, networks of Roma organizations and activists involved in the Romani movement, and development brokers at the local level.
7. In this position, I was simultaneously part and coproducer of the mechanism that I criticize. My involvement with the anthropology of development literature has allowed me to take some distance from practices of which I am now critical. This is not the space to expand on the ethical and methodological dimensions of recount-

ing my experience here, but I want to stress that I find it intellectually and morally important to rework post facto my insider's experience in critical terms, even while acknowledging my past connivance with the system that I now criticize.

8. Their book was translated into English in 2011 by Andrew Goffey, and published at Palgrave Macmillan under the title *Capitalist Sorcery: Breaking the Spell.*

References

Abu Lughod, Lila. 1990. "The Romance of Resistance: Tracing Transformations of Power through Bedouin Women." *American Ethnologist* 17 (1): 41–55.

Acton, Thomas, and Ilona Klímová-Alexander. 2001. "The International Romani Union: An East European Answer to a West European Question?" In *Between Past and Future: The Roma of Central and Eastern Europe,* edited by Will Guy, 157–219. Hatfield: University of Hertfordshire Press.

Acton, Thomas, Iulius Rostas, and Andrew Ryder. 2014. "The Roma in Europe: The Debate over the Possibilities for Empowerment to Seek Social Justice." In *Hearing the Voice of Gypsies, Roma and Travellers: Inclusive Community Development,* edited by Andrew Ryder, Sarah Cemlyn, and Thomas Acton, 177–96. Bristol: Policy Press.

Agarin, Timofey. 2014. "Introduction." In *When Stereotype Meets Prejudice: Antiziganism in European Societies,* edited by Timofey Agarin, 11–25. Stuttgart: Ibidem.

Appadurai, Arjun. 1988. "Putting Hierarchy in Its Place." *Cultural Anthropology* 3 (1): 36–49.

———. 2000. "Grassroots Globalisation and the Research Imagination." *Public Culture* 12 (1): 1–19.

———. 2013. *The Future as Cultural Fact: Essays on the Global Condition.* London: Verso.

Beck, Sam, and Carl Maida, eds. 2015. *Public Anthropology in a Borderless World.* New York: Berghahn Books.

Blum-Le Coat, Jean-Yves, and Christine Catarino. 2003. *Bilan critique des études et documents concernant les "Gens du Voyage"* [Critical appraisal of studies and documents on the "Gens du Voyage"]. Paris: Ministère de l'Équipement, du Transport et du Logement.

Boden, Rebecca, and Debbie Epstein. 2006. "Managing the Research Imagination? Globalisation and Research in Higher Education." *Globalisation, Societies and Education* 4 (2): 223–36.

Bodewig, Christian, and Akshay Sethi. 2005. *Poverty, Social Exclusion and Ethnicity in Serbia and Montenegro: The Case of the Roma.* Washington, DC: World Bank.

Casa Nova, Maria J. 2012. "Citoyenneté, ethnicité et dialecticité du pouvoir dans les relations du genre" [Citizenship, ethnicity and power dialectics in gender relations]. *Cahiers du genre* 53: 121–44.

Cooper, Frederick, and Packard M. Randall, eds. 1997. *International Development and the Social Sciences: Essays on the History and Politics of Knowledge.* Berkeley: University of California Press.

Cossée, Claire. 2000. "Tsiganes et politiques: Vers quelles représentations?" [Gypsies and policies: toward which representations?]. *Recherche Sociale* 155: 57–72.

Das, Veena, and Shalini Randeria. 2015. "Politics of the Urban Poor." An Introduction to Supplement 11. *Current Anthropology* 56: S3–S14.

Edelman, Marc, and Angelique Haugerud, eds. 2005. *The Anthropology of Development and Globalisation: From Classical Political Economy to Contemporary Neoliberalism.* Oxford: Blackwell Publishing.

Engebrigtsen, Ada. 2014. "Roma 'Activism,' the Media and the Space between the Devil and the Deep Blue Sea." *Acta Ethnographica Hungarica* 59 (1): 197–208. doi: 0.1556/AEthn.59.2014.1.9.

Escobar, Arturo. 1995. *Encountering Development: The Making and Unmaking of the Third World.* Princeton, NJ: Princeton University Press.

Fassin, Didier. 2012a. "Introduction: Toward a Critical Moral Anthropology." In *A Companion to Moral Anthropology,* edited by Didier Fassin, 1–18. Oxford: Wiley-Blackwell.

———. 2012b. *Humanitarian Reason: A Moral History of the Present Times.* Berkeley: University of California Press.

Fassin, Didier, and Richard Rechtman. 2009. *Empire of Trauma: An Inquiry into the Condition of Victimhood.* Princeton, NJ: Princeton University Press.

Ferguson, James. 1994. *The Anti-Politics Machine: Development, Depoliticization, and Bureaucratic Power in Lesotho.* Minneapolis: University of Minnesota Press.

———. 1997. "Anthropology and Its Evil Twin: Development in the Constitution of a Discipline." In *International Development and the Social Sciences: Essays on the History and Politics of Knowledge,* edited by Frederick Cooper and Packard M. Randall. Berkeley: University of California Press.

Fosztó, László, and Marian V. Anăstăsoaie. 2001. "Romania: Representations, Public Policies and Political Projects." In *Between Past and Future: The Roma of Central and Eastern Europe,* edited by Will Guy, 351–69. Hatfield: University of Hertfordshire Press.

Gardner, Katy, and David Lewis, eds. 2015. *Anthropology and Development: Challenges for the Twenty-First Century.* London: Pluto Press.

Gheorghe, Nicolae, and Gergő Pulay. 2013. "Choices to Be Made and Prices to Be Paid: Potential Roles and Consequences in Roma Activism and Policy-Making." In *From Victimhood to Citizenship: The Path of Roma Integration; A Debate,* edited by Will Guy, 41–100. Budapest: Kiadó.

Grignon, Claude, and Jean-Claude Passeron. 1989. *Le savant et le populaire: Misérabilisme et populisme en sociologie et en littérature* [The scholar and the popular: Miserabilism and populism in sociology and literature]. Paris: Seuil.

Hage, Ghassan. 2015. *Alter-Politics: Critical Anthropology and the Radical Imagination.* Melbourne: Melbourne University Press.

Hancock, Ian. 2000. "Standardisation and Ethnic Defence in Emergent Non-Literate Societies: The Gypsy and Caribbean Cases." In *Language, Blacks and Gypsies: Languages without a Written Tradition and Their Role in Education,* edited by Thomas Acton and Morgan Dalphinis, 9–23. London: Whiting and Birch.

Hobart, Mark. 1993. "Introduction: The Growth of Ignorance?" In *An Anthropological Critique of Development: The Growth of Ignorance,* edited by Mark Hobart. London: Routledge.

Ivasiuc, Ana. 2014. "Empowering the Roma: Lessons from Development Practice." Ph.D. dissertation, National School of Political Science and Public Administration, Bucharest, Romania.

Kóczé, Angéla. 2008. "Ethnicity and Gender in the Politics of Roma Identity in the Post-Communist Countries." In *Violence and Gender in the Globalized World: The In-*

timate and the Extimate, edited by Sanja Bahun-Radunović and Julie Rajan, 175–88. London: Ashgate.

———. 2009. "The Limits of Rights-Based Discourse in Romani Women's Activism: The Gender Dimension in Romani Politics." In *Romani Politics in Contemporary Europe,* edited by Nando Sigona and Nidhi Trehan, 133–55. New York: Palgrave Macmillan.

———. 2011. "Gender, Ethnicity and Class: Romani Women's Political Activism and Social Struggles." Ph.D. dissertation, Central European University, Budapest, Hungary.

Kóczé, Angéla, and Nidhi Trehan. 2009. "Racism, (Neo-) Colonialism and Social Justice: The Struggle for the Soul of the Romani Movement in Post-Socialist Europe ." In *Racism Postcolonialism Europe,* edited by Graham Huggan and Ian Law, 50–76. Liverpool: Liverpool University Press.

Kovats, Martin. 2001. "Problems of Intellectual and Political Accountability in Respect of Emerging European Roma Policy." *Journal of Ethnopolitics and Minorities Issues in Europe* 1 (Autumn) 1–9.

Lee, Ken. 2000. "Orientalism and Gypsylorism." *Social Analysis: The International Journal of Social and Cultural Practice* 44 (2): 129–56.

Marushiakova, Elena, and Veselin Popov. 2011. "Between Exoticization and Marginalization." *Behemoth* 4 (1): 51–68.

Matras, Yaron. 2013. "Scholarship and the Politics of Romani Identity: Strategic and Conceptual Issues." *European Yearbook of Minority Issues* 10 (1): 209–47.

———. 2015. "Europe's Neo-Traditional Roma Policy: Marginality Management and the Inflation of Expertise." In *Romani Worlds: Academia, Policy and Modern Media,* edited by Eben Friedman and Victor A. Friedman, 29–47. Cluj-Napoca: Editura Institutului pentru Studierea Problemelor Minorităților Naționale.

Matras, Yaron, Daniele V. Leggio, and Mirela Steel. 2015. "'Roma Education' as a Lucrative Niche: Ideologies and Representations." *Zeitschrift für internationale Bildungsforschung und Entwicklungspädagogik* 38 (1): 11–17.

Mile, Saimir. 2014. "Nous sommes une espèce en expansion" [We are an expanding species]. In *Avava-ovava,* edited by Anina Ciuciu, Pierre Chopinaud, Lise Foisneau, Valentin Merlin, and Saimir Mile, 51–62. Paris: Al Dante.

Mosse, David. 2005. *Cultivating Development: Ethnography of Aid Policy and Practice.* London: Pluto Press.

———, ed. 2011. *Adventures in Aidland: The Anthropology of Professionals in International Development.* New York: Berghahn Books.

Murray Li, Tania. 2007. *The Will to Improve: Governmentality, Development, and the Practice of Politics.* Durham, NC: Duke University Press.

———. 2016. "Fixing Non-market Subjects: Governing Land and Population in the Global South." In *Governing Practices: Neoliberalism, Governmentality, and the Ethnographic Imaginary,* edited by Michelle Brady, and Randy K. Lippert, 80–101. Toronto: University of Toronto Press.

Olivier de Sardan, Jean-Pierre. 2005. *Anthropology and Development: Understanding Contemporary Social Change.* London: Zed Books.

Ortner, Sherry. 1995. "Resistance and the Problem of Ethnographic Refusal." *Comparative Studies in Society and History* 37 (1): 173–93.

———. 2006. *Anthropology and Social Theory: Culture, Power, and the Acting Subject.* Durham, NC: Duke University Press.

———. 2016. "Dark Anthropology and Its Others: Theory since the Eighties." *HAU: Journal of Ethnographic Theory* 6 (1): 47–73.

Powell, Ryan. 2011. "Gypsy-Travellers and Welfare Professional Discourse: On Individu-
    alization and Social Integration." *Antipode* 43 (2): 471–93.
Pulay, Gergő. 2014. "Staging Ethnicity: Cultural Politics and Musical Practices of Roma
    Performers in Budapest." *Acta Ethnographica Hungarica* 59 (1): 3–24. doi: 10.1556/
    AEthn.59.2014.1.2.
Ringold, Dena, Michael A. Orenstein, and Erika Wilkens. 2005. *Roma in an Expanding
    Europe: Breaking the Poverty Cycle.* Washington: The World Bank.
Robbins, Joel. 2013. "Beyond the Suffering Subject: Toward an Anthropology of the
    Good." *Journal of the Royal Anthropological Institute* 19: 447–62.
Rorke, Bernard, and Andre Wilkens. 2006. *Roma Inclusion: Lessons Learned from OSI's
    Roma Programming.* New York: Open Society Institute.
Rose, Nikolas. 1999. *Powers of Freedom: Reframing Political Thought.* Cambridge: Cam-
    bridge University Press.
Rostas, Iulius. 2009. "The Romani Movement in Romania: Institutionalization and
    (De)mobilization." In *Romani Politics in Contemporary Europe,* edited by Nando
    Sigona and Nidhi Trehan, 159–85. New York: Palgrave Macmillan.
Routledge, Paul. 1996. "The Third Space as Critical Engagement." *Antipode* 28 (4):
    399–419.
Rövid, Márton. 2012. "Options of Roma Political Participation and Representation."
    Roma Rights: Journal of the European Roma Rights Centre, 9–17.
Said, Edward. 1979. *Orientalism.* New York: Vintage.
———. 1989. "Representing the Colonized: Anthropology's Interlocutors." *Critical In-
    quiry* 15 (2): 205–25.
Saul, Nicholas. 2007. *Gypsies and Orientalism in German Literature and Anthropology of
    the Long Nineteenth Century.* London: Legenda.
Schneeweis, Adina. 2015. "Communicating the Victim: Nongovernmental Organizations
    Advocacy Discourses for Roma Rights." *Communication, Culture and Critique* 8:
    235–53. doi:10.1111/cccr.12077.
Shore, Cris, and Susan Wright, eds. 1997. *Anthropology of Policy: Critical Perspectives on
    Governance and Power.* London: Routledge.
Sigona, Nando, and Lorenzo Monasta. 2006. *Imperfect Citizenship: Research into Patterns
    of Racial Discrimination against Roma and Sinti in Italy.* Florence: OsservAzione.
Solimene, Marco. 2013. "Undressing the Gağé Clad in State Garb: Bosnian Xoraxané
    Romá Face to Face with the Italian Authorities." *Romani Studies* 23 (2): 161–86.
Spolu International Foundation, and CEGA. 2000. *Breaking the Vicious Circle: Lessons
    Learned from Experience in Social Inclusion of Roma Communities through Participa-
    tion.* Sofia: Spolu; CEGA.
Stengers, Isabelle, and Philippe Pignarre. 2005. *La sorcellerie capitaliste: Pratiques de désen-
    voûtement* [Capitalist sorcery: practices of disenchantment]. Paris: La Découverte.
Stewart, Michael. 1997. *The Time of the Gypsies.* Boulder, CO: Westview Press.
Strathern, Andrew, and Pamela J. Stewart. 2001. "Introduction: Anthropology and Con-
    sultancy: Ethnographic Dilemmas and Opportunities." *Social Analysis: The Interna-
    tional Journal of Social and Cultural Practice* 45 (2): 3–22. Accessed 10 January 2016.
    http://www.jstor.org/stable/23170108.
Surdu, Mihai. 2015. *Expert Frames: Scientific and Policy Practices of Roma Classification.*
    Budapest: Central European University Press.
Synková, Hana. 2017. "Reformists and Revolutionists: Social Work NGOs and Activist
    Struggles in the Czech Republic." In *Cultures of Doing Good: Anthropologists and*

NGOs, edited by Amanda Lashaw, Christian Vannier, and Steven Sampson, 75–93. Tuscaloosa: University of Alabama Press.

Szalai, Júlia, and Violetta Zentai. 2014. *Faces and Causes of Roma Marginalization in Local Contexts.* Budapest: Center for Policy Studies, Central European University.

Thin, Neil. 2005. "Happiness and the Sad Topics of Anthropology." WeD Working Paper 10 ESCR Research Group on Well-Being in Developing Countries. Accessed 10 February 2016. http://www.welldev.org.uk/research/workingpaperpdf/wed10.pdf.

Timmer, Andria. 2010. "Constructing the 'Needy Subject': NGO Discourses of Roma Need." *PoLAR: Political and Legal Anthropology Review* 33 (2): 264–81.

Toninato, Paola. 2014. *Romani Writing: Literacy, Literature and Identity Politics.* London: Routledge.

Trehan, Nidhi. 2001. "In the Name of the Roma? The Role of Private Foundations and NGOs." In *Between Past and Future: The Roma of Central and Eastern Europe,* edited by Will Guy, 134–49. Hatfield: University of Hertfordshire Press.

———. 2009. "The Romani Subaltern within Neoliberal European Civil Society." In *Romani Politics in Contemporary Europe,* edited by Nando Sigona and Nidhi Trehan, 51–71. New York: Palgrave Macmillan.

Trubeta, Sevasti. 2013. "Roma as Homines Educandi: A Collective Subject between Educational Provision, Social Control and Humanism." In *Roma Education in Europe: Practices, Policies and Politics,* edited by Maja Miskovic, 15–28. London: Routledge.

United Nations Development Programme. 2002. *The Roma in Central and Eastern Europe: Avoiding the Dependency Trap.* Bratislava: UNDP.

van Baar, Huub. 2011. *The European Roma: Minority Representation, Memory and the Limits of Transnational Governmentality.* Amsterdam: F&N.

———. 2013. "Travelling Activism and Knowledge Formation in the Romani Social and Civil Movement." In *Roma Education in Europe: Practices, Policies and Politics,* edited by Maja Miskovic, 192–203. London: Routledge.

Vermeersch, Peter. 2005. "Marginality, Advocacy, and the Ambiguities of Multiculturalism: Notes on Romani Activism in Central Europe." *Identities* 12: 451–78.

Williams, Patrick. 1989. "Dans le lieu et dans l'époque" [In place and in time]. In *Tsiganes: identité, évolution,* edited by Patrick Williams. Paris: Syros Alternatives.

PART III

❋ ❋ ❋

RENEWING ACTIVISMS

CHAPTER 7

✻ ✻ ✻

POLICY INPUT ON THE FRONT LINE
Dilemmas of the Ethical Academic
Margaret Greenfields

This chapter sets out to discuss the ways in which academic-activists can most effectively and ethically engage with the development of public policy. In particular, it focuses on methodological challenges and the risk of unintended consequences when policy recommendations are poorly thought out or delivered. For many academics, the craft and practice of policy formulation is considerably outside their theoretical knowledge or disciplinary training, such that they often lack awareness of the ways in which their research may translate into potentially flawed policy. Accordingly, there may be a mismatch between intent and outcome, both in terms of the techniques academics use when seeking to engage with and influence policy professionals, and in how findings are ultimately translated into policy guidance. While it is widely accepted that there is an absolute necessity for ethical coproduction of policy recommendations in partnership with Romani and other communities directly impacted by enactments, this chapter argues that there is also a requirement for closer collaboration with the policy community, including the development of shared understanding of policy paradigms and techniques. An example is provided from the author's own pedagogic practice of the ways in which skills-based training which uses innovative, practical, policy-making processes, co-delivered by community members and those tasked with enacting policies, can greatly enhance the effectiveness of commissioners, service users, and academics. Such collaborative design and delivery, it is argued, may effectively deliver appropriate and reflexive solutions to tenacious social challenges. In order to comprehend the pitfalls and opportunities open to the scholar intent on influencing policy (regardless of whether they are themselves of Romani heritage or concerned *Gadjé*), it is important to outline both the various categories of engagement that are potentially open to leverage, and the challenges that frequently face the academic activist who may be unfamiliar with the processes of policy construction.

Activism, defined as "action undertaken on behalf of a cause which goes beyond that which is routine or conventional" (Martin 2007: 19), requires the analysis of the professional expectations of an "academic," in order to contextualize the debate on what constitutes an academic-activist and sketch out the desirable role for activism within the professional academic environment. Given the increasing administrative regulations and duties that require an academic's activities to fall within the rubric of departmental, faculty, and institutional priorities, it would appear that little scope exists for the radicalism and passionate commitment associated with activism, and defined by Martin (2007) as "[going] beyond conventional politics, typically being more energetic, passionate, innovative, and committed." However, I argue that for those whose primary orientation is academic (rather than those who consider themselves primarily as activists merely earning their income as academics, or those who seek to strategically use their role in the academy to support their activism), there is space within their professional role to support or engage in activism in several ways.

First, a researcher may utilize action research as their primary method of investigation, a model that consciously sets out to validate community experience and empower nonacademic participants through sharing knowledge. Second, teachers may critically challenge and engage with normative discourse, interpretations of findings, and theoretical models. This approach can lead to life-changing impacts on student understanding, their future career paths, and engagement with sociopolitical activities. Finally, and increasingly common (albeit in some cases driven by funders' insistence on assessable impact and community engagement pathways), research may be designed from the outset to engage with communities and service users. Depending on the skills, confidence, and approach of the principal investigator, such engagement may, however, range from the merely tokenistic, lowest stage[1] on Arnstein's (1969: 217) "ladder of participation," to fully collaborative sharing of a range of research tasks, analysis, and coproduction of outputs (SCIE 2012). The higher rungs of the ladder, designated as "citizen control" by Arnstein (1969: 222–224), range from partnerships working through delegated power over actions, to perhaps the most utopian—that of citizen control.

For academics involved in such policy-engaged work, which may sit anywhere along a continuum of conscious academic activism to funder-driven community collaboration, it can be argued that to operate at the most effective level, a mode of practice is utilized that takes account of multiple (and potentially conflicting) needs of parties, while retaining a pragmatic yet ethical commitment to ensuring recommendations are feasible enough to acquire recognition within the sphere of policy influence. As Flood et al. (2013) discuss, academic-activists may be subject to a significant degree of peer (and external) criticism and attempts to limit their activities through mechanisms ranging from dismissal of interpretation of data as propaganda, to resistance to publication of findings seen as controversial and hence potentially contrary to institutional interests. However, if contentious politicized outputs are developed, it is recommended that the researcher maintains a pragmatic stance, ensuring that colleagues and senior staff are kept appraised of research activities and the range of potential external responses to recommendations at all stages of the process, creating space to enable reflective review of impact. Thus, institutional protection from hostile challenges can be claimed, enabling the activist-academic to simultaneously use their professional expertise and operationalize the core academic claim of freedom of speech, backed up by internal peer review of findings and recommendations. In this way, counterarguments to criticisms can be rehearsed in advance, while the authors are also able to gain awareness of the likely stance of institutional management teams to critiques. Such practices enable collaborative working with university media professionals to productively and effectively present findings in a manner that can foreground key recommendations.

These processes can be used also as a way of meeting the benchmark of an even-handed review of evidence, such that outputs enable critical engagement with the more complex question of how best to meet the simultaneous—and at times conflicting—needs of policy makers and end users.[2] On this latter point, it is worth reminding the activist-scholar that a degree of watchful critical awareness must be retained when considering the purposes of policy and the standardized "rules" of policy-making, a point expressed by a number of academics who are highly critical of normative approaches to policy-making, and who argue that policy as enacted typically maintains the status quo rather than challenging unjust social hierarchies (Okely 1983: 232; Powell 2011; van Baar 2005; 2011; 2012).

Powell (2011), in a study of how professional discourse and perceptions of British Gypsies and Travellers inform the activities of welfare agencies, emphasizes the need for both researchers and policy makers to pay attention to the impact of social processes on minority cultures, stressing both the complexity of power dynamics and the subtle ways in which power can be exercised, leading to repressive outcomes when professional discourse translates into policy enactments or procedures. Similarly, van Baar (2012) persuasively argues, through the use of case studies from the Czech and Slovak republics, that Roma "policy," as enacted, can essentially become the equivalent of policing Roma populations. He argues that top-down evaluation criteria may create a narrative of self-improvement, and the development of projects that are only counted as successful and worthy of achieving repeat funding if the outcomes produce subjects who are perceived of—in normative terms—as responsible, self-controlling, and increasingly independent of the state (van Baar 2005). In an elaboration of this thesis, van Baar (2011) explores how widespread reliance on experts with limited knowledge of local contexts, or the standardization of techniques and milestones presented as politically neutral technologies that improve Roma socioeconomic status, have actually resulted in controversial forms of Romani internalized governance and a hierarchization of behaviors and subjects that can lead to the dehumanization of some of the most marginalized Roma populations.

Despite these highly pertinent concerns, raised, it is respectfully argued, predominantly by academics who operate outside of the practical policy-making domain, and who may thus be unfamiliar with some concerns and constraints under which policy formulation occurs (Gaudreau and Saner 2014), scope does still exist to make recommendations that use classic policy-making processes. Use of models that are familiar to the policy community (Sabatier and Weible 2014) but which also include in-built reevaluation phases and checks and balances so as to ensure that localized and nuanced interpretations occur, ensures that community actors are provided with mechanisms that create opportunities to engage with the higher levels of Arnstein's (1969) ladder of participation outlined above (Marsh and McConnell 2010).

In the light of the above salient reminders of the dangers that unnuanced (and indeed incautious) policy advice can represent to communities framed as disempowered or nonnormative, we turn now to the issue of how best to deliver guidance that meets the needs of the policy community in fulfilling their primary mandated role of delivering initiatives that engage with perceived social problems and seek to improve the quality of community life (Spicker 2014). In so doing, however, recommendations must include mechanisms and controls that offer some realistic chance of delivering effective and life-enhancing interventions, rather than merely creating space for the recycling of negative tropes and social control of Roma people (Surdu and Kovats 2015; see also Ivasiuc, this volume).

Becoming a Policy "Inexpert" and Collaborative Working on Roma Policy Development

While academics from a relatively broad range of disciplines have in recent years become more actively engaged in policy development on Roma issues, it can be seen that this shift has directly arisen from Europe-wide governance and concern over the collective condition of Roma populations, and—to no small extent—the release of funding and opportunities for policy expertise to be recognized in a transnational context. Subsequent to the Council of Europe's formal recognition of the plight of Roma minorities throughout the EU in the early years of the twenty-first century, and the concerted drive that followed to improve the situation of this most marginalized of populations, there has been an explosion of academic interest in the field of Romani studies.[3] Not only has the number of academics commissioned to undertake research activities and engage in delivering policy advice to EU agencies expanded exponentially in recent years, but a simple search for academic publications on Roma reveals that between the years 2000/01 and 2015/16, the annual rate of publication had grown from approximately 360 papers per annum to approximately 2000 per year.

Similarly, a web review reveals that funded Ph.D. studentships and post-doctoral fellowships that focus on the field of Roma "integration" or specific aspects of Roma health, gender, migration, history, linguistics, etc. have expanded dramatically. Throughout Europe, numerous higher education institutes, which in 2010 had no identified staff working in the field of Romani studies, or which did not appear to offer supervision to students in such a field, were frequently, some seven years later, offering relatively substantial doctoral funding and providing specialist advice in such areas of research.

Thus, for example, a discussion network founded at King's College London in 2014, which consisted initially of only U.K.-based graduate students and supervisory staff engaged in Romani studies, has grown from nine invited members to in excess of forty participants from a number of European countries in under three years, with new members joining prior to each meeting, often funded by their European institutions to present at the sessions. During the past two years alone, a not insignificant number of academic supervisors of doctoral candidates (often from elite institutions and typically supervising their first student in the field of Romani studies), have also joined the regular discussion sessions during which students present on their research findings and debate emergent trends in Romani studies.

Moreover, the author's analysis of the membership data pertaining to the European Academic Network of Romani Studies (EANRS) bears out this picture of ever increasing interest in the field of Romani studies. EANRS is a network for academics and doctoral students working in this field funded by the Council of Europe between 2011 and 2015, with a stated aim of "facilitating intercultural dialogue and raising the visibility of existing research outside the academic community in order to foster cooperation with policy-makers and other stakeholders" (see also Ryder, this volume).

As of June 2016 (drawn from materials provided by the EANRS secretariat), the network had 420 members in forty countries, of which 249 full members hold Ph.D.'s in a range of subject areas, predominantly related to social sciences such as anthropology, sociology, or cultural studies. Overall, just under 10 percent of members (twenty-six members) either held a doctorate or were studying at doctoral level with a specialization in political science, while 5 percent held a terminal (doctoral or higher) degree in legal studies. A mere seven members (all holding doctorates) were trained in social policy or public policy administration.

An in-depth analysis of membership data undertaken by the secretariat some three years previously (EANRS 2013) reported that of the (then) 395 members, 194 were of postdoctoral standing, of which a large majority (144) had received their doctorate after the year 2000. The (at that time) remaining 201 members were associate members studying for a higher research degree in the broad interdisciplinary field of Romani studies, with a particular emphasis on anthropology or sociology. In the three years between the time the earlier analysis was published and the latest membership list was received in June 2016, the proportions of full (holding a doctorate) to associate (studying for a doctorate or holding a master's degree) members of the network had remained relatively static, reflecting both an increasing interest in the broad field across time, and the successful completion of doctoral study by former "associate" members. In terms of specialist disciplines embraced by members, these remained broadly similar, although with a slight shift in disciplinary fields, with a small decline in the percentage of those working in anthropology and sociology and a mild increase in numbers working in the disciplines of human rights law, legal studies, and political science. There was, however, no increase in the number of those members claiming training in social and public policy analysis or administration.

Given that both the 2013 analysis and available data from 2016 reveal that the academic disciplines (in descending order) from which the greatest number of EANRS members were drawn were anthropology, sociology, history, and ethnology, with political science, human rights/legal studies, and social policy/administration nearer the bottom of areas of expertise, it would appear that there is something of a mismatch in terms of numbers of members who have received academic training in those areas potentially most pertinent to policy development. The claim for particularity and special relevance of certain disciplines to policy engagement is made not in an attempt to reify specific subjects, but to highlight the fact that academics engaged in research with Roma are noticeably unlikely to come from either specialist policy backgrounds or practice-oriented disciplines such as law, social work, or health sciences. These latter specialisms have long grappled with the implications of the interface between policy and practical outcomes for client groups (Adams 2002; Laverack 2012), a form of engagement removed both from microlevel ethnographic studies and "high theory" political science (Druckman et al. 2011).

If the EANRS membership is taken as a representative "snapshot" of academics engaged in the field of Romani studies, as evidenced in the document mapping the membership of the network (EANRS 2013: 2), a substantial proportion of members have engaged in the provision of policy advice to national or international agencies, or undertaken expert review of policy documents pertaining to Roma minorities. Accordingly, it can be seen that despite the expertise that can accrue through practice and close engagement with Roma populations, there is something of a mismatch between members' policy-related activities and their professional orientation and training. It is therefore likely that those academics who work most closely with Roma minorities and who are deeply committed to their wellbeing may have a lacuna in specialist training or expert knowledge in relation to policy-making processes and cycles, which may potentially hamper the effective delivery of policy advice (Cairney 2015).

Given the preponderance of certain disciplines among EANRS members, the majority of Roma "specialists" or those undertaking doctoral training with a focus on Romani studies are less likely than "practitioners" to be required to actively and theoretically engage with issues of both coproduction (as expounded by Ryder 2015) or the "nuts and bolts" of policy development, until they find themselves working in the field of policy review, or employed to undertake research on behalf of agencies seeking to identify the support needs of marginalized Roma populations. In contrast (and, it can be argued, better fitting such professionals for the role of academic-activist), issues of the complex interplay of community empowerment, coproduction of research, and the practical implications of influencing and implementing policy enactments have been explored over several decades, and in some depth, in relation to professional practice among a number of public service–oriented disciplines. Social workers (Reeser and Epstein 1990; Gray and Webb 2009), teachers (Giroux 1991; Sachs 2000) and health professionals (Holter and Schwartz-Barcott 1993; Warner 2003; Laverack 2012) are thus all able to draw on a body of literature and practice that engages with the above germane issues.

While such outcome-focused (as opposed to research-oriented) models have only relatively recently been identified as pertinent to more "traditional" academic disciplines (as opposed to applied, translational health and social sciences), geographers and anthropologists have been at the forefront of much of the cutting-edge critical debate on the importance of embedding principles of social justice into field research. This is perhaps unsurprising, given their disciplinary emphasis on reflexive practice and frequently close, microlevel, embedded working relationships with communities (Beck 2001; Hale 2006; Kingsolver 2009; Watt 2010; Rogaly 2015). Indeed, as early as 1996, the geographer Paul Routledge drew on the work of postcolonialist theorist Homi Bhabha (1994) to reflect upon the notion of a liminal politicized "third space" in which "no simple opposition exists between academia and activism. Rather, occupying a third space of critical engagement enables research to become a personal and reflexive project of resistance" (Routledge 1996: 411).

Given the academic disciplines most common to the "older generation" of Romani studies scholars, a slender but persistent thread of postcolonial social theory and radical anthropology has (albeit controversially) influenced Romani studies since the late 1970s (see Ryder 2015 for an excellent critical review of the tensions between proponents of "scientism" and "activism/standpoint theory," and also Ryder, this volume). More recently, with the emphasis within EU policy documents—most specifically in relation to National Roma Integration Strategies (NRIS) and the EU Framework—on "partnership" activities and coproduction of outputs, including monitoring reports by academics, civil society organizations, and Roma peoples, discourse on community development and activism has attained significant prominence across a wider range of fields. Thus, the plethora of opportunities that in the last decade have opened up for academics (of both Roma and non-Roma ethnicities) to work with and be influenced by (and in turn to influence) Roma activists means that the terrain and discourse of "expertise" has rightly shifted. Accordingly, evaluations of findings and recommendations presented to agencies charged with policy development, at both EU and nation-state level, typically and correctly require evidence of consultation and coproduction in order to be granted credence.

While the question of just how meaningful such collaborative research techniques may be (or whether mere "lip service" has been paid to the community or to practice-derived knowledge of nonacademic partners) is beyond the scope of this chapter, it is critically important to note that even in circumstances where impeccable attention has been paid to participatory research methods and the "voice" of hitherto marginalized populations is clearly presented in outputs, there is a very real danger that reports will languish on the shelf. Similarly, recommendations may often fail to win approval as a result of the authors' lack of knowledge of the realities of the policy-making terrain and the constraints under which bureaucrats must labor. This would ultimately nullify the efforts of engaged researchers to concretely make a difference in the lives of the communities they work with, and would relegate research back to its ivory tower.

While there is an accepted recognition of the value and necessity of academics "becoming inexpert"—recognizing the limitations of their own

world-view and drawing upon the lived community experience and expertise of Roma populations to coproduce data (see further Ryder et al. 2014;
Lane et al. 2014)—it can be argued that these specialist knowledge producers on Roma matters frequently misunderstand (and hence misrepresent)
the processes involved in the craft of policy-making (Cairney 2015). Predominantly, this occurs when academics fail to recognize the critical importance of theoretical and practical models inherent in, and fundamental
to, the design of policy activities. Particular gaps in understanding between
academics and policy makers arise from limited awareness by academics and
activists of the type of information required to support policy, how such information should be packaged, and the appropriate timing of input. In turn,
policy makers are frequently dismissive of abstract theoretical argument and
terminology that appears irrelevant to the case in question (Marble 2006:
3). It can be credibly argued that the "three legs" of the tripod that supports
Roma inclusion are empowerment ("voice"), high quality research and data
to support moral and practical arguments for change, and appropriate policy design. However, in order to create a stable structure, it is critically important for activist-academics to have a solid knowledge of how to translate
research into policy outcomes (Goldstein 2009) that are protected from mis-
application or poor implementation leading to unintentional harm.

Bridging the Gap between Academics, Activists, and Policy Makers

In the special edition of *Asia Policy* published in 2006, which was devoted
to a consideration of how best academics could be supported in delivering
policy-relevant outputs, contributors (Goldman 2006; Marble 2006; Vogel
2006) highlighted a number of excellent practice points. These essays on influencing policy design and outputs are as highly relevant to readers of this
chapter as to the initial target audience, even if they do not specifically focus
on Roma. Key elements flagged by authors concerned the necessity of understanding common policy dilemmas, being familiar with upcoming time-
tables, and foreseeing (so far as possible) crisis events that might have an
impact on decision-making. Contributors to the volume consistently noted
that recommendations must engage in a practical sense with such multifac-
torial issues. For instance, pertinent critiques that are phrased in terms that
may be perceived as offering too great a criticism of the administrative regime's actions were flagged as likely to lead policy makers to reject recommendations. It might well be added that so does a cavalier disregard for the
circumstances facing frequently overburdened policy professionals, a point
highlighted by Cairney (2015: 9), who proposes that academics "should

identify how the policy process works and seek to influence it on that basis—not according to how they would like it to be."

In the volume of *Asia Policy* referred to above, Goldman (2006: 20) recommends that academics should consider the use of case studies, problem-solving exercises, and simulations as tools for training students (and indeed activists) in policy design, noting that these techniques are used widely in professional policy training. As considered earlier in this chapter, certain professionals—such as lawyers, social workers, and medics—who are familiar with "on the ground" work are frequently acutely alert to both policy impacts on, and implications for, their practice. In part, this relates to both their practical activities and close engagement with "end users," but also perhaps to the fact that such methods form a core part of their training, as well as that of policy professionals who have undertaken a formal course of study in their chosen discipline.

To support this argument, I provide an example of the effective use of case studies, drawn from my own research and teaching. Feedback from participants and co-teachers in this program ("professionals" and "community members") all indicated that the methods utilized had been influential in changing their awareness, practice, and modes of policy input and collaboration. A cohort of public health students (master's degree level with feed-in pathway to M.Phil./Ph.D.), comprising policy staff and front-line practitioners working at both grassroots and strategic levels, took modules that I developed and co-delivered on the policy-making process. Students were overwhelmingly experienced practitioners, who in their professional lives were responsible for developing health commissioning and implementation policies, as well as—in some cases—delivering services.

In addition to standard "academic-led" sessions (for example on theoretical models and intervention cycles that occur when making policy), the program included an element that consisted of taught sessions and practice-based exercises focused on the use of pathways and network mapping. This set of activities focused on how best to design service delivery for "underserved groups," including Gypsies and Travellers, refugees and asylum seekers, and homeless people. This program element undertaken near the end of the year-long policy-making module took place over two months and was assessed through a series of short activities. The activities subject to assessment precisely reflected those elements with which policy practitioners engage throughout their working lives—for example, the production (and critique) of written policy justifications (including reflection on cost implications), network-development exercises (who to engage with, how to operationalize a network, and for what purpose), and the production of process-mapping papers. In addition, students were tasked with practical problem-solving exercises based on review and interrogation of data sets and policy options, and produced and made presentations to colleagues and examiners on selected themes.

Participants in the course were also supported in undertaking meetings with community groups led by Gypsy and Traveller (and homeless) activists, and experienced sessions led by health professionals working with the "underserved groups." These meetings enabled them to consider how best to ensure that policy was tailored to build in delivery flexibility such as might be required "on the ground" when working with groups experiencing particular challenges and rapid change in their circumstances. Sessions were also delivered on practical policy-making and policy interventions in which vignettes using anonymized "real life" policy and practice situations were embedded into the module. In addition, guest speakers from the communities took part in seminars (in some cases introduced as community members, and in other cases anonymized, so that their input was engaged with prior to their "outing" themselves as Gypsy or Traveller activists, once concerns over practice, stereotypical perceptions, and policy barriers had been discussed). Mutual sharing of understanding and knowledge thus took place in a respectful environment. In this way, we turned the model of typical policy analysis and engagement upside down, consciously creating a sense of disorientation and demonstrating that expertise is best created from co-production and sharing of knowledge and experience. Participants whose professional roles required them to actively design and implement health policy, outreach, and delivery of services were thus exposed to a 360-degree review of policy formation, implementation, and impact on service recipients. These learning experiences then had to be packaged as though for presentation to their employers, with the presentation subsequently subject to in-depth analysis and challenge in classroom settings by a range of audiences.

Based on my experiences, I would assert (as also noted by Goldman 2006) that awareness of practice-based approaches to critical thinking, requiring reflexive review of presumptions and practical engagement with policy tools, can make students and academics better producers of policy outputs. To this, it is worth adding that awareness of the potential for conjunctions of knowledge (i.e., gained from nonacademic or policy professionals) and alertness to key opportunities for engagement with "irregular" syndromes of policy-making (Rockman 1981) may be equally important in terms of influencing recommendations and outcomes.[4]

The Unintended Consequences of Overthinking

As the above review of the academic specialisms of Romani studies scholars from the EANRS has shown, academic researchers whose work is drawn upon to underpin policy development that impacts Roma populations come from a wide range of disciplines, but few are practitioners or policy specialists. As such, their traditional academic training will typically have omitted to engage with such methods as are proposed by experienced policy professionals and considered by Goldman (2006) and Rockman (1981). Further, academic expertise (often a narrow but deep focus) may mean that those academic-activists making recommendations do not routinely undertake a 360-degree scan of contemporary politics, day-to-day circumstances of end users, and current affairs, obscuring surrounding trends or potential opportunities for rapid, low-cost interventions.

This latter, often overlooked, category ("off-the-shelf," transferable practice) may quite ethically be subject to effective wholesale policy transfer as appropriate, or reworked at various phases of the policy cycle, using existing tools and techniques (see Dolowitz 2010 on "stored knowledge"), such as are commonly preferred by policy makers (see the "punctuated equilibrium theory," Baumgartner and Jones 1993: 1–19, 285–290).[5] Crucially, there is now a distinct trend toward a "new space of politics" impacting policy formation, to the extent that Hajer and Wagenaar (2003: 8) suggest that "concrete challenges to the practices of policy-making and politics [are emerging] from below." This "new space" is leading to expanded networks of policy influence, and greater scope for interpretation and the development of bottom-up narratives, which in turn permits engagement with the values and belief systems of those most impacted by enactments.

In itself, this apparent democratization of policy inputs must be seen as positive and offering valuable scope for the researcher to work closely with activists to craft a narrative that impacts policy formation. However, care must always be taken to ensure that the implications of greater "openness" are benign and not driven or overborne by factional concerns or "hobbyhorses" of more vocal or articulate proponents of a single view—circumstances that might lead to unforeseen negative consequences for the group concerned.

To give but one example, in the academic year 2014–15, on two separate mailing lists, one academic and one activist, intense and at times heated debates took place on the nature and precise formulation of the term "Roma," and who should be included within policy formulations such as the NRIS. These fascinating discussions focused (among other themes) on presumptions of "elective choice" of identity versus externally (or group-internal) imposed recognition; whether or not there was a necessity for a distinct Roma policy and if so, whether only individuals who were "Roma" (rather than of Traveller heritage) should be incorporated in enactments. A significant number of academic and activist commentators on both threads held academically precise but highly polarized views on the situation, cultures, and future direction of people from Roma and Irish Traveller populations.[6]

In the United Kingdom, although the full implications of this example are outside this chapter's focus, it was noted by a number of activists that Irish Travellers, while culturally distinct from Roma people, often find themselves closer in many ways to Romany Gypsies (who typically state a preference to living in culturally appropriate "caravan" accommodation and who are often highly resistant to house-dwelling and "assimilation") than they do to (migrant) Roma, who overwhelmingly seek a multicultural, rights-based recognition of their identity and ethnicity, but within a sedentarized context.

While for the academic or Roma activist the differences between the communities are self-evident, stark, and debated in full awareness of the exclusion and discrimination faced by "Roma," the policy practitioner is less concerned with the ethnicity and history of Travellers, Romany Gypsies, and Roma. The policy professional working within the context of government (and hence engaged with many diverse communities) will typically seek merely to create a category that provides protection for people subject to marginalization and racism, and who in the popular mind and discourse are all part of the same group of "nomads." While in the online forums it was debated whether creating a "convenience" policy category that incorporated nomadic Romany Gypsies, Travellers, and sedentarized Roma was scientifically pertinent, the concern of policy-alert commentators lays elsewhere.

This latter group argued that tampering with existing categories—which, while perhaps anthropologically, linguistically, or ethnically make little sense, nevertheless "work" in policy practice—potentially worsened the plight of many of the people currently contained within the rubric of "Roma," who share a status of marginalization associated with perceptions of nomadism and racist "othering," contaminated with arguments pertaining to the "cultures of poverty" narrative. This one small example, if carried to the logical conclusion of subdividing the groups to the extent that some would be "in" and others "out" of policy protection, would potentially overturn legislative "wins"—for example, the recognition in the United Kingdom of Irish and Scottish Travellers, as well as Romany Gypsies, as ethnic minorities with a right, in certain circumstances, to dwell in caravans and on "Gypsy/Traveller sites."

Moreover, such fragmentation of definitions could also offer succor to right wing or regressive political and media elements, determined to emphasize that long-established cultural practices held by all three "groups" are merely "lifestyle choice" and thus should not be afforded the dignity of policy protection. Accordingly, there are many pitfalls to the presentation of theoretical (and in such contexts highly relevant) debates, which can be confusing for the influential concept broker not fully au fait with the heightened passions afforded by what can, to the outsider, appear to be relatively irrelevant concerns. Similarly, a danger exists that the policy maker may be misled into believing that differences of opinion or an insistence on discrete scientific classifications equates to a lack of concern for social justice issues, or demonstrates a broad failure of consensus on anti-oppressive or antiracist action.

Exposing such complex minutiae of the academic and activist gaze to the public (political) observer or policy end user can thus have significant unintended negative consequences. Indeed such debates may, if only partially understood by the policy community, influence policy design or lead to refinements of targeted intervention in a manner frequently (and dangerously) outside the awareness of those researchers whose work directly feeds into outputs that impact the daily lives of millions of Roma and Traveller people. Moreover, Cohen et al. (2007) highlight that a dilemma often exists in terms of engaging with policy. Enactments and guidance are created with the best possible intentions: to alleviate a perceived problem identified by researchers and policy makers. However, front-line practitioners may then be placed under increased pressure (leading to a disengaged tick-box mentality in daily practice) as the instruments designed to encourage implementation are often imposed on staff whose capacity to challenge top-down expectations— or their own weak political position—means that they are required to deliver target-driven outcomes, regardless of potentially negative impacts on communities receiving services.

Accordingly, the effective realization of policy depends in practice on the fit between resources and the capacity and capabilities of those charged with delivering "change." The more the aims substantially outstrip capabilities, the less likely is the chance that implementation will take place successfully. As such, yet another danger exists for the unwary academic-activist: that of attempting to create a utopian policy, or one that is beyond the reach of those on the "front line" of service implementation and delivery. Inevitably, in such cases, an inability of staff to effectively undertake mandated tasks will lead to a culture of mistrust, avoidance, and resentment. Then policy activities targeted at improving lives may be regarded by overworked practitioners as merely an administrative burden: something to be fulfilled to the minimal standard or avoided as much as possible.

Conclusion

While this contribution offers a whistle-stop tour of the interaction between policy-making and research, as a former legal practitioner turned policy officer (prior to becoming an academic), I feel able to comment with some confidence on the distinct approaches and needs of the policy specialist, concluding this chapter by suggesting certain factors that need to be borne in mind by the activist-academic engaged in policy advice. One element that is often disregarded or misunderstood by activists and academics alike is the sheer pressures of time on policy professionals and their inability to own specialist knowledge across a broad range of areas. This role limitation impacts not only the daily role of the policy maker, but also the processes of data selection, as well as the purposes to which research or activist briefings are subject. Vogel (2006: 31–32), referring to the "luxury of academia," notes that policy makers are constantly under pressure to hold several portfolios of knowledge, often expected to respond (or preempt) the next emergent "crisis" or topic area, and typically have limited windows of opportunity to engage with a range of materials. As such, selection of data used to support policy development and decision-making will be subject to a degree of randomness.

Ginsburg and Gorostiaga (2001: 174–75) highlight that research can be used by policy makers in the following ways: instrumentally, to solve problems; interactively, essentially as one element combined with practice experiences; and/or to add enlightenment to shape general thinking. Further, research can function politically, to selectively provide support to predetermined actions; it may serve a tactical purpose, where policy practitioners use research to enhance their credibility or justify their nonactions; or it may be used promotionally, to disseminate and promote the implementation of policy decisions to individuals not actively involved in policy-making processes. As such, it can be seen that the complex ways in which data is used, the number of "network" members, the influences that variously foreground the voices of particular individuals or groups under the rubric of democratization—coupled with the intense pressures under which policy practitioners are placed to devise effective outcomes that still offer flexibility for responsive amendment (Weible et al. 2012)—all hold the potential for a toxic situation to develop. Accordingly, when mishandled, the group dynamics and politics associated with using research to influence policy design has the potential to lead to sclerotic turpitude and a desperate worsening of the situation of vulnerable groups.

Given that the selection of key policy themes and targets to measure and evaluate member state responsibilities toward national Roma minorities and other vulnerable or migrant populations are overwhelmingly formulated in response to research findings at both the national and EU level, it is imperative that both activists and academics remain supraconscious of the ethical weight of their activities, pronouncements, and recommendations to policy makers. While "impact assessments" are carried out prior to the implementation or adoption of policy and legislation at the EU level, inevitably these *also* are dependent upon the state of knowledge available to those undertaking the impact assessment and the quality of responses received from civil society and other agencies.[7] Accordingly, at all stages of the process of policy formation and implementation, the validity of research findings and the research teams' underlying philosophy, paradigmatic approach, and quality of relationship with "grassroots" civil society are all key (but typically unremarked) elements that feed into policy frameworks and the policy-making process. I have expounded elsewhere upon the symbiotic relationship between effective policy development, Roma empowerment, and ethical research predicated upon knowledge-sharing between Roma communities, policy makers, academics, and activists (Greenfields 2015). It is, however, worthwhile reiterating that for all those engaged in such a project, our collective priority must be to ensure that policy is based firmly upon the highest quality, most credible, and unbiased research evidence, supported by knowledgeable policy advice. When activists (both Roma and non-Roma), academics, and policy makers can base thoughtful, practical, and "deliverable" recommendations on incontrovertible substantive evidence, it is to be hoped that we will be able to identify (and ethically use) the tools that empower and deliver the greatest positive impact on the lives of those whose wellbeing may at least partially lie in our hands.

Margaret Greenfields worked as a researcher before training as a community lawyer with a particular interest in homelessness, migration, and gender issues. After some years working as a legal policy officer, she completed a Ph.D. and moved into academia. She is currently director of the Institute for Diversity Research (IDRICS) at Buckinghamshire New University, where she is Professor of Social Policy and Community Engagement. Greenfields has worked and published extensively in the field of social inclusion, ethnicity, equalities, and social justice, with emphasis on undertaking collaborative research with communities at risk of marginalization, racism, and "othering."

Notes

1. This lower stage has been classified as manipulative or therapeutic engagement, in which the objective is less to enable community members to participate in planning or to actively collaborate in projects than to provide scope for those who hold power to "educate," or that provides a therapeutic context in which those impacted by decisions can vocalize their concerns.
2. It is perhaps worth stating that outputs should by definition pass the first hurdle of fulfilling the basic standards for policy guidance—i.e., that they preclude bias en-

abling core or obvious issues to be dismissed in the interests of the authors' political stance. Moreover, they must not fail to engage with adequate and transparent arguments to justify a particular recommendation. In this way, potentially conflicting views can be presented, analyzed, and explored prior to recommendations being made that both satisfy the activist-academic's commitment to social justice and are fully supported, justifiable, and "deliverable."

3. Implemented via such mechanisms as the Decade of Roma Inclusion 2005–15 and the EU Framework for National Roma Integration Strategies up to 2020. Supporting documentation, case studies, and activities initiated and undertaken by the twelve member states participating in the Decade can be accessed by undertaking a country-by-country search. In addition, some regional initiatives (Roma Integration 2020; Regional Cooperation Councils) have been developed following the end of the Decade of Roma Inclusion (see, for example, "Documents," Roma Integration 2010: Regional Cooperation Council website, accessed 27 November 2017, http://www.rcc.int/romaintegration2020/docs_archive?search_type=3). The EU Framework for National Roma Integration Strategies (NRIS) is a policy framework that was strongly influenced by the underpinning activities of the Decade of Roma Inclusion and was adopted by European member states (MS) on 5 April 2011 (European Commission, 2011a and 2011b). Under the Framework, each member state was required to deliver an integration strategy pertinent to the circumstances of its Roma populations by the end of 2011, a deadline missed by a significant number. The Framework and resultant NRIS have been subject to widespread significant criticism for failing to deliver change (ERRC 2013), as illustrated by the monitoring reports required from each member state on a regular basis. Civil society monitoring documents pertaining to national reports were formerly lodged at a single website location hosted by the Decade of Roma Inclusion website, but since the ending of the Decade initiative these monitoring reports must now be accessed on a country-by-country basis. One core criticism leveled at the NRIS and associated outputs concerns the fact that individual MS have been permitted to adopt or develop policies that often failed to address pressing issues, even though they were aimed at ensuring that Roma (and members of other communities included within this rubric—e.g., Travellers, Sinti, Manouche, etc.) have equal access to employment, education, healthcare, and housing (including essential services) (ERRC 2013). Instead, they merely highlight limited ongoing activities that have been criticized by civil society "on the ground" as inadequate, poorly funded, or cost-neutral to the state in question, despite the availability of EU funding to support new initiatives. NRIS, as prepared and submitted by MS, have been identified as typically inadequate in scope (European Roma Policy Coalition 2012), while protective activities or strategies for inclusion have been frequently found to be lacking enforcement processes or adequate development. Indeed, NRIS often merely reiterate policies in place prior to the implementation of the Framework (see further European Commission 2012). Other commentaries suggest that, in practice, "new" outputs emerging from adopted strategies have tended to concentrate funding in the hands of NGOs or agencies that may be inexperienced in working with Roma. Concerns have also been articulated that agencies are subject to claims of corruption (see further Feffer 2013; Fontanella-Khan and Eddy 2014), with activities typically benefiting only a small (often elite) proportion of the population in need. In any event, progress has been slow, resources have typically been available on a short-term basis, there is lack of

sustainability, and many NRIS activities have been found to make very little difference to the daily lives of marginalized Roma populations (Commissioner for Human
Rights 2012; Guy 2012; Moisă et al. 2016).

4. Rockman (1981), in an astute "insider" review of the processes of policy-making in
the U.S. and European institutions, reviews the role of noncareer, "irregular" special advisors or experts in a particular field, who are external to traditional minis-
terial or departmental roles. These advisors, selected for their in-depth knowledge
of a particular field or set of networks, but typically not engaged on a career basis
with the "nuts and bolts" of direct policy implementation and design, may work
closely with lawmakers and politicians; as a result, particular expert knowledge or
approaches may become embedded in the knowledge of decision makers, leading to
the opportunity to influence outcome-focused policy design. In this way, Rockman
(1981: 913) notes the advantages of impact enjoyed by "irregulars," resulting from
their detachment from operational responsibilities and the more "entrepreneurial"
or "ideologically" driven approach that can appeal to lawmakers and politicians.

5. Punctuated equilibrium theory posits that political systems can be both dynamic
and stable. While the majority of policies may remain stable for relatively lengthy
periods of time, they can also shift dramatically, typically in reaction to the election of a new government wedded to a particular form of ideology, or triggered by
an apparent crisis that focuses political or public attention on a subject, leading to
urgent attempts to implement new forms of policy response. When this occurs, professional policy makers—under pressure to deliver a solution in a short time frame—
will typically rely on prior learning or methods with which they are familiar.

6. In the context of this debate, the Roma are identified as those with historically Indic
origins, thus including— in European Policy Centre terms—U.K. Romany Gypsy
groups, but excluding other "Traveller" groups. However, in U.K. terminology,
"Roma" is used only to designate European migrants with Indic origins, while British-
born Romani populations will overwhelmingly use the term "Romany Gypsy," "English Gypsy," or "Romany" to describe themselves, a practice followed in British
policy documents.

7. See further "Impact Assessments," European Commission website, accessed 27
October 2017, http://ec.europa.eu/smart-regulation/impact/index_en.htm; and,
explaining the processes undertaken prior to adoption and implementation of
policy, "Better Regulation: Guidelines and Toolbox," European Commission website, accessed 27 October 2017, http://ec.europa.eu/smart-regulation/guidelines/
toc_guide_en.htm.

References

Adams, Robert. 2002. *Social Policy for Social Work*. Basingstoke: Palgrave Macmillan.
Arnstein, Sherry R. 1969. "A Ladder of Citizen Participation." *Journal of the American Planning Association* 35 (4): 216–24.
Baumgartner Frank R., and Bryan D. Jones. 1993. *Agendas and Instability in American Politics*. Chicago: University of Chicago Press.
Beck, Sam. 2001. "Radicalizing Anthropology? Toward Experiential Learning." *Anthropology of Work Review* 22: 1–6.
Bhabha Homi. 1994. *The Location of Culture*. London: Routledge.

Cairney, Paul. 2015. *The Politics of Evidence-Based Policymaking*. Basingstoke: Palgrave Pivot.

Cohen, David K., Susan L. Moffitt, and Simona Goldin. 2007. "Policy and Practice: The Dilemma." *American Journal of Education* 113 (4): 515–48.

Commissioner for Human Rights. 2012. *Human Rights of Roma and Travellers in Europe*. Strasbourg Cedex: Council of Europe Publications. Accessed 13 September 2015. http://www.coe.int/t/commissioner/source/prems/prems79611_GBR_CouvHumanRightsOfRoma_WEB.pdf.

Dolowitz, David. 2010. "Learning, Information and Policy Transfer Process: What Do Governments Learn When Shopping for Ideas." Paper presented at the Royal Society of Edinburgh seminar on Policy Learning and Policy Transfer in Multilevel Systems, Scottish Policy Innovation Forum and University of Aberdeen, Edinburgh, 22 January 2010.

Druckman, James N., Donald P. Green, James H. Kuklinski, and Arthur Lupia, eds. 2011. *Cambridge Handbook of Experimental Political Science*. New York: Cambridge University Press.

EANRS (European Academic Network for Romani Studies). 2013. "Mapping the Network and Presenting Its Potentials." EU and Council of Europe. Accessed 3 August 2015. http://romanistudies.eu/wp-content/uploads/2015/02/mapping_Romani_Studies_network_sept2013.pdf.

European Commission. 2011a. "An EU framework for National Roma Integration Strategies up to 2020." COM(2011)173. Accessed 3 August 2015. https://ec.europa.eu/info/strategy/justice-and-fundamental-rights/discrimination/roma-and-eu/roma-integration-eu-countries_en#nationalromaintegrationstrategies.

———. 2011b. *Working Together for Roma Inclusion*. Luxembourg: Publications Office of the European Union. Accessed 30 April 2018. http://romani.humanities.manchester.ac.uk/virtuallibrary/librarydb/web/files/pdfs/190/VL-105.pdf.

———. 2012. "Communication from the Commission to the European Parliament, the Council, the European Economic and Social Committee and the Committee of the Regions: National Roma Integration Strategies: A First Step in the Implementation of the EU Framework." COM(2012)260. Accessed 30 April 2018. https://publications.europa.eu/en/publication-detail/-/publication/3b9bfed7-c6b5-4713-89f0-e1465ae16ac3.

———. 2015. "Better Regulation Guidelines." Commission Staff Working Document. Accessed 1 October 2016. http://ec.europa.eu/smart-regulation/guidelines/docs/swd_br_guidelines_en.pdf.

European Roma Policy Coalition. 2012. *Analysis of the National Roma Integration Strategies*. N.p.: European Roma Policy Coalition.

European Roma Rights Centre. 2013. "National Roma Integration Strategies: What Next?" Special issue, *Roma Rights: Journal of the European Roma Rights Centre*.

Feffer, John. 2013. "The Failure of Funding Roma Inclusion." *Foreign Policy in Focus*, 28 January 2013. Accessed 13 June 2016. http://fpif.org/the_failure_of_funding_roma_inclusion/.

Flood, Michael G., Brian Martin, and Tanja Dreher. 2013. "Combining Academia and Activism: Common Obstacles and Useful Tools." *Australian Universities Review* 55 (1): 17–26.

Fontanella-Khan, James, and Eddy Kester. 2014. "Roma: Moving Target." *The Financial Times*, 25 February 2014. Accessed 15 June 2014. http://www.ft.com/cms/s/2/27e2aa22-995f-11e3-91cd-00144feab7de.html#axzz3kgY8jj95.

Gaudreau, Matthew, and Marc Saner. 2014. "Researchers Are from Mars; Policymakers Are from Venus." Policy Brief Series: Science/Policy Interface no. 1. Institute for Science, Society and Policy. Accessed 10 June 2016. http://issp.uottawa.ca/sites/issp.uottawa.ca/files/issp2014-spibrief1-collaboration.pdf.

Ginsburg, Mark B., and Jorge Gorostiaga. 2001. "Relationships between Theorists/Researchers and Policy Makers/Practitioners: Rethinking the Two-Cultures Thesis and the Possibility of Dialogue." *Comparative Education Review* 45 (2): 173–96.

Giroux, Henry. 1991. *Border Crossings: Cultural Workers and the Politics of Education.* New York: Routledge.

Goldman, Emily O. 2006. "Closing the Gap: Networking the Policy and Academic Communities." *Asia Policy* 1 (1): 16–24.

Goldstein, Harold. 2009. "Translating Research into Public Policy." *Journal of Public Health Policy* 30 (Supplement 1: *Connecting Active Living Research to Policy Solutions*): s16–s20.

Gray, Mel, and Stephen A. Webb. 2009. "The Return of the Political in Social Work." *International Journal of Social Welfare* 18: 111–15.

Greenfields, Margaret. 2015. "Policies for Roma Inclusion: The Contribution of Academic Research." Opening Statement: Showcase Event, Strasbourg, 22 April 2015.

Guy, Will. 2012. "Roma Inclusion at the Crossroads: Can the Lessons from PHARE be Learned?" *Roma Rights: Journal of the European Roma Rights Centre* 5. Accessed 3 September 2015. http://www.errc.org/article/roma-rights-2011-funding-roma-rights-challenges-and-prospects/4062/1.

Hajer, Maarten A., and Hendrik Wagenaar, eds. 2003. *Deliberative Policy Analysis: Understanding Governance in the Network Society.* Cambridge: Cambridge University Press.

Hale, Charles R. 2006. "Activist Research v. Cultural Critique: Indigenous Land Rights and the Contradictions of Politically Engaged Anthropology." *Cultural Anthropology* 21 (1): 96–120.

Holter, Inger M., and Donna Schwartz-Barcott. 1993. "Action Research: What Is It? How Has It Been Used and How Can It Be Used in Nursing?" *Journal of Advanced Nursing* 128: 298–304.

Kingsolver, Anne E. 2009. "Learning from Activist Anthropologists' Praxis." *New Proposals: Journal of Marxism and Interdisciplinary Inquiry* 2 (2): 73–77.

Lane, Pauline, Siobhan Spencer, and Adrian Jones. 2014. *Gypsy, Traveller and Roma: Experts by Experience: Reviewing UK Progress on the European Union Framework for National Roma Integration Strategies.* Cambridge: Anglia Ruskin University. Accessed 1 October 2016. https://www.birmingham.ac.uk/Documents/college-social-sciences/social-policy/iris/2014/Experts-by-Experience--JRTF-Report-Oct-2014.pdf.

Laverack, Glenn. 2012. "Health Activism." *Health Promotion International* 27 (4): 429–34.

Marble, Andrew D. 2006. "Bridging the Gap with Market Driven Knowledge: Launching Asia Policy." *Asia Policy* 1 (1): 2–6.

Marsh, David, and Allan McConnell. 2010. "Towards a Framework for Establishing Policy Success." *Public Administration* 88 (2): 564–83.

Martin, Brian. 2007. "Activism, Social and Political." In *Encyclopedia of Activism and Social Justice,* edited by Garry L. Andersen and Kathryn G. Herr, 19–27. London: Sage.

Moisă, Florin, Daniela Tarnovschi, Ivan Claudiu, Adrian Marin, Diana Lăcătuş, and Radu Lăcătuş. 2016. *Strategies–YES, Funding–NO: Financing Mechanisms for Roma Public Policies in Romania*. Cluj-Napoca: Resource Center for Roma Communities.

Okely, Judith. 1983. *The Traveller-Gypsies*. Cambridge: Cambridge University Press.

Powell, Ryan. 2011. "Gypsy-Travellers and Welfare Professional Discourse: On Individualization and Social Integration." *Antipode* 43 (2): 471–93.

Reeser, Linda C., and Irwin Epstein. 1990. *Professionalization and Activism in Social Work*. New York: Columbia University Press.

Rockman, Bert A. 1981. "America's Departments of State: Irregular and Regular Syndromes of Policy Making." *The American Political Science Review* 75 (4): 911–27.

Rogaly, Ben. 2015. "Disrupting Migration Stories: Reading Life Histories through the Lens of Mobility and Fixity." *Environment and Planning D: Society and Space* 33 (3): 528–44.

Routledge, Paul. 1996. "The Third Space as Critical Engagement." *Antipode* 28 (4): 399–419.

Ryder, Andrew, Sarah Cemlyn, and Thomas Acton, eds. 2014. *Hearing the Voice of Gypsies, Roma and Travellers: Inclusive Community Development*. Bristol: Policy Press.

Ryder, Andrew. 2015. "Co-producing Knowledge with Below the Radar Communities: Factionalism, Commodification or Partnership? A Gypsy, Roma and Traveller Case Study." Third Sector Research Centre Working Paper, Discussion Paper G, University of Birmingham. Accessed 26 August 2016. http://www.birmingham.ac.uk/generic/tsrc/documents/tsrc/discussion-papers/2015/gtr-discussion-paper-g-ryder-28janfinal.pdf.

Sabatier, Paul A., and Weible Christopher M., eds. 2014. *Theories of the Policy Process*. 3rd ed. Chicago: Westview Press.

Sachs, Judyth. 2000. "The Activist Professional." *Journal of Educational Change* 1 (1): 77–94.

Social Care Institute for Excellence. 2012. *Towards Co-production: Taking Participation to the Next Level*. SCIE Report 53. London: Social Care Institute for Excellence.

Spicker, Paul. 2014. *Social Policy: Theory and Practice*. Bristol: Policy Press.

Surdu, Mihai, and Martin Kovats. 2015. "Roma Identity as an Expert-Political Construction." *Social Inclusion* 3 (5): 5–18.

van Baar, Huub. 2005. "Romany Counter-Governmentality through Transnational Networking." Conference paper, Oxford Symposium on (Trans-) Nationalism in South East Europe, St. Antony's College, University of Oxford, UK, 17–19 June 2005.

———. 2011. "Europe's Romaphobia: Problematization, Securitization, Nomadization." *Environment and Planning D: Society and Space* 29 (2): 203–12.

———. 2012. "Socio-Economic Mobility and Neoliberal Governmentality in Post-Socialist Europe." *Journal of Ethnic and Migration Studies* 38 (8): 1289–304.

Vogel, Ezra F. 2006. "Some Reflections on Policy and Academics." *Asia Policy* 1 (1): 31–41.

Warner, Joanne R. 2003. "A Phenomenological Approach to Political Competence: Stories of Nurse Activists." *Policy, Politics, and Nursing Practice* 4 (2): 135–43.

Watt, Paul. 2010. "Unravelling the Narratives and Politics of Belonging to Place." *Housing, Theory and Society* 27 (2): 153–59.

Weible, Christopher M., Tanya Heikkila, Peter deLeon, and Paul A. Sabatier. 2012. "Understanding and Influencing the Policy Process." *Policy Sciences* 45 (1): 1–21.

CHAPTER 8

✻ ✻ ✻

BETWEEN GLOBAL SOLIDARITY AND NATIONAL BELONGING
The Politics of Inclusion for *Romanlar* in Turkey

Danielle V. Schoon

In late May 2013, hundreds of demonstrators gathered in Istanbul's Gezi Park to resist its demolition by one of the Turkish government's infamous redevelopment projects. After a sit-in of several days and the growth of the demonstration to include thousands of people, the police raided the park and dispersed demonstrators with tear gas, attracting worldwide attention to the cause. In the early days of June, tens of thousands of protestors gathered in Gezi Park and adjacent Taksim Square and experienced violent clashes with police that left several dead and hundreds wounded. This aggressive display of state power set off a countrywide protest movement against President (then Prime Minister) Erdoğan and the AKP (Justice and Development Party) that lasted for several months and continues to reverberate today. International public media and scholars noted the diversity of ideologies and identities represented in the Occupy Gezi movement—Kurds, LGBTQ people, nationalists, anarchists, environmentalists, Islamists, and even *futbol* (soccer) clubs were united by their frustration with the heavy-handed response of the government (Gruber 2013: 33).

It was this sense of solidarity among usually disparate groups that captured international interest. Zeynep Tufekci wrote at the time, "In Gezi, one thing that struck me . . . was the spirit of tolerance and diversity. Gezi protests participation included people ranging from nationalist/traditional Kemalists to Kurdish political parties, from the 'internet generation' youth

... to feminists, from 'revolutionary muslims' to many ordinary citizens who do not fit into any of these categories" (Tufekci 2013).

There were various interpretations of the meaning of such solidarity, but most agreed that the reasons were complex (see David and Toktamış 2015). One article noted, "The majority of those taking part are middle class and secular, but the participation of working-class people, practicing Muslims, and ethnic and religious minorities belies any simplistic attempt to characterize this movement as a simple reiteration of existing divisions between secular and religious, urban and rural, Turkish and non-Turkish, and so forth" (Hammond and Angell 2013). Britta Ohm described the dynamic interactions of the protestors thusly:

> Inadvertently, the protestors showed the limits of media and representation in contrast to the active, physical togetherness of hitherto deeply divided groups of people in the real public space, the direct getting-to-know each other, seeing each other, speaking with each other, learning about and from each other, organising things together, and, increasingly, suffering together, helping each other during relentless attacks of teargas and water cannon and, also, joining in burying and commemorating the dead. (Ohm 2013)

Ohm goes on to propose that Gezi was about discovering a tentative "common-ness through the very defense of the commons." El-Kazaz (2013) takes a similar interpretation: tracing the right-to-the-city cause back to the passing of the "Renewal and Preservation Law" in 2005, which allows municipalities to designate urban renewal areas for demolition or transformation, she notes that the first such project was implemented in a *Roman* (Gypsy)[1] neighborhood in central Istanbul known as Sulukule. The Sulukule project prompted a coalition of civil society organizations called the Sulukule Platform to protest the demolition. Although the neighborhood was ultimately demolished, the networks that were formed in the Sulukule Platform were later galvanized in the Gezi Park protests, and Sulukule remains a touchstone example of the ills of neoliberal urban governance for right-to-the-city activists in Istanbul. Urban renewal projects that are displacing *Roman* populations in Istanbul and other Turkish cities have catalyzed a sense of solidarity among the *Romanlar* (Schoon 2014).

It is not surprising, then, that Ohm and others included the *Romanlar* when listing the diverse groups thought to be represented in the Occupy Gezi movement. However, with the exception of a few individuals acting on their own behalf, *Roman* spokespersons did not participate.[2] In fact, not only were the representatives of *Roman* associations (*dernek*) not in conspicuous attendance at the Gezi Park protests in Istanbul or elsewhere, several such leaders participated in Erdoğan's "respect for the national will" counterrallies for AKP supporters and publicly disassociated the *Romanlar* from the

Occupy Gezi movement (*Türkiye Gazetesi* 2013). A young *Roman* activist from Edirne, with whom I conducted research, attended the protests but was disillusioned to discover that she was one of very few. She sent me a message from Gezi Park: "Other *Romanlar* are not here, they are against us" (electronic correspondence, June 2013).

This chapter addresses the challenges posed to scholars and activists in understanding the dynamics of Romani rights in Turkey today, exemplified first of all by the absence of *Roman* representatives from the Occupy Gezi movement and second by their presumed presence. An analysis of the absence of Romani rights representation in the protest movement offers insights into the challenges that Turkey's *Romanlar* face as they find themselves between local discourses of national belonging and those of global solidarity with the larger Romani rights movement. If the Occupy Gezi movement was indeed made up of diverse groups that found common ground in their rejection of the AKP's strategies of urban governance, then the absence of *Roman* representatives tells us something about how they define their cause and its place in the current political climate. Just as important, because both the participants and outside observers interpreted the Occupy Gezi movement as a manifestation of civil society resistance against state power and an example of democracy at work, the presumed presence of the *Romanlar* alongside other underrepresented or marginalized citizens in Turkey hints at expectations that Romani rights would be central to such a movement.

First, I explain the absence of *Roman* spokespersons in Gezi Park by describing the development of Romani rights in Turkey as it has been shaped by a particular politics of inclusion. Second, I discuss the reasons why the *Romanlar* were assumed to be present in Gezi Park by most accounts. Turkey's position on the European periphery is mirrored by the position of Turkey's *Romanlar* on the periphery of the Romani rights movements; a combination of Islamism and nationalism makes Turkey and the *Romanlar* seem foreign to activists from EU member countries. I argue that, in order to be effective, it is essential for Romani rights activists to understand the political discourses and practices internal to *Roman* communities in Turkey, rather than impose outside interpretations and agendas. Similarly, the study of Romani identity and political participation in the European periphery ought to be central to the considerations of engaged scholarship in Romani studies.

Why Were the *Romanlar* Absent from the Gezi Park Protests? The Politics of Inclusion in Turkey

Turkey's relationship with its minorities emerged out of particular historical circumstances. As the Ottoman Empire was shrinking from the late eighteenth century until the early twentieth century, an estimated ten million Ottoman Muslim citizens (or *muhacir*) emigrated to Anatolia to escape persecution, including Romani Muslims. Although they were accepted because they would help recover the diminished population, there were not official policies for the integration of *Romanlar,* unlike for other *muhacir*; they were considered a threat to law and order and therefore subjected to surveillance and state control. Instead of being settled in small groups dispersed among the Turkish population, like other emigrants were, Romani Muslims were settled in large groups according to their skills, and their movements were restricted (Gürboğa 2016). Although they had been called "Turks" in the Ottoman Balkans, they were not officially recognized as ethnically or culturally Turkish, but as "Copts" (*kıpti*), or Egyptians, living within the Turkish nation. Nurşen Gürboğa's research (2016) found that these *Romanlar* identified themselves as *mübadil* (emigrants) and demanded the same treatment as other Muslim emigrants, demonstrating a long history of efforts by the *Romanlar* to be accepted as equal citizens based on their status as Muslims.

The reconfiguration of empires after World War I brought about the independence of the Turkish Republic in 1923 (see Göçek 2002: 20–21). Greeks and Armenians in this new nation-state were perceived as internal enemies who wanted to partition the state, and so were not incorporated into its imaginary (Akçam 2004: ix–x and 1). The Republic, although secular, was defined by its new demographic as Turkish-Muslim[3] (see Adak and Altınay 2010), subsuming all heterodox Muslims (like Alevis) and non-Turkish Muslims (like Kurds and Laz) under one national identity that was to be defined by a common language, race, and religion. Under the republican ethos, Turkish citizenship was supposed to represent everyone equally. The Lausanne Treaty of 1923[4] defined only non-Muslim religious groups as minorities in Turkey and non-Greek Orthodox Christians in Greece, so that Jews and Armenians became minorities in both. Muslim ethnic minorities were not legitimized and hence did not exist (Kieser 2006: 180; Göner 2010: 112). A common history was constructed as part of the national narrative so that other nations were detached and emerged as alien (Akçam 2004: xi). With the population exchanges between Turkey and Greece, more *Romanlar* emigrated to Anatolia. As Muslims, they were incorporated into the Turkish imaginary; they were assimilated into the nation via a rejection of any ethnic or linguistic differences. Modernization in the early Republican period was a top-down project (see Bozdoğan and Kasaba 1997) that not only defined the boundaries of Turkish citizenship according to language and religion, but also intervened in the lives of Turkish citizens to ensure they constituted a modern, secular nation. As Özyürek (2006: 90) states, "Turkish citizenship has corresponded more to a classical model than a liberal one, according to a popular way of categorization wherein citizens are defined through their duties toward the state rather than their rights." Turkey's constitution still defines Turkish as the only official language. Furthermore, religion is still the only officially recognized basis for minority status, so that Muslim minorities are not recognized as such by the state.

The globalization of Turkey's society and political economy in the 1980s opened the way to critiques of the official national narrative and new examinations of the past. During the 1990s, Turkey's policies of homogenization were increasingly questioned (Tambar 2014) against the backdrop of violent conflicts between the state and the PKK (Kurdistan Worker's Party), inquiries into the cultural history of the Rum (Turkey's Greek Orthodox Christians), and international pressure to recognize the Armenian genocide. Any mobilization of Romani rights in Turkey must take into account the generations-long armed conflict between the Turkish state and the PKK, which intensified Turkish nationalism (see Açıksöz 2014: 247) and is the backdrop of identity politics in Turkey. Turkey's Kurds have made some progress in pressuring the state to recognize their ethnic and linguistic differences, but the perception of Kurds as traitors to the state remains prevalent among non-Kurdish members of Turkish society, and this perception has been encouraged by state discourses and practices. For example, in 1994, President Demirel asserted that the Turkish Republic's constitution did not specify origin, belief, or language as the basis for citizenship or "national belonging." Accordingly, a Turk was anyone who was a citizen of Turkey and there would be no need for the recognition of a Kurdish minority and the granting of minority rights since full rights had already been bestowed upon them as citizens of Turkey (Kirişçi and Winrow 1997: 2).

The election to power of the AKP in 2002 brought about the acceleration of reforms aimed at liberalization and democratization (although the party has become increasingly authoritarian in recent years). Social movements that seek to redefine the terms and limits of collective identity have also been aided by new communication networks, which have become a means for contesting and accommodating different conceptions of national and global belonging (Yavuz 1999: 180; Tambar 2014: 83). Despite transformations in the public sphere, the republican approach to difference, which is perceived as divisive and threatening to the unity of the nation, still holds a lot of power in Turkey. Ultranationalists repeatedly accuse international organizations working in Turkey, particularly the Soros-sponsored Open Society Foundation, of "Balkanization" (*balkanlaşma*), referring to the supposed attempt of "the West" to fragment the unity of the Turkish nation in order to weaken its power. When, in 2004, the prime minister's Human Rights Advisory Board adopted the report of its Working Group on Minority and Cultural Rights as part of Turkey's endeavor to abide by the human rights provisions of the Copenhagen political criteria required for Turkish accession to the EU (European Commission 2007), the author of the report and the president of the board were prosecuted for "insulting state institutions" and "inciting people to hatred and enmity" (Oran 2007: 2). Although the defendants were eventually acquitted, the trial brought to light the tensions between republican conceptions of civil rights and liberal conceptions of minority rights introduced via EU harmonization (see Babül 2017).

Nationalism and the politics of "Turkishness" go partway in explaining the trajectory of Romani rights in Turkey.[5] *Roman* political participation in Turkey is also being shaped by the increasing presence of international civil society organizations (CSOs). I turn to the relationship between the state and civil society in Turkey and its impact on the *Romanlar.*

Romani Rights in the European Periphery

In 2013, the *New York Times* reported that there were 2.75 million *Romanlar* in Turkey (*New York Times* 2013). However, population estimates are unreliable because the Turkish census does not account for ethnicity. Furthermore, until recently, the *Romanlar* rarely possessed identity cards, and they are still not designated an official minority. As elsewhere, some individuals may have Romani origins but do not identify as *Roman.* Likely due to the suppression of linguistic and ethnic designations in Turkey, the term *Roman* is more often used to distinguish territorial, occupational, or cultural differences (Oprişan 2006: 165–66; also see Eren 2008).[6] The most common *Roman* occupations in Turkish cities are in semiformal economies, particularly entertainment and flower selling. They are also involved in informal occupations as scrap iron recyclers (*hurdacı*), garbage collectors, shoe shiners, vendors, buskers, and beggars, making them highly visible in the streets, but socially marginal. As in many parts of Europe, the *Romanlar* are associated with music and dancing; although this is generally a positive association, it also leads to exotic stereotypes and contributes to a process of distancing them from "normal" society (see Silverman 2012).

The term *Roman* in current Turkish rights discourses should be understood as part of the larger Romani political mobilization across Europe (see Vermeersch 2006: 13).[7] The European Romani rights movement began in the early 1990s after the neoliberal capitalist penetration of formerly communist central and eastern Europe, at which time increasing attention was given to minority rights issues (see van Baar 2011; see also the chapter by van Baar in this volume). Since then, Romani rights activists and organizations have been on the rise (Vermeersch 2006: 2), as has what van Baar (2012: 287) refers to as "the Europeanization of Roma representation." In the past decade, the European Commission has directed resources toward raising awareness and fighting the discrimination and marginalization of the Roma in EU member countries. As a candidate to the EU since 1999, Turkey has been under pressure to improve its poor human rights record, particularly for ethnic and religious minorities. Minority Rights Group International tracks the progress of Romani rights in Turkey. According to them, Turkey fails to meet international standards for human rights by not recognizing certain ethnic groups as minorities, particularly the *Romanlar* (Minority Rights Group, n.d.).

The mobilization of Romani rights groups and the organization of *dernek* led by *Romanlar* has increased since Turkey's Associations Law (*Dernekler Kanunu,* no. 5253) was significantly revised in 2004 to comply with the Copenhagen Criteria (Arkilic 2008). The revisions enabled their cooperation with international organizations and introduced opportunities for funds from the EU. While the law clearly outlines the right of Turkish citizens to found associations and makes it more difficult for the state to monitor their activities, it explicitly prohibits engagement in "political" activities, and associations must notify the government if they are to receive or use foreign funds. Furthermore, it prevents associations from being established solely on the basis of religious, ethnic, or racial affiliations, although in practice many CSOs do manage to serve particular communities (Kuzmanovic 2012: 9–11). *Roman* associations must walk a fine line between these stipulations and "doing the rights thing" (Osanloo 2004; also see Asad 2000) in order to secure funding from EU agencies.

EdRom (the Edirne *Roman* Association) is the most prominent *Roman* association in Turkey[8] and has been involved in several collaborations with the European Roma Rights Centre (ERRC), a public interest law organization. Together with the Helsinki Citizens' Assembly, it developed and implemented between 2005 and 2008 the Promoting Roma Rights in Turkey project, funded by the European Commission and the Open Society Foundation–Turkey. The objectives of the project included the collection of data regarding the *Romanlar,* as well as their empowerment for political mobilization (Uzpeder et al. 2008). The project combined the twin objectives of promoting democracy (which involves the mobilization of the *Romanlar* themselves, as well as efforts to persuade the government to reform state institutions toward their inclusion as ethnic minorities) and identifying the *Romanlar* as citizens of the nation with specific social problems that must be documented and addressed.

The initial stages of a government initiative for *Roman* inclusion also began in 2005, when Prime Minister Erdoğan, responding to accusations that the government was not doing enough to recognize its minorities, offered a reformulated (yet familiar) conception of identity in Turkey. He distinguished between *üst kimlik* (supra-identity), which is citizenship in the Turkish Republic, and *alt kimlik,* which refers to subidentities such as Kurdish, Alevi, or *Roman*. Public intellectuals in Turkey noted that by proposing the Kurdish "subidentity" as merely a cultural difference that is ultimately subsumed within the unity of the nation, Erdoğan elides the suppression of Kurdish language and culture and the state's history of violent oppression of its Kurds and other minorities (Yavuz 2009; İnce 2012). Nonetheless, this approach resurfaced in 2009, when the AKP declared a "Democratic Opening Process" (*Demokratik Açılım Süreci*) that would supposedly improve the country's standards of democracy and respect for human rights. The initiative includes a Romani Opening (*Roman Açılımı*) alongside openings for Kurds, Alevis, Armenians, women, and other so-called "disadvantaged groups" in Turkey, but avoids the term "minority" (*azınlık*).[9]

When the Romani Opening was announced at a public event at Istanbul's Abdi İpekçi Sports Hall in 2010, it was well received. Erdoğan addressed a large crowd of thousands of *Romanlar*, saying, "Nobody in this country can be treated as 'half' a person."[10] He went on: "Today we are heading towards the destination. We call this road the 'national unity and brotherhood project.' We are taking up the issues one by one—the Kurds, the Laz, the Roma, the Circassians—all Turkish citizens are our brothers. Their problems are our problems. We have taken the first steps. But we expect support from you as well" (*Today's Zaman* 2010). Erdoğan referred to the Kurds and the *Romanlar* as Turkish citizens and brothers, and charged them with the responsibility of supporting the initiative. This double move reminded the *Romanlar* to model "correct" citizenship while denying the right to ethnic difference for Turkey's Kurds. It also highlighted an essential aspect of *Roman* inclusion in Turkey under the AKP: their status as Muslims. Religious identity has gained salience under the Islamist party, alongside a neo-Ottoman nostalgia for the Islamic past (Aktürk 2018). The Kurds and the *Romanlar* are incorporated into this narrative as "brothers" in Islam and as groups that have been present in Anatolia since before the founding of the nation state. The Turkish state, by not addressing Roma-ness as a source of ethnic difference, redirects attention and resources to their exclusion vis-à-vis class. This is appealing to many *Roman* community leaders, who see the potential for new policies that make a quantifiable difference in their lives.

Via the Romani Opening, the *Romanlar* emerged as a "disadvantaged group" in public discourse for the first time in Turkey. As part of the initiative, a workshop was held with *dernek* leaders from Istanbul, Edirne, and other major cities, and a report was drafted about their most significant problems: discriminatory language, with reference to the term "*çingene*," was highlighted along with their exclusion from education, employment, healthcare, and housing. They proposed to add information about the *Romanlar* to school textbooks and eliminate insulting expressions, provide state identity cards, and implement social programs aimed at combating drug abuse and the prevention of early marriage (Gençoğlu-Onbaşı 2012). The initiative

also specifically addressed housing rights for the *Romanlar* (which were receiving a lot of media attention in Turkey and abroad at the time, due to
the demolition of Sulukule and of other *Roman* neighborhoods in Istanbul).
Erdoğan publicly declared, "I don't want to see my Roma brothers in tents
any more. I want them to enjoy a decent standard of living." He went on to
promise "there will be no Roma living in shanty houses anymore" (*Today's
Zaman* 2010). A few months later, Turkey's Housing Administration (TOKİ)
announced it was launching projects for over two thousand residential units
for *Romanlar* in eleven cities around Turkey.

Responses to the Romani Opening have been mixed. Scholars point out
that Erdoğan's statements wrongly suggest that the *Romanlar* are itiner-
ant, when many communities have been settled in urban neighborhoods
for decades, and stigmatize them as dependent on government assistance
(Gençoğlu-Onbaşı 2012; Özerdem and Özerdem 2013; see also Timmer
2010). Right-to-the-city activists told me that the Romani Opening might be
little more than a justification for urban renewal projects and the dislocation
of urban *Roman* communities to state housing units. Although the initiative
was originally met with enthusiasm on the part of *Roman dernek* leaders,
my interviews in 2011–12 recorded ambivalence. One *dernek* leader from
Izmir expressed resentment that, although the initiative promised to "open
the government to our issues," in truth Turkey's *Romanlar* have been tasked
with "opening our issues up to the government" (interview, August 2012).
Despite these critiques, none of my informants suggested that the government should treat them as ethnic minorities. In fact, they recognized the
contradictory effects of officially recognizing the *Romanlar* as full citizens
with the same rights and responsibilities as other Turkish citizens, while simultaneously establishing a state-led program that targeted the *Romanlar* as
a separate group. A young *Roman* man in Bergama told me,

> There was no need for a Romani Opening. The Kurdish Opening makes sense
> as Kurdish people have problems. I say that we are Turkish. Our grandfathers
> were Ottoman. We don't want differentiation among *Çerkez* [Circassian], Roma,
> etcetera. . . . Turkey is a nice mosaic, all together. Atatürk said, "Peace at Home,
> Peace in the World." There is a political aim behind discussions about ethnicity.
> There are some people who run the world. They want to create divisions and take
> over control. They are the ones who are racist. When you look up *çingene* [Gypsy]
> in the dictionary, it means "brings bad luck; thief; nomadic." But according to
> Islam, the rule is that everybody is equal, no matter where they are from or who
> they are. Everybody has to respect Allah. That's the final word. (interview, August
> 2012; translation from Turkish by Funda Oral)

This points to a common attitude about identity among the *Romanlar*: they
do not, as a rule, associate themselves with other marginalized groups, nor

do they define themselves according to European conceptions of ethnic difference, even with incentives to do so.[11] In fact, *Romanlar* are generally indifferent or opposed to the aims of international Romani rights organizations and do not self-ascribe as an ethnic minority. The majority of *Romanlar* are Muslims and speak Turkish as their first language (Oprişan 2006: 164–65). When asked, they emphasize their Muslim Turkish identity and refer to *Roman* identity as secondary.[12]

"How Happy Is the One Who Calls Himself a Turk"

I attended a number of Romani rights events in Turkey in 2011–12, at which *Roman* association leaders professed loyalty to Turkey and proclaimed nationalist phrases such as "How happy is the one who calls himself a Turk." At the celebration of International Romani Day in 2012, visiting Romani rights activists were frustrated when they heard such phrases. A representative of the ERRC told me after the event, "This is why Romani rights does not succeed in Turkey. They can't stop talking about how happy they are to be Turkish!"

Other researchers experienced similar encounters. Strand (2006) found that the *Roman* aspect of identity in Istanbul is located in associations with local communities or neighborhoods (*mahalle*) and family origins (also see Mischek 2006: 157–62). She heard the *Romanlar* identify themselves in contradistinction to the Kurds, whom they described as separatists (Strand 2006: 99–100).[13] Several *Romanlar* told Strand about their experiences with non-Turkish Roma attempting to recruit them to Romani rights activism. They not only turned them away, claiming that they already have "a nation," but they referred to the non-Turkish Roma as *yabancı* ("foreign"), implying that they were non-Muslims. Strand (2006: 101) writes, "I believe that here lies the crucial difference between the *Romanlar* of Turkey and the Roma in Europe. A Muslim *Roman* identifies himself/herself more with a Turkish Muslim, albeit he/she is *gadjo* [non-Roma], and less with a foreign (Christian) *yabancı* Rom." She asserts that Romani rights activists misinterpret the absence of Romani ethnonationalism in Turkey as false consciousness. This leads her to question whether the Romani rights movement is truly transnational and can accommodate Turkish Muslim *Roman* identity, or if the movement will miss opportunities to include the *Romanlar* due to its emphasis on ethnic difference (Strand 2006: 101–103).

Similarly, Somersan (2007) found that, despite the influence of right-to-the-city activists, the *Romanlar* of Sulukule consistently emphasized their Islamic identity over their *Roman* identity. She attributes this to the structural violence that they have experienced in Turkey over the centuries; social and economic exclusion, forced evictions, poverty, and stigmatization have produced both shame and fear regarding *Roman* identity. Furthermore, advertising one's *Roman* origins in Turkey, as elsewhere, typically results in discrimination; being Muslim, on the other hand, offers status and respect in Turkey (Somersan 2007). The Islamic concept of *umma* (a supranational community of Muslims) encompasses all Muslims despite ethnic or national identities, at least ideally.

I have so far described the context for the development of *Roman* identity and political participation in Turkey. In much the same way that Turkey is expected to meet human rights standards that EU member nations often fail to meet themselves, Turkey's *Romanlar* are expected to participate in civil society acts of protest and resistance against an oppressive state. Yet, the state and civil society initiatives work in tandem to intervene upon *Roman* identity in Turkey, and upon the terms of their political participation. The *Romanlar* must either appeal to the state's notion of Turkish Islamic identity or the EU definition of ethnic difference and minority status; a combination of fear of state reprisal and several recent successes in politics[14] means the *dernek* leaders tend to favor the first option. In light of this, it is understandable that *Roman* representatives did not participate in the Occupy Gezi movement. Their loyalty to the AKP vis-à-vis their Islamic identity also precludes their participation in protest movements.[15]

Romani rights mobilization was shaped by a particular political context (namely postcommunist Eastern Europe) wherein the rise of civil society was central to the process of democratization and capital penetration. The treatment and status of the Roma in these nations was used as a "litmus test" to measure the growth of civil society and, hence, the progress of democratic development (O'Nions 2007: 1). Indeed, the Turkish government has several times made public statements claiming that they are doing a better job of addressing Romani rights than the rest of Europe (see Aydoğan 2015). Along this line of analysis, the question would be whether the *Romanlar* are being effectively integrated into civil society, and, subsequently, resistant to hegemonic state discourses or representative of Turkey's democratic transition. However, I propose to shift the focus toward examining how and why they do not meet such expectations; this move invites us to reframe scholarship on Romani identity and political participation in order to account for the dynamics of the Turkish case.

Why Were the *Romanlar* Assumed to Be Present at the Gezi Park Protests? A New Framework for Engaged Scholarship in Romani Studies

> Poverty and identity are not parallel problems—if we aren't poor, is identity still an issue? In Turkey, this is more about class discrimination than ethnic difference. (interview with a young *Roman* man from Istanbul, February 2012)

Identity can be a trap for people. It is only useful if it provides opportunities, rather than limitations. There are only brief instances of solidarity and unity because its needs shift and change. (interview with a Turkish Romani rights activist in Istanbul, October 2011)

Both of these interviews suggested that the *Romanlar* and Romani rights activists in Turkey are skeptical of the politics of identity. The young man confirms O'Nions's (2007: 222–24) observation that identity politics can distract from structural inequalities and the realities of marginalization on the ground.[16] The activist recognizes that identity is not static and is often strategic. The opposition between the universal ideals of national or global belonging and the particular demands of identity is at the heart of the politics of recognition in Turkey and elsewhere. Instances of ambivalence over narratives of ethnic belonging are products of this context (Chatterjee 2004: 7). Ironically, while Romani rights activism battles essentializing discourses that characterize the Roma using sweeping generalizations, the movement advocates a unified, global, Romani ethnic identity. Scholars of Romani studies actively debate the usefulness of representing the Roma as an autonomous, distinct group with internal coherence (see Stewart 2013: 415). Historians and linguists have definitively proved a common origin of Romani speakers (and their descendants) in India, and this is the basis for designating the Roma as an ethnic group (see Fraser 1995; Hancock 2002; Matras 2012). The International Romani Union (IRU) also used this as a basis for designating a Romani "nation without a territory." This approach has been countered by social scientists that insist on the importance of local ties over concerns with origins (see Acton 1974; Okely 1983) and who turn attention, instead, to ethnic mobilization in the struggle for recognition (Stewart 2013: 419). However, as Silverman (2012) points out, recognizing that Romani identity is not essential or universal does not discredit its importance for particular communities or for the sake of mobilization. Drawing from Spivak's (1988) concept of "strategic essentialism," she reminds scholars that we have the luxury to critique essentialized identities, while those who use them are considered misguided (Silverman 2012: 53). She writes, "For Roma, identity has always been construed in relation to hegemonic powers such as patrons of the arts, socialist ideologues, European Union officials, and NGO funders" (Silverman 2012: 55).

The discourses and practices of the European Romani rights movement and Romani studies scholars, when they delineate the boundaries of Romani identity and the terms of political engagement, can be hegemonic (see Sigona and Trehan 2009). The concept of a unified and singular *Roman* identity is political and, as such, it is always and everywhere shaped by power. Mayall (2004: 3) suggests that instead of trying to definitively answer the question "Who are the Gypsies?," we might consider who is asking that question and why. This shifts the focus from a debate about identity to a concern with subjectivity. How are the *Romanlar* made the subjects of the state and civil society? And how are they simultaneously objectified via what Foucault (1982: 777) called "dividing practices," turning them into a population that is targeted for intervention and improvement?

The "Politics of the Governed"

Social scientists have recently begun to question Enlightenment categories and how they might be "renewed from and by the margins" (Chakrabarty 2000: 16). Murray Li (2007: 1) interrogates the "logic of improvement," or programs that set out to improve the condition of the population in a deliberate manner by shaping "landscapes, livelihoods, and identities." She argues that these programs also set the conditions for particular "social problems." To understand the rationale of improvement schemes, we must ask what they seek to change and analyze the calculations they apply; however, we must also pay attention to the gaps between what is attempted and what is accomplished, as "subjects are produced as much by the failures, exclusions, or misrecognitions of the improvement programs as by their successes" (Murray Li 2007: 12). Some scholars in Romani studies have also turned attention to the way that Western concepts used by CSOs and activists (such as self-actualization, social integration, and resistance) ignore local concepts of community and culture and can even be used to further marginalize the Roma (see Sigona and Trehan 2009; Powell 2011; see also Fosztó, this volume).

In Turkey, international CSOs insist that the *Romanlar* give precedence to their "Roma-ness" over national, religious, or communal ties. Furthermore, Romani rights initiatives rely on the assumption that "civil society" exists as a domain that is accessible, or can be made accessible, to the *Romanlar,* and that in order to demonstrate that Turkey is a true democracy, they must be brought into this domain. However, civil society actors are not necessarily "nongovernmental," nor do they function outside of hierarchies of power (Agnew 2002; Adak and Altınay 2010: 7; see also Tvedt 1998). Navaro-Yashin (2002) argues that public life in Turkey is a site for the generation of the political, and that there is, in reality, no distinction between domains of power and resistance. Similarly, Kuzmanovic (2012: 2) found that, despite the political discourse of the EU and the World Bank, there is no easily discernible bounded sphere of civil society in Turkey that is distinct from the market and government. However, international policy actors and donors who draw on dominant ideas of civil society continue to impact the "makings of civil society" in Turkey (ibid.: 4).

The amendment to Turkey's Law of Associations was enacted alongside a decision by the EU that allowed Turkish CSOs to access EU money under the Instrument for Pre-Accession Assistance (IPA). As the availability of local funding is very limited and competitive, Turkish CSOs working in the area of human and minority rights must generally look to foreign funds for support, and therefore adhere to the norms of rights discourses. *Roman dernek* leaders are shut out of such lines of support because they rarely have the ability to write a grant in English. Their exclusion from the international rights scene thereby occurs at several levels simultaneously.

I do not propose that scholars take it at face value when the *Romanlar* say they privilege their Turkish Islamic identity over their *Roman* identity. As Strand (2006: 102) aptly observed, the *Romanlar* activate multiple identities under different conditions. Furthermore, structural inequalities at the levels of the state and society mean that, even if the *Romanlar* deny any ethnic difference, they do not escape the experiences of marginalization and exclusion. Somersan's (2007) point that structural violence is an incentive for the *Romanlar* to emphasize other aspects of their identity is important.[17] However, although their self-designation as Muslim Turks affords them symbolic inclusion in the Islamic community and Turkish nation, respectively, their class position vis-à-vis the larger society makes it difficult, if not impossible, to achieve equal citizenship in practice (see Ceyhan 2003; Akkan et al. 2011). They are still perceived as *Roman* by others, and this is due to latent racism and classism. *Dernek* leaders must therefore rely on local affiliations and implement reforms in their communities by appealing to familiar conceptions of identity and difference predicated on notions of Turkish or Muslim solidarity. When they can, *dernek* leaders also selectively and strategically mobilize their limited agency, using human and minority rights concepts and institutions (see Rajagopal 2003). As "subalterns"[18] who have been excluded from the established structures for political representation for much of their history, they make temporary, calculated alliances, engage in local conflicts for resources, and display contradictory loyalties. These forms of "doing politics" are not perceived as "civil." However, as Chatterjee (2004: 41) suggests, democratization does not consist of the strengthening of civil society as much as the increasing entry of marginal populations into political society, where they negotiate for what they are entitled to from the state.

As the *Romanlar* are being repositioned within a new citizenship regime in Turkey, they are laying claim to political subjectivity by articulating their rights as citizens in the idioms available to them (Secor 2004: 352). The multiple ways in which Turkey's *Romanlar* are defined and targeted by the state and civil society actors increasingly form the parameters within which they elaborate Romani rights. The *Romanlar* are being interpellated[19] into a new kind of political subjectivity, or the "politics of the governed" (Chatterjee

2004): just as nationalism in Turkey has shaped *Roman* identity, so too is it shaped by the politics of the country's EU harmonization and the critical role that minority rights discourses and practices play in that process. In this shifting context, such discourses both enable and limit the boundaries of *Roman* participation in politics (Timmer 2010) and the *Romanlar* find themselves caught in a "double bind" (Vermeersch 2006: 181) between national belonging and global solidarity. As the AKP has embraced state-led pluralism as a governing ideal, and the other major parties (the CHP, or Republican People's Party, and the MHP, or Nationalist Movement Party) have followed suit, minorities remain dependent upon the state's authority to define the conditions of political articulation (Tambar 2014: 4–5). At the same time, a movement toward solidarity among *Roman* communities across Turkey is growing in direct relation to civil society initiatives, and attention to Romani rights in Turkey is creating new contexts for the *Romanlar* to participate in politics. Therefore, Romani rights in Turkey emerges via a process by which the *Romanlar* are "learning to practice politics" (Murray Li 2007: 23), or what Anna Secor (2004: 352) has referred to as "becoming political."

Rather than assume any kind of essential identity of which the *Romanlar* must become conscious, let us ask what are the political, economic, and social processes that make *Roman* identity visible and potent in the current political climate. This approach sheds light on the ambiguous reactions of the *Romanlar* when civil society projects seek integration while targeting them as different or separate from the "majority." It also accounts for the limited yet agentive role of the *Romanlar* in this process, rather than as victims or passive subjects of power. Tambar (2014: 8) explains, "The discourses of pluralism and liberalization are not simply about augmenting minority freedoms; rather, the political liberties they support are elements of a new mode of regulating social difference." As Tamblar argues, the tensions between nationalism and the politics of difference have not been resolved, only reconfigured.

Conclusion

In this chapter, I have described the development of *Roman* identity as it has been shaped by a particular politics of social inclusion and ethnic difference in Turkey. I have also tried to address the misunderstandings between European civil society activists and local *Roman* community leaders regarding the agenda for Romani rights in Turkey. *Roman* identity has a particular history and context and, with EU harmonization, aspects of identity are highlighted that may not have been salient before. Class, religion, and ethnicity intersect in Turkey's *Roman* communities in interesting and specific ways, and deserve more focused attention. Theoretical accounts of Romani identity and political participation in the academic study of the Roma must be revised in order to account for the Turkish case. Activists and scholars must understand the political discourses and practices internal to *Roman* communities in Turkey, rather than impose outside interpretations and agendas. There cannot be one Romani rights paradigm or a universal prescription for solving Romani exclusion; the multiple Rom/Dom/Lom identities represented in even just one country, like Turkey, is a case in point.

Questioning our categories invites us to recognize how they shape the possible directions for social and political inclusion, and how they can be oppressive and limiting. For example, the *Romanlar* are targeted by the state as a population and by international rights organizations as a minority group, and in both cases the *Romanlar* are treated as homogenous and in need of intervention and improvement. Although it may appear that civil society is working to resist state hegemony, in fact the state and society are not at odds in the project of identifying the *Romanlar*. Civil society initiatives do not inherently free minorities from state power (see Crowe 2008); rather, they reconfigure the power relations that govern marginalized populations like the *Romanlar*. They are not passive subjects of these new configurations; the ways that the *Romanlar* engage in politics demonstrates their agency, as well as the specific ways in which their agency is limited by the social and political environment in which they live.

Many *Romanlar* believe that their path to inclusion is via the Turkish state, and that full citizenship is available to them. Their agency is shaped by participation in the state apparatus. *Dernek* leaders demand equal treatment by the state, claiming their right to Turkish citizenship as it is promised. This in itself is a radical position: they are taking the state to task on the definition of citizenship. If a Turkish citizen is one who speaks Turkish and is a Muslim, then the *Romanlar* should have full rights just as any other citizen. If their "subculture" is to be celebrated, not as a marker of unassimilable difference but as a contribution to Turkey's plural society, then it should not also be used as a basis for discrimination. This version of identity politics seems to recognize, at face value, the contradictions of liberal versus republican conceptions of identity as they intersect in Turkey. The *Romanlar* are practicing politics within the parameters of a particular social and political context. Romani rights, then, emerges not via resistance against a hegemonic state, but by learning to practice the politics of inclusion, between the global solidarity movement and Turkish national belonging.

Danielle V. Schoon is a lecturer in the Department of Near Eastern Languages and Cultures (NELC) at The Ohio State University. She earned a master's degree in dance from UCLA and a dual Ph.D. in anthropology and Middle Eastern studies from the University of Arizona. Her ethnographic research was funded by Fulbright-Hays and the Institute of Turkish Studies, and examines the politics of Romani ("Gypsy") identity and civic engagement in contemporary Turkey. She is an associate editor of the *Journal of Gypsy Studies.*

Notes

I extend gratitude to: Brian Silverstein, Salih Can Açıksöz, Anne Betteridge, Zehra Aslı Iğsız, and Carol Silverman. This research was funded by Fulbright-Hays, the Institute of Turkish Studies, several Foreign Language and Area Studies (FLAS) fellowships, and many intramural grants from the University of Arizona. A version of this paper was presented at the annual meeting of the American Anthropological Association in 2015. Special thanks to Funda Oral for collaborating on this project and Hikmet Kocamaner for checking my Turkish translations. Many thanks to Sam Beck, Ana Ivasiuc, and Victor A. Friedman for their helpful edits. Any remaining errors are my own.

1. I use the Turkish *Roman* (singular, or adjective) and *Romanlar* (plural) to refer to urban and politically active Roma in Turkey, as that is the term they use to refer to themselves. I use Roma or Romani to refer to the global Romani movement, or to refer to Roma living in Europe, or when the terms appear in quotes. My fieldwork was conducted in 2011–12 among urban *Romanlar.* This chapter does not reflect the politics of identity among rural *Romanlar* or Dom and Lom communities in Turkey.

2. An important exception was the presence of some young *Romanlar* from Sulukule (Schoon 2014).

3. The diversity of the empire was no longer part of the new nation's reality: with rising nationalism in the Balkans and the dissolution of the Ottoman Empire after World War I, Turkish-Muslim immigrants flooded into Anatolia; most of the Christian population had been exchanged (as with the Greek-Turkish population exchange) or killed (as with the Armenian genocide); and most of the Jews had left.

4. A peace treaty that officially settled the conflict between the Ottoman Empire and the Allies at the end of World War I, the Lausanne Treaty of 1923 defined and recognized the borders and sovereignty of the modern Turkish Republic and provided for the protection of the Greek Orthodox Christian minority in Turkey and the Muslim minority in Greece.

5. For a more extensive discussion of this history and its relevance to *Roman* identity, see Uzpeder et al. 2008, Arkilic 2008, and the prolific work of Dr. Adrian Marsh on this subject.

6. In Turkey, local names are often used to designate the *Romanlar,* such as *abdal, kıpti,* and others (Oprişan 2006). Non-*Roman* Turks often use the derogatory word *çingene.* The majority of Turkey's *Romanlar* are Sunni Muslims (Kolukirik and Toktaş

2007). The older generations often speak *Kıptici*, a Romani dialect mixed with Turkish, Kurdish, Greek, or Persian (Oprişan 2006). Younger generations may know a few words but mostly speak Turkish (Kolukirik and Toktaş 2007). The majority of the *Romanlar* live in the western regions of Turkey.

7. Note that the terms *Dom* and *Lom* are rarely used in public discourse.

8. Edirne's *Roman* population has historical connections with other Balkan minorities, given their geographic location. EdRom's connection to non-Turkish agencies and funding sources is a point of contention among other *dernek* leaders.

9. The Romani initiative has been the least contentious of these, as the *Romanlar* do not have a history of conflict with the state. They are the "'safe face' of cultural/political pluralism" in Turkey (Potuoğlu-Cook 2010: 101) in supposed contrast to the Kurds, who are portrayed as violent and dangerous to the unity of the nation.

10. Erdoğan was referencing a Turkish proverb: "*Türkiye'de altmışaltı büçük millet var*" (there are sixty-six and a half nationalities in Turkey, the "half" being the Roma).

11. Tambar (2014) describes a parallel situation, in which the category of minority applied to Turkey's Alevi Muslims spurs internal debates. Like the *Romanlar*, Alevi spokespersons position themselves within the official state narrative rather than emphasizing minority status. Tambar (2014: 7) explains this as a "reckoning of pluralism"—caught between state-building projects and liberal claims to difference, "democratic politics in the modern state contends with the legacies of a historical contradiction."

12. A new generation of Turkish *Roman* youth is becoming more interested in global solidarity with the Romani rights movement, and they are more readily embracing the idea of ethnic difference as they are influenced by the interventions of international CSOs.

13. Also see Önen 2013 for a discussion of the relationship between *Roman* and Turkish identity in contradistinction to the Dom, who are associated with Kurds.

14. When Turkey held general elections in June 2015, the main political parties all fielded *Roman* candidates for Parliament, which is unprecedented in Turkish history, resulting in the first self-identified *Roman* Parliamentarian in Turkish history being elected. In April 2016, a "Strategy Document for Roma Citizens" and a "First Phase Action Plan" were published by the Turkish Ministry of Family and Social Policies to launch an action plan against the discrimination of *Romanlar* (*Hürriyet Daily News* 2016).

15. This is true for the most part; a major exception is the *Roman* associations in Izmir, which tend to go for the Republican People's Party, or CHP.

16. Thanks to Victor A. Friedman for pointing out that this may be true only for linguistically assimilated Roma who do not have a distinct marker of ethnic difference, and for suggesting that an interesting comparison could be made between Turkey's *Romanlar* and Spain's *Gitanos*.

17. For an account of exclusionary violence against the *Romanlar,* see Özateşler 2014.

18. In postcolonial theory, "subaltern," derived from Antonio Gramsci's work, refers to populations that are socially, politically, and geographically outside the hegemonic power structure.

19. I refer to interpellation in the sense of being hailed or called, as defined by Althusser (1971), particularly for its emphasis on the subject as an effect of social relations.

References

Acton, Thomas. 1974. *Gypsy Politics and Social Change: The Development of Ethnic Ideology and Pressure Politics among British Gypsies from Victorian Reformism to Romany Nationalism.* London: Kegan Paul.

Açıksöz, Salih C. 2014. "Ghazis or Beggars: The Double Life of Turkish Disabled Veterans." *Ethnologie Française* 2014 (2): 247–56.

Adak, Hülya, and Ayşe G. Altınay. 2010. "Guest Editors' Introduction: At the Crossroads of Gender and Ethnicity: Moving Beyond the National Imaginaire." *New Perspectives on Turkey* 42: 9–30.

Agnew, John. 2002. "Democracy and Human Rights after the Cold War." In *Geographies of Global Change: Remapping the World,* edited by R. J. Johnston, Peter J. Taylor, and Michael Watts, 117–29. Oxford: Blackwell Publishing.

Akçam, Taner. 2004. *From Empire to Republic: Turkish Nationalism and the Armenian Genocide.* London: Zed Books.

Akkan, Başak A., Baki D. Mehmet, and Mehmet Ertan. 2011. *Poverty and Social Exclusion of Roma in Turkey.* Istanbul: EdRom; Boğaziçi University; Anadolu Kültür.

Aktürk, Şener. 2018. "One Nation Under Allah? Islamic Multiculturalism, Muslim Nationalism and Turkey's Reforms for Kurds, Alevis, and non-Muslims." *Turkish Studies* 3: 1–29.

Althusser, Louis. 1971. *Lenin and Philosophy and Other Essays.* Translated from the French by Ben Brewster. New York: Monthly Review Press.

Arkilic, Ayca. 2008. "The Romani Mobilization in Turkey." Master's thesis, Central European University, Budapest, Hungary.

Asad, Talal. 2000. "What Do Human Rights Do? An Anthropological Enquiry." *Theory and Event* 4 (4). Accessed 7 May 2018. https://muse.jhu.edu/article/32601.

Aydoğan, Merve. 2015. "Turkish Government Continues Reforms for Roma as EU Struggles To Find Solution." *Daily Sabah,* 19 April 2015. Accessed 2 May 2018. http://www.dailysabah.com/politics/2015/04/19/turkish-govt-continues-reforms-for-roma-as-eu-struggles-to-find-solution.

Babül, Elif M. 2017. *Bureaucratic Intimacies: Translating Human Rights in Turkey.* Stanford, CA: Stanford University Press.

Beck, Sam. 1984. "Ethnicity, Class and Public Policy: Ţiganii/Gypsies in Socialist Romania." In *Papers for the V. Congress of Southeast European Studies, Belgrade,* edited by Kot Shangriladze and Erica Townsend, 19–38. Columbus, OH: Slavica Publishers.

Bozdoğan, Sibel, and Reşat Kasaba. 1997. *Rethinking Modernity and National Identity in Turkey.* Washington, DC: University of Washington Press.

Ceyhan, Selin. 2003. "A Case Study of Gypsy/Roma Identity Construction in Edirne." Master's thesis, Middle East Technical University, Ankara, Turkey.

Chakrabarty, Dipesh. 2000. *Provincializing Europe: Postcolonial Thought and Historical Difference.* Princeton: Princeton University Press.

Chatterjee, Partha. 1984. *The Land Question: Bengal, 1920–1947.* Calcutta: K.P. Bagchi and Co.

———. 2004. *The Politics of the Governed: Reflections on Popular Politics in Most of the World.* New York: Columbia University Press.

Crowe, David. 2008. "The Roma in Post-Communist Eastern Europe: Questions of Ethnic Conflict and Ethnic Peace." *Nationalities Papers* 36 (3): 521–552.

Dalton, Bronwen. 2014. "Civil Society: Overlapping Frames." *Cosmopolitan Civil Societies: An Interdisciplinary Journal* 6 (2): 40–78. Accessed 2 May 2018. https://epress .lib.uts.edu.au/journals/index.php/mcs/article/view/3918/4349.

David, Isabel, and Kumru F. Toktamış. 2015. *Everywhere Taksim: Sowing the Seeds for a New Turkey at Gezi.* Amsterdam: Amsterdam University Press.

El-Kazaz, Sarah. 2013. "It Is about the Park: A Struggle for Turkey's Cities." *Jadaliyya,* 16 June 2013. Accessed 2 May 2018. http://www.jadaliyya.com/pages/index/12259/it-is-about-the-park_a-struggle-for-turkey percentE2 percent80 percent99s-citie.

Eren, Zeynep C. 2008. "Imaging and Positioning Gypsiness: A Case Study of Gypsy/ Roma from Izmir, Tepecik." Master's thesis, Middle East Technical University, Ankara, Turkey.

European Commission. 2007. *Turkey 2007 Progress Report.* Brussels: European Commission. SEC 1436.

Foucault, Michel. 1982. "The Subject and Power." *Critical Inquiry* 8 (4): 777–95.

Fraser, Angus. 1995. *The Gypsies.* 2nd ed. The People of Europe series. Oxford: Wiley-Blackwell.

Fraser, Nancy. 2000. "Rethinking Recognition." *New Left Review* 3: 107–20.

Gençoğlu-Onbaşı, Funda. 2012. "The Romani Opening in Turkey: Antidiscrimination?" *Turkish Studies* 13 (2): 599–613.

———. 2013. "What Went Wrong with the 'Romani Opening' in Turkey?" In *Turkey and Human Security: Challenges for the Twenty-First Century,* edited by Alpaslan Özerdem and Füsun Özerdem, 56–70. London, New York: Routledge.

Göçek, Fatma M. 2002. "Decline of the Ottoman Empire and the Emergence of Greek, Armenian, Turkish and Arab Nationalisms." In *Social Constructions of Nationalism in the Middle East,* edited by Fatma M. Göçek, 15–83. New York: SUNY Press.

Göner, Özlem. 2010. "The Transformation of the Alevi Collective Identity." *Cultural Dynamics* 17 (2): 107–34.

Gruber, Christiane. 2013. "The Visual Emergence of the Occupy Gezi Movement." *Jadaliyya.* Accessed 2 May 2018. http://www.jadaliyya.com/Details/28971/The-Visual-Emergence-of-the-Occupy-Gezi-Movement,-Part-One-Oh-Biber.

Gürboğa, Nurşen. 2016. "'Being Intrinsically, Hereditarily, Racially and Morally Gypsy': The 1923 Population Exchange and the State Policies towards the Exchanged Muslim Roman/Gypsy Groups." Paper presented at the Turkish Migration Conference, University of Vienna, Austria, 12–15 July 2016.

Hammond, Timur, and Elizabeth Angell. 2013. "Is Everywhere Taksim? Public Space and Possible Publics." *Jadaliyya.* Accessed 2 May 2018. http://www.jadaliyya.com/ pages/index/12143/is-everywhere-taksim_public-space-and-possible-pub.

Hancock, Ian. 2002. *We Are the Romani People.* Hatfield: University of Hertfordshire Press.

Hürriyet Daily News. 2016. "Action Plan against Roma Discrimination Launched." 2 May 2016. Accessed 3 September 2016. http://www.hurriyetdailynews.com/ac tion-plan-against-roma-discrimination-launched.aspx.

İnce, Başak. 2012. *Citizenship and Identity in Turkey: From Atatürk's Republic to the Present Day.* London: I.B. Tauris.

Kieser, Hans-Lukas, ed. 2006. *Turkey beyond Nationalism: Towards Post-Nationalist Identities.* London: I.B. Tauris.

Kirişçi, Kemal, and Gareth M. Winrow. 1997. *The Kurdish Question and Turkey: An Example of a Trans-State Ethnic Conflict.* London: Frank Cass.

Kolukirik, Suat, and Şule Toktaş. 2007. "Turkey's Roma: Political Participation and Organization." *Middle Eastern Studies* 43 (5): 761–77.

Kuzmanovic, Daniella. 2012. *Refractions of Civil Society in Turkey.* New York: Palgrave Macmillan.

Marsh, Adrian, and Elin Strand, eds. 2006. *Gypsies and the Problem of Identities: Contextual, Constructed and Contested.* London: I.B. Tauris.

Matras, Yaron. 2012. "The Role of Language in Mystifying and De-mystifying Gypsy Identity." In *The Role of the Romanies: Images and Counter-Images of "Gypsies"/Romanies in European Cultures,* edited by Nicholas Saul and Susan Tebbutt, 53–78. Liverpool: University of Liverpool Press.

Mayall, David. 2004. *Gypsy Identities 1500–2000: From Egipcyans to Moon-men to the Ethnic Romany.* London: Routledge.

Mercer, Claire. 2002. "NGOs, Civil Society and Democratization: A Critical Review of the Literature." *Progress in Development Studies* 2 (1): 5–22.

Minority Rights Group International. n.d. "Turkey Overview: Minorities." Minority Rights Group International website. Accessed 2 May 2018. http://minorityrights .org/country/turkey/.

Mischek, Udo. 2006. "Mahalle Identity: Roman (Gypsy) Identity under Urban Conditions." In *Gypsies and the Problem of Identities: Contextual, Constructed and Contested,* edited by Adrian Marsh and Elin Strand, 157–62. London: I.B. Tauris.

Murray Li, Tania. 2007. *The Will to Improve: Governmentality, Development, and the Practice of Politics.* Durham, NC: Duke University Press.

Navaro-Yashin, Yael. 2002. *Faces of the State: Secularism and Public Life in Turkey.* Princeton: Princeton University Press.

New York Times. 2013. "A Diaspora of 11 Million." 19 October 2013. Accessed 2 May 2018. http://www.nytimes.com/interactive/2013/10/20/sunday-review/a-diaspora-of-11-million.html.

O'Nions, Helen. 2007. *Minority Rights Protection in International Law: The Roma of Europe.* Aldershot: Ashgate.

Ohm, Britta. 2013. "A Public for Democracy: Overcoming Mediated Segregation in Turkey." Open Democracy website. 22 July 2013. Accessed 2 May 2018. https:// www.opendemocracy.net/britta-ohm/public-for-democracy-overcoming-mediated-segregation-in-turkey.

Okely, Judith. 1983. *The Traveller-Gypsies.* Cambridge: Cambridge University Press.

Oprişan, Ana. 2006. "An Overview of the Romanlar in Turkey." In *Gypsies and the Problem of Identities: Contextual, Constructed and Contested,* edited by Adrian Marsh and Elin Strand, 163–70. London: I.B. Tauris.

Oran, Baskın. 2007. "Minority Report Affair in Turkey." *Regent Journal in International Law* 5: 1–95.

Osanloo, Arzoo. 2004. "Doing the 'Rights' Thing: Methods and Challenges of Fieldwork in Iran." *Iranian Studies* 37 (4): 675–84.

Önen, Selin. 2013. "Citizenship Rights of Gypsies in Turkey: Roma and Dom Communities." *Middle Eastern Studies* 49 (4): 608–22.

Özateşler, Gül. 2014. *Gypsy Stigma and Exclusion in Turkey, 1970: The Social Dynamics of Exclusionary Violence.* London: Palgrave Macmillan.

Özerdem, Alpaslan, and Füsun Özerdem, eds. 2013. *Turkey and Human Security: Challenges for the 21st Century.* London: Routledge.

Özyürek, Esra. 2006. *Nostalgia for the Modern: State Secularism and Everyday Politics in Turkey.* Durham, NC: Duke University Press.

Pogány, István. 2006. "Minority Rights and the Roma of Central and Eastern Europe." *Human Rights Law Review* 6 (1): 1–25.

Potuoğlu-Cook, Öykü. 2010. "The Uneasy Vernacular: Choreographing Multiculturalism and Dancing Difference Away in Globalised Turkey." *Anthropological Notebooks* 16 (3): 93–105.

Powell, Ryan. 2011. "Gypsy-Travellers and Welfare Professional Discourse: On Individualization and Social Integration." *Antipode* 43 (2): 471–93.

Putnam, Robert D., Robert Leonardi, and Raffaella Y. Nanetti. 1994. *Making Democracy Work: Civic Traditions in Modern Italy.* Princeton: Princeton University Press.

Rajagopal, Balakrishnan. 2003. *International Law from Below: Development, Social Movements, and Third World Resistance.* Cambridge: Cambridge University Press.

Schoon, Danielle. 2014. "'Sulukule Is the Gun and We Are Its Bullets': Urban Renewal and Romani Identity in Istanbul." *CITY* 18 (6): 720–31.

Secor, Anna. 2004. "'There Is an Istanbul That Belongs to Me': Citizenship, Space, and Identity in the City." *Annals of the Association of American Geographers* 94 (2): 352–68.

Sigona, Nando, and Nidhi Trehan, eds. 2009. *Romani Politics in Contemporary Europe: Poverty, Ethnic Mobilization, and the Neoliberal Order.* New York: Palgrave Macmillan.

Silverman, Carol. 2012. *Romani Routes: Cultural Politics and Balkan Music in Diaspora.* Oxford: Oxford University Press.

Somersan, Semra. 2007. *Swapping Identities in Sulukule.* Paper presented in 2007 at Inter: A European Cultural Studies Conference, Linköping, Sweden.

Spivak, Gayatri. 1988. "Can the Subaltern Speak?" In *Marxism and the Interpretation of Culture,* edited by Cary Nelson and Lawrence Grossberg, 271–313. Urbana: University of Illinois Press.

Stewart, Michael. 2013. "Roma and Gypsy 'Ethnicity' as a Subject of Anthropological Inquiry." *Annual Review of Anthropology* 42: 415–32.

Strand, Elin. 2006. "Romanlar and Ethno-Religious Identity in Turkey: A Comparative Perspective." In *Gypsies and the Problem of Identities: Contextual, Constructed and Contested,* edited by Adrian Marsh and Elin Strand, 97–104. London: I.B. Tauris.

Tambar, Kabir. 2014. *The Reckoning of Pluralism: Political Belonging and the Demands of History in Turkey.* Stanford: Stanford University Press.

Timmer, Andria. 2010. "Constructing the 'Needy Subject': NGO Discourses of Roma Need." *PoLAR* 33 (2): 264–81.

Today's Zaman. 2010. "National Prime Minister Tells Roma 'Your Sufferings Are Mine.'" 14 March 2010. Accessed 1 May 2015. http://www.todayszaman.com/national_prime-minister-tells-roma-your-sufferings-are-mine_204361.html.

Tufekci, Zeynep. 2013. "'Come, Come, Whoever You Are': As a Pluralist Movement Emerges from Gezi Park in Turkey." Accessed 3 September 2016. http://technosociology.org/?p=1421.

Türkiye Gazetesi. 2013. "Duran Adam'a karşı 'göbek atan roman'" ["Dancing Roma" oppose the standing man], 20 June 2013. Accessed 2 May 2018. http://www.turkiyegazetesi.com.tr/gundem/46775.aspx.

Tvedt, Terje. 1998. *Angels of Mercy or Development Diplomats? NGOs & Foreign Aid.* Trenton, NJ: Africa World Press; Oxford: James Currey.

Uzpeder, Ebru, Savelina Danova/Roussinova, Sevgi Özçelik, and Sinan Gökçen, eds. 2008. *Biz Buradayız! Türkiye'de Romanlar, Ayrımcı Uygulamalar ve Hak Mücadelesi* [We Are Here! Discriminatory Exclusion and Struggle for Rights of Roma in Turkey]. Istanbul: Mart Matbaacılık Sanatları.

van Baar, Huub. 2011. *The European Roma: Minority Representation, Memory, and the Limits of Transnational Governmentality*. Amsterdam: F&N.

———. 2012. "Towards a Politics of Representation beyond Hegemonic Neoliberalism: The European Romani Movement Revisited." *Citizenship Studies* 16 (2): 285–94.

Vermeersch, Peter. 2006. *The Romani Movement: Minority Politics and Ethnic Mobilization in Contemporary Central Europe*. Oxford: Berghahn Books.

Yavuz, Hakan M. 1999. "Media Identities for Alevis and Kurds in Turkey." In *New Media in the Muslim World,* edited by Dale F. Eickelman and Jon W. Anderson, 180–99. Bloomington: Indiana University Press.

———. 2009. *Secularism and Muslim Democracy in Turkey*. Cambridge: Cambridge University Press.

CHAPTER 9

❀ ❀ ❀

"BE YOUNG, BE ROMA"
Modern Roma Youth Activism in the Current Panorama of Romani Affairs

Anna Mirga-Kruszelnicka

This chapter aims to shed light on the current panorama of Romani affairs,[1] alongside existing Roma policies, paying special attention to the emergence of Roma youth activism as a dynamic and rising stakeholder. The first section of the chapter analyzes the arena of Romani affairs, marked by increasing opportunities for civil society actors to become involved; the growth of funding opportunities attracts new actors, leading to a greater expansion and diversification of stakeholders involved in Roma inclusion. This section also examines the arena of Romani affairs as a field of interaction, pointing to existing tensions and competition between Roma and non-Roma/pro-Roma stakeholders. The second section of the chapter deals with the phenomenon of Roma youth activism and its significance as a new facet of Romani ethnic mobilization. Through specific examples, I will outline some noticeable tendencies, its forms and prospects, as well as implications for the Roma movement in general. Rather than providing a comprehensive picture of the landscape of Romani affairs today (in absolute terms), this chapter aims to shed light on a number of emerging trends.

Current Landscape of Romani Affairs: Diversification, Tensions, and Implications for Civil Society

There are different views about what has prompted the interest resulting in policy programs targeting the Roma in Europe. Some see it as an outcome of

Roma mobility: especially after 1989 and subsequently as a result of EU en-largement, westward Romani migration intensified, raising concerns among majority societies and politicians and prompting policy responses (Kóczé and Rövid 2012; Matras 2013; Rövid 2013; Vermeersch 2013). Others may argue that numerous violations of Roma rights led intergovernmental or-ganizations to scrutinize Roma's situation more closely (Vermeersch 2006). While in the first situation, governments were mobilized to find a response to Roma migrations, in the latter, Romani activists worked to raise interest in Roma among national governments and international actors.

In fact, intergovernmental organizations have been a reference within which various concerns regarding this population were raised. Following on their specific mandates, they have played a significant role, especially after 1989: they developed programs and activities targeting Roma, produced a body of recommendations and commitments on Roma, and encouraged, fa-cilitated, and supported the design and adoption of governmental programs. With the European Union enlargement process, the center of gravity for Roma issues has quite understandably shifted to the European Union and its institutions. The "minority conditionality" for EU accession placed the in-clusion of Roma among the political criteria and spelled out requests for im-provement in their social and economic standing; the preaccession PHARE[2] program for Roma communities was also a determining factor in developing Roma national strategies. With the completion of the fifth enlargement wave in 2007, the EU policy toward the Roma shifted from being an item of ex-ternal relations toward a key priority of internal EU policies (Sobotka and Vermeersch 2012; Vermeersch 2012). Eventually, the EU acknowledged a need for coordinated responses to Roma on a pan-European level, leading in 2011 to the adoption of the EU Framework for National Roma Integration Strategies up to 2020 (European Commission 2011).[3]

The development of Roma-targeted policies, most notably the EU Roma Framework, opened up a "window of opportunity" for civil society actors as part of the so-called "deliberative turn" (Goodin 2008; Steffek 2014) in European governance, a trend that places nonstate actors at the heart of pro-cesses of policy-making and implementation. "Involvement of civil society" and "active participation of Roma" became important components of the EU Roma Framework and of the overall policy-making on Roma, with a par-amount implication: funding.[4]

The emergence of Roma-targeted policies, together with increasing bud-get made available for their implementation, generated heightened interests in Roma issues among a variety of nonstate actors. Consequently, there has been an unprecedented growth and proliferation of various types of actors ready to join the task of implementing Roma-related policies, ranging from Roma-led civil and political organizations, pro-Roma advocacy groups (composed principally by non-Roma but with a clear and targeted mission of working for the benefit of Roma communities), non-Roma organizations (with a broader mission of fighting poverty or assisting vulnerable communities, but not an exclusive focus on Roma, such as, for example, Amnesty International or the Red Cross), and development agencies (for example, the United Nations Development Program, or UNDP), to scholars and experts, both dominated by non-Roma.[5]

On the one hand, the fall of communism in Europe marked the rapid growth of Roma civil society, especially in former communist countries (Mirga and Gheorghe 1997); a process that some scholars refer to as the "NGO boom" (Marushiakova and Popov 2005) or the "Roma awakening" (McGarry 2010). This trend is also visible in some countries of the West.[6] No doubt that availability of funding, especially for civil society actors in former communist countries, supported this growth (Sigona and Trehan 2009; van Baar 2011; Kóczé 2012). Within this variety of mobilizing structures, Roma NGOs became the principal organizational vehicles thought to represent Roma collective interests and claims (Marushiakova and Popov 2005; Vermeersch 2006; Sigona and Trehan 2009; Rostas 2012). The rapid growth of Romani structures has highlighted numerous challenges stemming from issues of legitimacy, transparency, internal fragmentation, accountability or donor dependency, co-optation, and self-interest; it was also argued that Romani organizations maintain weak links with grassroots communities and their interests. These challenges that some Roma organizations have faced weakened their performance, their impact over communities, and/or their influence on Roma policies and policy makers (Mirga and Gheorghe 1997; McGarry 2010; Kóczé 2012; Rostas 2012; Guy 2013; Acton, Rostas, and Ryder 2014; Mirga 2015).

On the other hand, during the same period, the arena of Romani affairs became greatly diversified.[7] Simultaneously to the proliferation of Roma-led civil society, other actors became increasingly involved in Romani issues as well: non-Roma/pro-Roma organizations, charitable organizations, and development agencies emerged as stakeholders in Romani policies as project implementers, service providers, or, in many cases, as voices representing Romani interests. Such non-Roma/pro-Roma actors, most notably the Catholic Church, have frequently been involved in Roma issues at least since the late 1950s; and in some countries, such as Spain, they preceded Roma self-organization (Méndez López 2005). Over the last two decades, however, a "pro-Roma microcosm" (Kóczé and Rövid 2012) emerged, marked by the rise of global non-Roma/pro-Roma civil society. Furthermore, availability of financial resources continues to attract new actors in the field of non-Roma/pro-Roma interventions. A study conducted by UNDP on the use of the European Social Fund in Slovakia, for example, found that an increasing number of organizations, with no previous experience in working with Roma, specialize in writing projects and often become implementing entities (Hurrle et al. 2012: 83).[8] Engagement of nonprofit organizations, even those without relevant expertise in the field of Roma inclusion, seemingly becomes a widespread phenomenon from East to West. Moreover, the rising demand for expertise and knowledge on Roma issues, especially among intergovernmental organizations, governmental agencies, and policy makers, heightens the influence of "experts on Roma" and especially those associated with academia. The role of "experts," however, has often been regarded as ambiguous or problematic. Latour (2011: 13) notes that "the expert was never a coherent figure: neither a researcher, nor a political representative, nor an activist, nor an administrator in charge of the protocol of the experiment, but playing a bit all of those roles at once without being able to fulfill any of them satisfactorily." Okely (1997: 234), with regards to Romani affairs, further argues that the very term "expert" refers to a certain category of power related to a glorified notion "of detached knowledge and political neutrality," and that it "also presumes that other lay people, including ordinary members of an ethnic group are not themselves expert witnesses" (see also Ryder, this volume).

The rise in the number of non-Roma/pro-Roma organizations engaged in Romani affairs is not in itself negative; after all, it contributes to legitimizing Romani claims and adds political leverage on policy makers or governments to act. On the other hand, however, the proliferation of actors involved in Roma policy has dire consequences for this field and for Roma civil society. Romani affairs is dominated by professional pro-Roma civil society, "while Romani associations remain weak and fragmented" (Kóczé and Rövid 2012). Some critics point to the "NGOization of human rights" (Trehan 2001; 2009); others denounce the emergence of the so-called "Gypsy industry" (Trehan 2001; Marushiakova and Popov 2005; Sigona and Trehan 2009), with profound implications for the Roma communities. A general critique of this dynamic draws from "Third World" literature on developmental policies (Kóczé 2012: 17), arguing that "development experts are misusing the concept of 'human development,' and instead of increasing choices and creating opportunities and more freedoms for the socially excluded groups, they are increasing their control over financial resources and misusing their powerful positions." Other scholars demonstrate how the Romani identity has been framed through scholarly and expert knowledge, often producing frames that tend to reinforce existing stereotypes (Surdu 2016). Furthermore, Rövid (2013: 385) argues that the case of pro-Roma involvement of non-Roma experts reveals power relations in which "solidarity can easily turn into hegemony." These authors have been raising the important question of legitimacy and motivation of those who enter into the field of interventions for the Roma, often seeking funding opportunities rather than being committed to resolving the Roma plight (Rostas 2012).

With the expansion and diversification of actors involved, the arena of Romani affairs gradually becomes an overpopulated field, and, consequently, it increasingly becomes a site of tensions between Roma and non-Roma stakeholders. These tensions become obvious when comparing resources of both types of actors. Although both Roma and non-Roma/pro-Roma organizations are included under the label of "CSOs" (civil society organizations) in European policy-making, some substantial differences can be detected: Roma organizations, especially smaller grassroots entities, are less skilled and resourced, and are losers in comparison with non-Roma/pro-Roma ones; they also frequently face difficulties in accessing EU funds and "have recurrently contested the position of the EU as a donor and the distribution of the funds allocated to Roma integration-related activities. The difficult access to and excessive bureaucratization of the EU funding mechanisms tend to facilitate global pro-Roma CSOs thus disadvantaging smaller Roma organisations operating at the grassroots" (D'Agostino 2014). As a result, the non-Roma/pro-Roma organizations often become dominant actors and principal beneficiaries of funding destined for Roma inclusion (ERRC 2011).[9]

This dynamic led to two interrelated consequences: the establishment of elite networks of non-Roma/pro-Roma organizations, and a weakening of Roma grassroots organizations (D'Agostino 2014). Furthermore, for some of the latter, accessing funding has become a matter of survival, which alters their role and character: they become more dependent on donor's funding and agendas, which may differ from articulated interests of their constituencies (see also Ivasiuc's chapter in this volume). Some Roma scholars express their discontent with current Roma civil society practice for becoming "a society of professional service delivery NGOs, which mainly concentrate on grant application and report writing, instead of mobilizing communities and developing a participatory democracy with the involvement of the Roma community" (Kóczé 2012: 15). My own research also points to the weakness of Roma organizations as "mobilizing structures" (McAdam et al. 1996): rather than mobilizing constituencies, they tend to target the authorities and are more accountable to the donors than to their local communities (Rostas 2009: 166). The struggle for grants also affects the relationship between Roma organizations; as the field becomes increasingly more competitive and resources are limited, the Roma organizations necessarily enter into competition with each other. This often leads to rivalry and tensions that effectively hinder cooperation, consolidation, and strategic alignment, and ultimately weakens Roma civil society as a whole.

For Romani actors, maintaining an influential voice in Roma policy issues vis-à-vis other voices has become a challenge. Roma civil society has been criticized for being an elite-driven endeavor, lacking legitimacy, detached from grassroots communities, and without a representative mandate (Kóczé 2012; McGarry 2010; Rostas 2012; Acton et al. 2014). Internal fragmentation, the existence of overlapping structures that claim representation of Roma (pan-European but also at national level), and occasional in-fighting among Romani actors only magnify the impression of shortage of legitimate Romani partners. For this reason, policy makers often turn to non-Roma/pro-Roma organizations or non-Roma independent experts, perceived as more reliable and professional partners due to their qualified staff and administrative capacity (Rostas 2012).

Despite claims of securing "Romani participation," this principle is often fulfilled only symbolically through what could be coined as "rituals of participation" or tokenistic involvement of Roma. This dynamic has been denounced most notably in the framework of the EU Roma Platform (Acton and Ryder 2013) and over the years became a constant topic. In 2014, following the third EU Roma Summit held in Brussels in April, the European Roma Grassroots Organizations Network (ERGO) denounced the lack of Romani involvement. Nonetheless, and despite repeated complaints regarding the lack of participation of Romani actors, the field of Roma policy and implementation continues to be dominated and shaped by non-Roma/pro-Roma stakeholders. It seems that for the EC this phenomenon is not perceived as problematic, even when it contradicts the motto "Nothing for the Roma without Roma": in a written response to ERGO, the EC made clear that "the fact that in [Roma] debates the majority of formal speakers are not Roma is certainly an advantage, and a major one" (ERGO 2014).

A similar struggle among Roma and non-Roma/pro-Roma actors over who maintains the dominant position is also present in national settings (Law 2014; Renouard 2014). This kind of often antagonistic relationship between Roma and non-Roma/pro-Roma actors goes beyond political activism. The tensions between non-Roma experts (often regarded as more objective and skilled) and, as these experts named it, "self-proclaimed" Roma voices, have made their way to the world of academia.[10] Beyond disputes of academic nature, these tensions should also be regarded as a power struggle of sorts in which the status quo is questioned by emerging Romani scholarship and the emergence of a critical Romani studies approach (Mirga-Kruszelnicka 2015; Ryder 2015; see also Kóczé, this volume).

Consequently, it seems that the current arena of Romani affairs is in a gridlock: despite existing political commitments, the expansion of the field, the diversification and multiplication of actors involved, and continuous financial investment, the everyday reality of the vast majority of Roma has not significantly improved. Arguably, the current arena of Romani affairs emerges as a landscape marked by increasing competition between Roma

and non-Roma/pro-Roma stakeholders over funding and influence, effectively hindering the impact in its receiving end of Romani communities.

Emerging Roma Youth Activism:
"We Are Not the Future, We Are the Present!"[11]

In the current panorama, modern Romani youth activism represents a new
facet in the overall continuum of Romani activism, which during the past
decade has taken on an ever quickening pace.[12]

Roma youth emerged as an explicit target group since the 1990s, receiving special attention from the Council of Europe (since 1995), the OSCE
ODIHR,[13] the EU, and private donors. The investment in youth-targeted
projects was driven by the need to "break the poverty cycle" (Ringold et al.
2005), but also by the desire to train and promote a new cadre of "young Roma
leaders" who would eventually replace the older generation of not uncom-
monly traditional and poorly educated Roma leadership. Major initiatives of
mid-2000s, such as the "Decade of Roma Inclusion 2005–2015" or the Roma
Education Fund (REF), placed the Roma youth at the heart of their activities.

Initially, the youth were perceived and treated as passive beneficiaries, in
some cases as implementers of projects and activities, but seldom as equal
stakeholders. Over time, however, the Roma youth have emerged as a separate and conscious subject demanding their place within the structures
of Romani ethnic mobilization and at the policy table. Instead of joining
the ranks of existing structures of Romani leadership, many "young Roma
leaders" have begun to forge a distinct movement of their own, part of the
emerging Roma youth movement (Mirga 2014).

Roma youth organizations, especially networks and those with international outreach and agendas, such as the Forum of European Roma Young
People (FERYP) and ternYpe International Roma Youth Network, played an
important role in this process. Both organizations have come to existence
through different processes—FERYP as a fruit of Council of Europe activities and ternYpe through more grassroots action. Over the years, both entities have been vocal in advocating for the inclusion of the youth dimension
in all Roma policies and programs, aiming at producing a paradigm shift in
approaches to Roma youth. The rationale was based on the conviction that
"these policies should be developed based on a mutual dialogue between
young people and the policy-makers" (ternYpe 2010b) and that Romani
youth should be acknowledged as equal stakeholders in policy-making that
concerns them. ternYpe activities most notably increased visibility, helped
to galvanize Roma youth across Europe, and mobilized international organizations to respond to these demands. Since then, both youth networks have

not only contributed to the inclusion of the youth dimension in relevant policy documents on Roma, but have also brought recognition of Roma youth activism and youth agency.

Although much of the youth-oriented investment has been directed towards countries of central and eastern Europe as well as the Western Balkans, the involvement of intergovernmental organizations such as the Council of Europe, and especially the EU-funded project schemes Youth for Europe (1989–99), Youth Programme (2000–06), Youth in Action (2007–13) and Erasmus+ (2014–20), facilitated exchange, involvement, and cooperation with western European countries; international Roma youth networks also include member organizations from across the continent. Consequently, over the years, Roma youth activism proliferated and is widespread throughout Europe.[14] Today, as never before, one can observe a plethora of youth-oriented initiatives at the OSCE, Council of Europe, or the EU, which further contribute to the growth and expansion of Romani youth activism. Furthermore, Roma youth organizations are increasingly moving beyond the niche of youth activism and are beginning to play a role as recognized stakeholders, involved in policy-making processes alongside other structures of Romani ethnic mobilization.

Roma youth activism, both as a target for support and increasingly as a social movement on its own, has been a novelty. True, in the past there were young Roma activists present in the Roma movement—after all, many of the current senior Roma leaders and activists joined when they were young, and could, in that time, be considered "youth activists." Nonetheless, their "youth condition" did not bear significantly on their work—they participated as Romani activists, but not as youth leaders. By contrast, current Roma youth organizations and networks succeeded in constructing a "Roma youth identity" as a foundation and a mobilizing force: its members are not Roma activists who happen to be young; rather they build on their youth status, embrace it fully, and underline their difference from other Romani actors involved. They act based on a conviction that the youth "needs to speak with their own voice" (Fernández Jiménez 1996) and that their distinct claims, but also different methods and approaches in working for and with Romani young people, need to be recognized; they also differentiate their aims and forms of activism from their predecessors. The emergence of Roma youth activism, or what has been referred to as the "Roma youth movement" (Mack 2012), opens up a new chapter in Romani ethnic mobilization. An overview of Romani youth organizations and youth-led initiatives points to some shared characteristics that increasingly have become recognizable traits of Romani youth activism.[15]

First, unlike the earlier paradigm of Romani mobilization based on exposing discrimination and exclusion [so-called "injustice frames" (Benford

and Snow 2000)], Roma youth tend to mobilize around the affirmation of
Roma identity (Mirga 2014: 203). Although Roma youth recognizes discrimination as the everyday reality of Roma communities, they rather tend to
denounce the phenomenon of self-stigmatization that stems from the victimization perspective (ternYpe 2010). That is why Roma youth activists
construct a narrative that builds on shared identity but exposes its elements
of ethnic pride. The annual Roma Genocide Remembrance Initiatives clearly
show how youth activists aim to strengthen the collective Romani identity,
rooted in a common history of the Roma Genocide (Mirga-Kruszelnicka et
al. 2015).[16] Here, in particular, by picking up and celebrating the "Romani resistance" theme, the Roma youth reframed historical events and used them
as an empowerment tool instead of simply commemorating victims.[17] Similarly, campaigns such as the 2010 "Be young, be Roma" have built on positive
messages that work to raise self-esteem and strengthen the affirmation of
Roma identity.[18] Roma youth also draw from more youth-friendly aesthetics
and iconography straight from contemporary pop culture. For example, by
seeking inspiration in comic books and superheroes stories (Rodríguez and
Oleaque 2010), they construct new symbols of empowerment and youth
potential.[19] These kinds of messages are part of a narrative constructed by
Romani youth and reflect differences from older generations—unlike their
predecessors, who tried to build a movement on a "stigmatized identity"
(Vermeersch 2006), numerous youth-led initiatives aim at strengthening a
positive identity frame, which the youth can embrace and use as a resource
in their mobilization. This new narrative, based on ethnic pride and affirma-
tive discourse, has also begun to permeate other youth-oriented initiatives.[20]

Second, Roma youth increasingly concentrate on community participation and community-building at grassroots level (Šerek 2014). Many of
the newly created organizations are established through a process of critical
reflection regarding shortcomings of past and dominant Romani activism.
Acknowledging the detachment of Romani grassroots from their representatives, young Roma consciously focus on the potential of Roma communities
as a resource (Mack 2012: 79). Through a variety of actions, organizations
such as ternYpe strive to activate local communities and reconnect transnational movements back with the grassroots. This is regarded as a two-direc-
tional communication, in which local communities should also have input
in international agendas (Mack 2012: 53). In its 2011 strategy paper, ternYpe
argues:

> We have learned that as an international network we should not focus on the
> project management on international level, but strengthen our efforts on local,
> regional and national level. Participants of international exchanges and trainings
> often return with a great inspiration, but mostly do not have possibilities to en-

gage at home and to take responsibility, as long as there is no structure of a youth network or self-organization. (ternYpe 2011)

They recognized the limitations of previous efforts—for example, the experience of FERYP: while it did work to provide opportunities to individual Roma youth at the international level, it did not succeed in building a structure for young Roma long-term engagement and activism. This kind of reflection helped to define the mission of Roma youth and focus on the grassroots. Other national Roma youth-led initiatives, such as the Romano Avazi association in Macedonia, aim at mobilizing constituencies and community participation. This organization, led by a group of Roma university students, adapted theories of community-building to Roma communities and put them into practice, drawing from expert literature (Marshall Gantz tactics) and experiences of other minority struggles (the Afro-American civil rights movement in the United States). Through local campaigns and a structure based on local team leaders, Romano Avazi aims at creating a framework that enables community-building and local-level engagement. Although not all campaigns of Romano Avazi have brought the desired results, this new approach has already positioned the organization on the map of Macedonian Roma civil society and has become a promising alternative to how civil society should interact with local communities.

These examples of Roma youth actions share one common feature: the interaction with local Roma communities is not based on the principle of service provision but on community engagement. Usually, Roma organizations engage with communities by providing services of various kinds to their constituencies. While this is necessary and often positive, some scholars argue that such an approach fosters a patron-client relationship between the organization and their local communities, and does not encourage cooperation and reciprocity, undermining the potential mobilizing power of Roma organizations (Rostas 2009: 160). Roma youth organizations propose a different approach; instead of providing Roma with services, they want to provide them with an opportunity to engage actively themselves, building a sense of self-awareness and political and civic consciousness. While it is still too early to evaluate the impact of this strategy, it represents a paradigmatic shift in the way Romani organizations interact with constituencies. They view the community as a resource, concentrating on its human potential and agency, instead of focusing on the grassroots community's deficits. This approach offers a promising alternative to the previous one, though it is not yet seen as an emerging tendency: lack of funding, and difficulty in shifting the mindset—not only of CSOs but also of donors and scholars—from service-provision toward community empowerment, tend to be obstacles to this trend.

Third, many young Roma advocates aim at building durable relationships of partnership and cooperation with non-Roma, rather than feed into the existing competition and divide between Roma and non-Roma/pro-Roma actors. They are, of course, aware of the social divide between the Roma minority and non-Roma majority, but they tend to view this divide as an obstacle to achieving substantial progress. For ternYpe, for example, inclusion of non-Roma and partnership with them are defined as core values (Mack 2012: 42). By actively involving non-Roma, ternYpe managed to overcome the Roma–non-Roma divide and has crafted an identity based not so much on ethnic grounds but rather on shared goals and values. Thus "membership and participation in ternYpe depends less on the personal background, education, qualification or ethnicity, but on the shared beliefs and interests to engage for the common cause, creating a movement identity" (Mack 2012: 46). In this way, Roma youth organizations managed to create a broader frame for civic engagement by reconnecting the interests of young Roma to the general issues of a young generation and the youth movement as such (Mack 2012: 50). The organization Phiren Amenca provides a good example of this effort. Using the framework of European Voluntary Service (EVS) grants, Phiren Amenca provides volunteering opportunities to young Roma and non-Roma mainly in Roma organizations. They are guided by similar principles as those of ternYpe, namely the need for dialogue, mutual respect, and solidarity among Roma and non-Roma youth. Linking the interests of Romani youth with the broader youth movement, as well as inclusion of non-Roma in Roma youth organizations, opens up opportunities for reconnecting Roma youth organizations with mainstream youth initiatives: ternYpe, for example, encourages its members to join local, regional, or national-level youth councils; FERYP, Phiren Amenca, and ternYpe are also actively involved in the initiatives of the European Youth Forum.

These examples demonstrate a shift in mindset toward involvement in Romani issues: rather than dichotomization, competition, and divide based on ethnic background, these initiatives aim at building a generation of young people committed to similar goals and values. This approach represents a paradigmatic shift, which overcomes the essentialized frame of Roma identity, characteristic of the first wave of Roma activism (Vermeersch 2006), and builds broader identity frames as a foundation for activism. At the same time, however, these organizations maintain their Roma identity (as Roma youth organizations), but create a "welcoming environment" (Jennings et al. 2006) for non-Roma to participate based on joint action, common values, and shared ownership.

Furthermore, this kind of approach, based on the amplification of identity and interests frames, and in which diversity is perceived as a resource in itself (Mack 2012: 57), enables building solidarity ties across groups, countries, and, in fact, other movements. Various youth-led initiatives consciously construct such partnerships around commonly shared aims. Most notably, the topic of Holocaust remembrance has become a powerful premise of building solidarity ties across movements and people. Not only ternYpe but also other youth organizations embrace an interethnic approach to the commemoration of the Holocaust. Over the years, in the framework of the Roma Genocide Remembrance Initiative, ternYpe brought young people of diverse backgrounds (Roma, Jewish, but also young people from across Europe) to reflect together on the events of the past and contribute together to building inclusive, respectful, and tolerant societies in the present. Such interethnic dialogue rooted in past experiences helps to establish common values and shared interests, enabling closer cooperation—as, for example, the partnership between ternYpe and the European Union of Jewish Students (EUJS). Similarly, various organizations (among them ERGO and Phiren Amenca) organized a number of meetings that brought together young people of Roma, Jewish, and Armenian backgrounds. By reflecting on commonly shared realities of discrimination, exclusion, and experienced genocides, the youth construct a common understanding and joint response to present-day challenges. There are also evolving efforts of coalition-building across diverse collective struggles, most notably regarding LGBTQ movements. In Spain, for example, the informal network Ververipen, led by a Roma activist, reaches out to young LGBTQ, among them Roma and Muslim youth. Through seminars, international exchanges, and trainings, often combined with joint public actions or flash- mobs, young people of diverse national, ethnic, and religious backgrounds learn about each other, paving the way for acknowledging not only their different identities, but, most importantly, their similarities, common interests, and shared values.

The emergence of broader coalitions among Roma and other sectors of the society reconnects the Romani cause with diverse social and civic movements and bridges Romani issues with other themes and interests of mainstream society. While such initiatives could be identified in the past, they were isolated and sporadic and had not succeeded in building longer-term partnerships. Present-day youth-led initiatives are built on premises of youth activism and volunteerism, and although they are still relatively new, they are noticeable and evolving. After all, the literature on social movements points to the importance of alliance-building, arguing that "a set of actors with similar goals strengthen their position when coordinating their activities or even joining forces" (Rucht 2007: 202). In the case of Roma activism, this has been a strategy rarely practiced until recently. Roma youth-led initiatives may become an important step in building such strategic and potentially sustainable alliances.

Finally, the emergence of the "Roma youth movement" is a relatively new phenomenon, and although it is developing dynamically, both nationally and internationally, it is still early to evaluate the extent of its success or durability. Some of the known problems of the Romani ethnic mobilization (or civil society as such) also affect Roma youth organizations—such as lack of financial sustainability, donor dependency, the challenge of constructing enduring institutions, or the danger of co-option or instrumentalization. The existence of international networks facilitates the process of internal consolidation of Romani youth actors at the transnational level, but is yet to be accomplished in national contexts. After all, the increasing number of Roma youth organizations created locally may lead to fragmentation and internal divisions, thus strategic alignment of youth actors, especially in local and national contexts, is of paramount importance. Organizations such as ternYpe acknowledge this challenge and encourage its members to build up groups and networks. Similar to the Romani women's movement (Jovanović et al. 2015), the youth movement is also complex and involves a plethora of diverse forms, structures, and strategies. The Roma youth organizations, especially local and grassroots ones, vary in terms of objectives, scope of activities, and level of engagement with public policies or international structures; nonetheless, they are all founded on premises of active engagement of Roma youth, which serves as a basis for establishing joint platforms. Roma youth networks play an important role in cross-fertilization, promoting replication of their methods and narratives in national and local settings and enabling further internal consolidation. Despite the internal diversity of Roma youth actors, one emerging pattern of youth engagement shows that rather than joining existing structures of Roma representation, the youth prefer to establish their own independent organizations, where they themselves possess ownership of the processes and decision-making (Mirga 2014). Furthermore, as the Roma youth movement expands, it faces the challenge of positioning itself vis-à-vis already existing structures of power of Roma representation. As a salient new stakeholder, young Roma inevitably defy the dominant role of older generation of Romani leaders, occasionally leading to glitches and tensions.[21] Nonetheless, Roma youth organizations are generally enthusiastically supported by the older organizations, and showcased as a source of community pride. Yet, bridging across generations within Romani ethnic mobilization through articulated cooperation and strategic coordination in many cases remains a task to be undertaken.

Conclusion

The contemporary field of Romani affairs has become a densely populated battlefield where a plethora of diverse stakeholders, interests, and competing claims interact and clash. The increasing involvement of diverse types of actors, ranging from Roma or non-Roma grassroots local entities to global pro-Roma networks, charitable agencies, scholars, and so forth, may be seen as positive developments: they contribute to legitimizing Romani claims and provide political leverage to further advance the efforts to improve the situation of Romani communities. Some actors' engagement and interests in joining this field, however, can be questioned; they tend to blend in and benefit from an expanding "Gypsy industry."

As opportunities for funding and participation of nonstate actors increase, the question of which stakeholders retain the dominant position becomes an essential point of disagreement, especially in the context of Roma and non-Roma/pro-Roma involvement. Oftentimes, non-Roma/pro-Roma actors become competitors rather than strategic allies. Although examples of positive and effective Roma and non-Roma partnership can be mapped out throughout Europe, the increasing number of powerful non-Roma/pro-Roma actors and their salience as key stakeholders in Romani-related affairs challenges the premises of Roma-led change. Kóczé and Rövid (2012: 120) rightfully argue that non-Roma/pro-Roma actors should support Romani claims, but warn that "replacing or outweighing Roma activists is counterproductive; it can only result in the further marginalization and demobilization of Roma."

In the current panorama, the emerging Romani youth activism represents a new facet of Romani ethnic mobilization and becomes a promising alternative. After all, "youth activism has always played a central role in the democratic process and continues to forge new grounds for social change" (Ginwright et al. 2006: xiii). Furthermore, the youth have been recognized as a major force in social movements and have been at the forefront of the most important European political and social transformations in recent years (Flesher Fominaya 2012). The Roma youth are becoming an integral part of contemporary youth-led movements, and are also increasingly becoming empowered as agents of social change.

Roma youth activism is developing dynamically across Europe, creating important spaces for young Roma to practice leadership, develop a sense of democratic action, and discover the empowering potential of their own agency. By learning from the shortcomings of existing Romani civil society and by drawing inspiration from other youth movements, Roma youngsters propose a new approach to engagement in Romani-related affairs. Their commitment to building communities and grassroots focus, their pledge to inclusiveness and Roma–non-Roma shared ownership, and their emphasis on self-organization may contribute to a qualitative shift in overall Romani ethnic mobilization and a remaking of the Roma movement strategy. The potential of Roma youth activism lies in their approach to mobilize internally (downward, toward Romani communities) and externally (sideways, across movements and interests). The Roma youth movement should increasingly embrace another variable—that of consolidating across generations—in order to combine the experience and wisdom of senior Roma leadership with the knowledge and energy of younger activists.

Furthermore, in the context of the current landscape of Romani affairs being marked by rivalry and tensions, Roma youth initiatives provide a refreshing alternative. Some of the Roma youth organizations effectively overcome these existing discords between Roma and non-Roma actors: while they maintain a "Roma youth movement" identity, simultaneously they construct inclusive spaces for engagement and cooperation with non-Roma youth, based on joint action, collective values, and shared responsibility. Their approach represents an essential paradigmatic change: rather than feeding into the Roma versus non-Roma divide, they build inclusive Roma organizations based on the premise of Roma leadership and vital non-Roma partnership and their valuable contribution.

The phenomenon of increased youth activism signals a change in the existing strategy of Roma ethnic engagement, not only locally, but also throughout Europe, and may contribute to move Romani ethnic mobilization toward a process of sustainable growth and maturity. The youth are an essential building block of social movements, and, in the case of Roma mobilization, the youth may be the missing piece that helps to reconnect communities and their representatives toward a process of building a renewed Roma social movement or what some refer to as "reviving civil society" (Acton et al. 2014). Roma youth advocates have become increasingly recognized as significant and visible stakeholders, and are multipliers at the grassroots, contributing to the expansion of Roma youth activism both internationally and locally. In this context, the Roma youth should be regarded as a resource for Roma ethnic mobilization. After all, the youth are "agents of change, not simple subjects to change" (Ginwright et al. 2006: xviii), and emerging Roma youth activism is bound to bring a qualitative change in overall Roma mobilization, shaping a new generation of Romani social and political leaders.

Finally, it should be noted that scholarship on Roma youth activism is still scarce. Further research is needed to analyze emerging trends through the lens of youth movements, as well as by incorporating intersecting variables of age, gender, and social class, among others.

Anna Mirga-Kruszelnicka is an anthropologist and Roma activist, born in 1985 in Cracow, Poland. She earned her Ph.D. in social and cultural anthropology at the Universitat Autònoma de Barcelona (UAB) in 2016. Between 2013 and 2015, she was an Open Society Foundations Roma Initiatives Fellow, conducting a comparative study of the Roma associative movements in various countries of Latin America and Europe. Anna was a postdoctoral research fellow in Romani studies at the CEU between 2017 and 2018. As of January 2018, she is the deputy director of the European Roma Institute for Arts and Culture (ERIAC).

Notes

This chapter draws from my research conducted as part of a Roma Initiatives Office fellowship, which aims to analyze patterns of Roma ethnic mobilization in diverse geopolitical, social, legal, and cultural contexts, as well as my Central European University postdoctoral fellowship in Romani Studies.

 1. I use the term "Romani affairs" to delineate the field that engages with broadly-understood Roma-related issues. The "arena of Romani affairs" encompasses both Roma activism (Roma-driven, by Romani actors themselves) and Roma-targeted activism, including by non-Roma/pro-Roma actors. "Romani affairs" also engages states, intergovernmental organizations, and donors. Throughout the chapter, the term "Romani activism" refers only to Roma-driven endeavors in pursuit of Romani rights.
 2. Originally established in 1989 as the Poland and Hungary Assistance for the Restructuring of the Economy (PHARE), the program was later expanded to cover pre-accession countries in central and eastern Europe.
 3. These policies, recommendations, and resolutions issued by diverse intergovernmental organizations were not developed independently from each other, but followed a similar trend and influenced each other mutually. The development of the EU Roma Framework was influenced not only by the much older 2003 OSCE Action Plan but also by the Decade of Roma Inclusion 2005–2015. The EU Roma Framework also reflects broader changes in EU Roma policy priorities: the emergence of the "social inclusion" paradigm (Sobotka and Vermeersch 2012), on the one hand, and a shift in the language of European integration toward economic growth and social cohesion as mutually strengthening, on the other (Goodwin and Buijs 2013: 2041).
 4. Since the 2000s, the EU has invested billions of euros in social inclusion projects, including Roma inclusion (European Commission 2005; 2008; 2011); this commitment has been renewed for the 2014–20 period, opening up new funding opportunities (D'Agostino 2014).
 5. Kóczé and Rövid (2012: 111) define "pro-Roma NGOs" as "run by non-Roma but advocating on behalf of Roma." Generally, an entity can be considered "Roma" if more than half of its leadership structures (board and executive management) is constituted of individuals of Romani background.
 6. In Spain, for example, as of the 1990s, Gitano organizations began to grow considerably in number: between 1997 and 2004, from two hundred to around four hundred (Méndez López 2005).

7. Economic neoliberalizations influenced the development of NGOs (Haney 2002). This trend was characterized by the emergence of a large number of experts and developers who, besides the small number of Romani activists, got involved in Roma issues through consultancy or development work (Kóczé 2012: 16).

8. The same study argues that such "commercial contractors . . . consume considerable sums" for their services and their involvement is "often accompanied by a suspicion that the mediating site, frequently associated with powerful non-Roma mediating institutions, are benefiting from the projects more than the local Roma" (Hurrle et al. 2012: 72).

9. In Spain, for example, the Fundación Secretariado Gitano (FSG) receives annually more funding from the state than any other Roma organization or federation; FSG is also the main consumer of European Social Funds (ESF) on Roma. Numerous Roma CSOs in Spain have complained that the state is favoring FSG by providing it with more public funding, and criticized FSG for its focus on service provision rather than empowerment, its inability to employ Roma in higher ranks of management, and its weakness in criticizing the state.

10. As in the case of Roma participation in policy-making, it has been argued that Romani studies has also not done enough to facilitate Roma communities to express their voice through participatory research approaches (Ryder 2015; Mirga-Kruszelnicka 2015).

11. This is a paraphrase of the ternYpe statement during the OSCE Review Conference in 2010. The original phrase reads: "Although some people say that we young people are the future, let me tell you: we are also the present!" (ternYpe 2010b).

12. When speaking about Roma youth, it is easy to fall into generalizations. As a means of simplification, this chapter refers to "Roma youth" as a specific sector of the Roma community, which also tends to self-identify as such. However, the reader should bear in mind that the Roma youth is not a homogeneous entity. For more, see Mirga 2014.

13. Organization for Security and Co-operation in Europe (OSCE) Office for Democratic Institutions and Human Rights (ODIHR).

14. It is difficult to estimate the number of existing Roma youth organizations in Europe, but such structures can be found in most European countries. International Roma youth networks also include members from across Europe, bridging old and new EU member states as well as non-EU countries.

15. While not all Roma youth organizations and initiatives share these characteristics, they increasingly become recognizable trends, which influence a greater number of youth endeavors and are replicated in diverse settings. The role of youth networks is paramount, as it enables the "multiplier effect" locally.

16. See "Dikh he na Bister / Look and Don't Forget: Roma Genocide Remembrance Initiative." ternYpe: International Roma Youth Network website. Accessed 30 December 2017. http://2august.eu/.

17. Romani Resistance, celebrated on 16 May, commemorates the only documented act of insurgence that took place in the Auschwitz-Birkenau concentration camp in 1944.

18. The campaign, launched in 2010 by the International Roma Youth Network ternYpe, aimed at strengthening Roma identity and mobilizing active engagement of Roma and non-Roma youth. See also the network's website: http://www.ternype.eu/be-young-be-roma.

19. Comic books are full of Romani characters, as argued in this compiled list: "Religion of Comic Book Characters listed by religious Group: Gypsy/Roma Super-Heroes, Villains, and Other Characters." Comic Book Religion. Accessed 30 December 2017. http://www.comicbookreligion.com/?srch=religion-Gypsy_/_Roma __36. The existence of Romani fictional characters has been used most recently by Phiren Amenca to boost self-esteem in young Roma. For more information, see Irina Spataru, "Romani Resistance or How to Become a Roma Superhero." Phiren Amenca. Accessed 30 December 2017. http://phirenamenca.eu/romani-resistance-or-how-to-become-a-roma-superhero-2/.
20. The Open Society Foundations Roma Initiatives Office, for example, has supported *Barvalipe* ("pride") camps, which also focus on a positive identity-building process. Other initiatives across Europe also gradually shift toward a positive counterdiscourse that helps to minimize the impact of a stigmatized ethnic identity.
21. For example, Valeriu Nicolae noted controversies surrounding the 2003 conference Roma in an Expanding Europe, when "young Roma leaders" were invited, while some of the traditional leaders were excluded.

References

Acton, Thomas, Iulius Rostas, and Andrew Ryder. 2014. "The Roma in Europe: The Debate over the Possibilities for Empowerment to Seek Social Justice." In *Hearing the Voice of Gypsies, Roma and Travellers: Inclusive Community Development,* edited by Andrew Ryder, Sarah Cemlyn, and Thomas Acton, 177–96. Bristol: Policy Press.

Acton, Thomas, and Andrew Ryder. 2013. "Roma Civil Society." Third Sector Research Centre Working Paper, Discussion Paper F. Accessed 7 May 2018. https://www.birmingham.ac.uk/generic/tsrc/documents/tsrc/discussion-papers/discussion-paper-f-roma-civil-soc.pdf.

Benford, Robert D., and David A. Snow. 2000. "Framing Processes and Social Movements." *Annual Review of Sociology* 26 (1): 611–39.

D'Agostino, Serena. 2014. "The Missing Piece: Empowerment of Roma Grassroots Organisations in EU Roma Integration Policies." Policy Brief, Institute for European Studies, Vrije Universiteit Brussel. Accessed 25 February 2015. http://www.ies.be/files/PB_2014_10_0.pdf.

European Romani Grassroots Organizations. 2014. "European Roma Summit." ERGO Network News. Accessed 5 May 2016. http://www.ergonetwork.org/ergo-network/news/129/000000/European-Roma-Summit/.

European Commission. 2005. "Situation of Roma in an Enlarged European Union." Brussels: European Commission. Accessed 7 May 2018. https://publications.europa.eu/en/publication-detail/-/publication/b628783f-622a-4e33-9133-141329672d6e/language-en.

———. 2008. "European Roma Summit: MEMO/08/559." Brussels, 12 September 2008. Accessed 7 May 2018. europa.eu/rapid/press-release_MEMO-08-559_en.pdf.

———. 2011. "An EU Framework for National Roma Integration Strategies up to 2020." COM(2011)173. Brussels: European Commission Accessed 3 August 2015. https://www.eumonitor.eu/9353000/1/j4nvke1fm2yd1u0_j9vvik7m1c3gyxp/vkcwedwy32zz/v=s7z/f=/com(2011)173_en.pdf.

Fernández Jiménez, Diego L. 1996. "Young Roma, Gypsies and Travellers in Europe: Report from the Training course 'Situation and Perspectives of Young People from Roma, Gypsy and Travellers Background in Europe.'" Strasbourg: Council of Europe.

Flesher Fominaya, Cristina. 2012. "Youth Participation in Contemporary European Social Movements." Accessed 30 June 2015. http://pjp-eu.coe.int/documents/1017981/1668207/Youth_Participation_in_Contemporary_European_Social_Movements_Flesher_Fominaya_FinalPB_CFFPB_CFF_x2x.pdf/30c4dbcd-296e-411f-a338-ac033b3a98f6.

European Roma Rights Centre. 2011. "Funding Challenges: Roma Organisations." *Roma Rights: Journal of the European Roma Rights Centre.* Accessed 20 November 2015. http://www.errc.org/article/roma-rights-2011-funding-roma-rights-challenges-and-prospects/4062/4.

Ginwright, Shawn, Pedro Noguera, and Julio Cammarota. 2006. *Beyond Resistance! Youth Activism and Community Change.* New York: Routledge.

Goodin, Robert E. 2008. *Innovating Democracy: Democratic Theory and Practice after the Deliberative Turn.* Oxford: Oxford University Press.

Goodwin, Morag, and Roosmarijn Buijs. 2013. "Making Good European Citizens of the Roma: A Closer Look at the EU Framework for National Roma Integration Strategies." *German Law Journal* 14 (10): 2041–56.

Guy, Will, ed. 2013. *From Victimhood to Citizenship: The Path of Roma Integration; A Debate.* Budapest: Kiadó.

Hurrle, Jakob, Andrey Ivanov, Jan Grill, Jaroslav Kling, and Daniel Škobla. 2012. "Uncertain Impact: Have the Roma in Slovakia Benefited from the European Social Fund?" Roma Inclusion Working Papers. Bratislava: UNDP Europe and CIS: Bratislava Regional Centre.

Jennings, Louise B., Deborah M. Parra-Medina, DeAnne K. Hilfinger Messias, and Kerry McLoughlin. 2006. "Toward a Critical Social Theory of Youth Empowerment." *Journal of Community Practice* 14 (1/2): 31–55.

Jovanović, Jelena, Angéla Kóczé, and Lídia Balogh. 2015. "Intersections of Gender, Ethnicity and Class: History and Future of the Romani Women's Movement" Accessed 20 June 2016. http://fesbp.hu/common/pdf/Paper_Roma_women_Gender_Politics.pdf.

Kóczé, Angéla. 2012. "Civil Society, Civil Involvement and Social Inclusion of the Roma." Bratislava: United Nations Development Program.

Kóczé, Angéla, and Márton Rövid. 2012. "Pro-Roma Global Civil Society: Acting For, With or Instead of Roma?" In *Global Civil Society 2012: Ten Years of Critical Reflection,* edited by Mary Kaldor, Sabine Selchow, and Henrietta L. Moore, 110–22. London: Palgrave Macmillan.

Latour, Bruno. 2011. "From Multiculturalism to Multinaturalism: What Rules of Method for the New Socio-Scientific Experiments?" *Nature and Culture* 6 (1): 1–17.

Law, Ian. 2014. *Mediterranean Racisms: Connections and Complexities in the Racialization of the Mediterranean Region.* London: Palgrave Macmillan.

Mack, Jonathan. 2012. "The Social Movement of Roma in Europe: Chance and Problems of Transnational Social Movement Coalitions for Empowerment and Grassroots Mobilization: The Case Study of ternYpe International Roma Youth Network." Master's thesis, Freie Universität Berlin.

Marushiakova, Elena, and Veselin Popov. 2005. "The Roma: A Nation without a State?" In *Nationalismus across the Globe,* edited by Wojciech Burszta, Tomasz Kamusella, and Sebastian Wojciechowski, 433–55. Poznan: School of Humanities and Journalism.

Matras, Yaron. 2013. "Scholarship and the Politics of Romani Identity: Strategic and Conceptual Issues." *European Yearbook of Minority Issues* 10 (2011): 209–47.

McAdam, Doug, John D. McCarthy, and Mayer N. Zald. 1996. *Comparative Perspectives on Social Movements: Political Opportunities, Mobilizing Structures, and Cultural Framings.* Cambridge: Cambridge University Press.

McGarry, Aidan. 2010. *Who Speaks for Roma? Political Representation of a Transnational Minority Community.* New York: Continuum.

Méndez López, Carmen. 2005. "Por El Camino de La Participación: Una Aproximación Contrastada a Los Procesos de Integración Social Y Política de Los Gitanos Y Las Gitanas" [On the Way to Participation: A Comparative Approach to the Social and Political Integration Processes of Gitanos and Gitanas]. Ph.D. dissertation, Universitat Autónoma de Barcelona.

Mirga, Andrzej, and Nicolae Gheorghe. 1997. *The Roma in the Twenty-First Century: A Policy Paper.* Princeton: Project on Ethnic Relations.

Mirga, Anna. 2014. "Youth Engagement in Gitano Associative Movement in Catalonia." In *"Cadjan—Kiduhu": Global Perspectives on Youth Work,* edited by Brian Belton, 195–210. Rotterdam: Sense Publishers.

———. 2015. "The Re-emergence of Informal and Traditional Leaders (Bulibasha, Vajda) and the Role of Romanipen." *Roma Rights: Journal of the European Roma Rights Centre* 1: 31–37.

Mirga-Kruszelnicka, Anna. 2015. "Romani Studies and Emerging Romani Scholarship." *Roma Rights: Journal of the European Roma Rights Centre* 2: 39–46.

Mirga-Kruszelnicka, Anna, Esteban Acuña C., and Piotr Trojański, eds. 2015. *Education for Remembrance of the Roma Genocide: Scholarship, Commemoration and the Role of Youth.* Cracow: Libron.

Okely, Judith. 1997. "Some Political Consequences of Theories of Gypsy Ethnicity: The Place of the Intellectual." In *After Writing Culture: Epistemology and Praxis in Contemporary Anthropology,* edited by Allison James, Jennifer L. Hockey, and Andrew Dawson, 224–43. London: Routledge.

Renouard, Anne-Cécile. 2014. "Constructing a Roma Cause in Contemporary Finland and Italy: The Social and Cultural Significance of Roma and pro-Roma Mobilizations." In *From Silence to Protest: International Perspectives on Weakly Resourced Groups,* edited by Didier Chabanet and Frédéric Royall. London: Ashgate.

Ringold, Dena, Michael A. Orenstein, and Erika Wilkens. 2005. *Roma in an Expanding Europe: Breaking the Poverty Cycle.* Washington, DC: The World Bank.

Rodríguez, Vicente, and J. M. Oleaque. 2010. "Superhéroes Gitanos: Los Roma Y Sinti En La Novela Gráfica Americana." *Cuadernos Gitanos* 7: 38–41.

Rostas, Iulius. 2009. "The Romani Movement in Romania." In *Romani Politics in Contemporary Europe,* edited by Nando Sigona and Nidhi Trehan, 159–85. New York: Palgrave Macmillan.

———. 2012. "Roma Participation: From Manipulation to Citizen Control." *Roma Rights: Journal of the European Roma Rights Centre,* 3–7.

Rövid, Márton. 2013. "Solidarity, Citizenship, Democracy: The Lessons of Romani Activism." *European Yearbook of Minority Issues* 10 (2011): 381–96.

Rucht, Dieter. 2007. "Movement Allies, Adversaries and Third Parties." In *The Blackwell Companion to Social Movements,* edited by David A. Snow, Hanspeter Kriesi, and Sarah A. Soule, 197–217. London: Blackwell Publishing.

Ryder, Andrew. 2015. "Co-producing Knowledge with Below the Radar Communities: Factionalism, Commodification or Partnership? A Gypsy, Roma and Traveller Case Study." Third Sector Research Centre Working Paper, Discussion Paper G. Accessed 26 August 2016. http://www.birmingham.ac.uk/generic/tsrc/documents/tsrc/discussion-papers/2015/gtr-discussion-paper-g-ryder-28janfinal.pdf.

Sigona, Nando, and Nidhi Trehan, eds. 2009. *Romani Politics in Contemporary Europe.* New York: Palgrave Macmillan.

Sobotka, Eva, and Peter Vermeersch. 2012. "Governing Human Rights and Roma Inclusion: Can the EU Be a Catalyst for Local Social Change?" *Human Rights Quarterly* 34 (3): 800–22.

Steffek, Jens. 2014. "Civil Society Participation and Deliberative Democracy in the European Union." Accessed 20 November 2015. http://www.e-ir.info/2014/03/21/civil-society-participation-and-deliberative-democracy-in-the-european-union.

Surdu, Mihai. 2015. *Expert Frames: Scientific and Policy Practices of Roma Classification.* Budapest: Central European University Press.

Šerek, Jan. 2014. "Three Myths on Civic Engagement among Roma Youth." *EWC Statement Series* 4: 27–30.

ternYpe. 2010a. "European Roma Youth Summit: ternYpe."

———. 2010b. "Statement of 'ternYpe—International Roma Youth Network.'" Accessed 12 May 2014. http://www.osce.org/home/71774?download=true.

———. 2011. "ternYpe Strategy Paper."

van Baar, Huub. 2011. *The European Roma: Minority Representation, Memory and the Limits of Transnational Governmentality.* Amsterdam: F&N.

Vermeersch, Peter. 2006. *The Romani Movement: Minority Politics and Ethnic Mobilization in Contemporary Central Europe.* Oxford: Berghahn Books.

———. 2012. "Reframing the Roma: EU Initiatives and the Politics of Reinterpretation." *Journal of Ethnic and Migration Studies* 38 (8): 1195–212.

———. 2013. "The European Union and the Roma: An Analysis of Recent Institutional and Policy Developments." *European Yearbook of Minority Issues* 10 (2011): 341–58.

INDEX

� � �

www.ingramcontent.com/pod-product-compliance
Lightning Source LLC
Chambersburg PA
CBHW070921030426
42336CB00014BA/2486